ADDITIONS AND CORRECTIONS

TO THE

W.P.A.

INVENTORY

OF

LAKE COUNTY, OHIO:

PAINESVILLE

Jana Sloan Broglin

HERITAGE BOOKS
2025

HERITAGE BOOKS

AN IMPRINT OF HERITAGE BOOKS, INC.

Books, CDs, and more—Worldwide

For our listing of thousands of titles see our website
at
www.HeritageBooks.com

Published 2025 by
HERITAGE BOOKS, INC.
Publishing Division
5810 Ruatan Street
Berwyn Heights, MD 20740

(Originally Titled)
INVENTORY OF THE COUNTY ARCHIVES OF OHIO

Prepared by
The Ohio Historical Records Survey Project
Division of Community Service Programs
Work Projects Administration

No. 43. LAKE COUNTY (PAINESVILLE)

Columbus, Ohio
The Ohio Historical Records Survey Project
October 1941

International Standard Book Number
Paperbound: 978-0-7884-4837-9

County Offices and Their Records

       Minutes. Reports. Improvements. Fiscal accounts. Miscellaneous. Maps and photographs. Aid for the blind. Relief Administration: case records; work relief and CCC; correspondence
       Real property transfers: deeds; leases; mortgages; liens; registered lands; plats and maps. Personal property transfers. Corporations and partnerships. Grants of authority. Fiscal accounts. Miscellaneous.
       Dockets and general indexes. General court records: jury and witness records; bonds; sheriff's returns. Motor vehicles. Commissions and licenses. Partnerships. Elections. Accounts fiscal. Judicial statistics. Corner's inquests. Miscellaneous.
       Dockets. Court proceedings. Naturalization. Miscellaneous.
       District and circuit courts. Court of appeals.

TABLE OF CONTENTS

The Historical Records Survey Program

Sargent B. Child, National Director
Willard N. Hogan, Regional Supervisor
Lillian Kessler, State Supervisor
Ruth Sloan, District Supervisor

Division of Community Service Programs

Florence Kerr, Assistant Commissioner
Mary Gillett Moon, Chief Regional supervisor
Ruth Neighbors, State Director
Marion Wilson, District Director

WORK PROJECTS ADMINISTRATION

Howard O. Hunter, Acting Commissioner
George Field, Regional Director
Carl Watson, State Administrator
Frank Miskell, District Manager

Sponsors

The Ohio State Archaeological and Historical Society

The Board of County Commissioners of Lake County
Charles D. Clark
L. C. Hull
Emmett Sweeney

The *Inventory of the County Archives of Ohio* is one of a number of bibliographies of historical materials prepared throughout the United States by workers on the Historical Records Survey Program of the Work Projects Administration. The publication herewith presented, an inventory of the archives of Lake County, is Number 43 of the Ohio series.

The Historical Records Survey Program was undertaken in the winter of 1935 - 1936 for the purpose of providing useful employment to needy unemployed historians, lawyers, teachers, and research and clerical workers. In carrying out this objective, the project was organized to compile inventories of historical materials, particularly the unpublished government documents and records which are basic in the administration of local government, and which provide invaluable data for students of political, economic, and social history. The archival guide herewith presented is intended to meet the requirements of day-to-day administration by the officials of the county, and also the needs of lawyers, businessmen, and other citizens who require facts from the public records for the proper conduct of their affairs. The volume is so designed that it can be used by the historian in his research in unprinted sources in the same way he uses the library card catalog for printed sources.

The inventories produced by the Historical Records Survey Program attempt to do more than give merely a list of records– they attempt further to sketch in the historical background of the county or other unit of government, to describe precisely and in detail the organization and functions of the government agencies whose records they list. The county, town, and other local inventories for the entire county will, when completed constitute an encyclopedia of local government as well as a bibliography of local archives.

The successful conclusion of the work of the Historical Records Survey Program, even in a single county, would not be possible without the support of public officials, historical and legal specialists, and many other groups in the community. Their cooperation is gratefully acknowledged.

The Survey Program was organized by Luther H. Evans, who served as Director until March 1, 1940, when he was succeeded by Sargent B. Child, who had been Field Supervisor since the inauguration of the Survey. The Survey Program operates as a Nation-wide series of locally sponsored projects in the Division of Community Service Programs, of which Mrs. Florence Kerr, Assistant Commissioner, is in charge.

Howard O. Hunter
Acting Commissioner

In 1929 after the stock market crash along with the Great Depression which followed, President Herbert Hoover and his successor Franklin D. Roosevelt formulated relief projects, the most successful was the establishment of the Works Progress Administration (WPA).

Established as the Works Projects Administration in 1935, the WPA was the largest of the many programs developed during Roosevelt's "New Deal." In 1939, the agency's name was changed to Works Progress Administration, and continued as such until its demise in 1943.

The Federal Writers' Project, a division of the WPA (known as Federal Project Number One), created jobs for many unemployed librarians, clerks, researchers, editors, and historians. The workers went to courthouses, town halls, offices in large cities, vital statistics offices and inventoried records. Besides indexing works, many records were transcribed. One of these many projects was the *Inventory of the County Archives* which has benefitted genealogists and historians. The inventories listed the records, either by volumes or file boxes and years per record type, within the office. Although the WPA oversaw this project, the information for each volume of records may differ significantly by the information submitted.

The information herein is verbatim except for obvious spelling errors. Records listed may have met the requirement for retention and have been destroyed as per the records retention act, while other records are considered permanent records. (*See:* **https://codes.ohio.gov/ohio-revised-code**) Ohio Revised Code, sections 149.31 and 149.34). Records once considered "open" to the public, such as lunacy, idiotic, and juvenile cases, may be "closed" due to a revision of state laws. However, the records may be opened to family members with adequate proof of lineage.

The addresses and website section of this edition list an up-to-date location guide to each office mentioned.

This project was to encompass all of Ohio's 88 counties although approximately 30 of these inventories have been located while others may be missing or not done.

Jana Sloan Broglin
Fellow, Ohio Genealogical Society
Swanton, Ohio
2025

PREFACE
1st Edition

The Historical Records Survey of the Work Projects Administration began operation in Ohio in February 1936. The Project was organized and operated by the district supervisors of the Writers' Project until November 1936, when it became an independent part of Federal Project Number 1. With the termination of the Federal Projects in September 1939, the Ohio unit became the Ohio Historical Records Survey Project, sponsored by the Ohio State Archaeological and Historical Society.

The purpose of the Survey in Ohio has been the preparation of complete inventories of the records of the state and of each county, city, and other local governmental unit. The *Inventory of the County Archives of Ohio* will, when completed, consist of a set of 88 volumes numbered according to the position of the county name in an alphabetical list of Ohio counties. Thus, the inventory herewith presented for Lake County is Number 43. The inventory of the State Archives and of municipal and other local records will constitute separate publications.

The principle followed in the inventory of the county records has been to place a record in the office of origin rather than in the office of deposit. The records are arranged with those of the executive branch of government first, followed by judicial, law enforcement, fiscal, and miscellaneous agencies. Minor agencies are placed in the general arrangement according to function rather than according to constitutional or statutory responsibility to a major subdivision. The legal development of each office or agency has been treated in a preparatory section preceding the inventory of the records of the office. Although a condensed form of entry is used, information is given as to the limiting dates of all extant records, the contents of individual series, and the location of records in county courthouse, state house, or other depository.

The Ohio Historical Records Survey Project was inaugurated in Lake County in May 1936. Since July 1940, the project has been under the administration and technical supervision of Dr. Ruth Sloan. The whole-hearted cooperation of the county officials with the project workers has meant much in the thoroughness and completeness of the result. The board of county commissioners, serving as a contributing co-sponsor, made possible the publication of this volume. For the accuracy of the inventory the project personnel in Lake County, working under the direction of S. Leroy Ives, is entirely responsible. The Summit County office staff, under the immediate supervision of Mrs. Rosaline Irish, Project Technician, arranged, edited, and indexed the volume. Advice and assistance were rendered by the State office staff under the supervision of Miss Winifred Smith, Project Technician.

The various units of the *Inventory of the County Archives of Ohio* will be issued in mimeographed or printed form for free distribution to state and other public officials and to public libraries in Ohio, and to a limited number of libraries outside the state. Requests for information concerning particular units of the *Inventory* should be addressed to the Ohio Historical Records Survey Project, Room 216, Clinton Building, Columbus, Ohio.

Lillian Kessler
State Supervisor
Ohio Historical Records Survey Project

Columbus, Ohio
October 6, 1941

adm. . . . . administration
am.. . . . . amended
Arch.. . . . . Archaeological
Art. . . . . Article
bull. . . . . bulletin
c.. . . . . copyright
capias . . . . a warrant or order for arrest of a person,
                              typically issued by the judge or magistrate in a case.
CCC.. . . . . Civilian Conservation Corps
centiorari . . . . to be more fully informed
chap (s). . . . . chapter(s)
comp. . . . . compiler
Const. . . . . Constitution
ed(s). . . . . editor(s)
et al. . . . . (et alii), and others
(et) passim . . . . and here and there
ex officio . . . . as a result of one's status or position
et seq. . . . . and following
fee simple . . . . full and irrevocable ownership
G. C. . . . . General Code
habeas corpus . . . . protection against illegal imprisonment
ibid. . . . . the same reference
LL.D. . . . . Doctor of Laws
loc. cit. . . . . *(coco citato)*
N.P. . . . . The Ohio NISI PRIUS REPORTS
n.p. . . . . no place of publication shown
n. s. . . . . new series
nolle prosequi . . . . notice of abandonment by a
                              plaintiff or prosecutor of all or part of a suit or action
O.L. . . . . *Laws of Ohio*
op. cit. . . . . *(opere citato)* In the work cited
posse comitatus. . . . . a group of citizens called upon to assist the sheriff
praecipes. . . . . a written request for action
prima facie . . . . on the first impression

pro rata . . . . in proportion
procedendo . . . . sends case from appellate court to a lower court
pt. . . . . part
quo warranto. . . . . by what authority or warrant
replevins . . . . return of personal property
wrongfully taken or held by a defendant
R. . . . . River
rep. . . . . reporter
R.S. . . . . Revised Statutes
sec(s). . . . . section(s)
sic . . . . thus, following copy
supersedeas . . . . a stay of enforcement of a judgment pending appeal
v. . . . . versus
venires . . . . a group of people summoned for jury duty
vol(s). . . . . volume(s)
WPA . . . . Works Progress/Projects Administration
writ . . . . a formal, legal document, a decree
x . . . . by
— . . . . current, to date
4-H . . . . (Four - H)

Each chapter or section of "County Offices and Their Records" consists of an essay describing the legal status and functions of one department of county government and an inventory of the records of that department.

Each record constitutes a separate entry. Entries are arranged under topical headings and subheadings.

Each entry sets forth, insofar as applicable, the following:

1. Entry number. Entries are numbered consecutively throughout the inventory.

2. The exact title as it appears on the record, or if the record has no title a supplied title in brackets. If the title of the record is non-descriptive, misleading, or incorrect, an additional title (in capitals and lowercase letters), also enclosed in brackets, has been supplied.

3. Dates show inclusive years or parts of years covered by the record. Breaks in dates indicate that the record is missing or was not kept between dates shown. A dash in place of the final date indicates an open record. If no current entries have been made the date of the last entry is noted. Where no statement is made that the record was discontinued at the last date shown, it could not be definitely established that such was the case. Where no comment is made on the absence of prior and subsequent records, no definite information could be obtained.

4. Quantity, given in chronological order wherever possible.

5. Labeling. Numbers and letters within parentheses indicate labeling on volumes, file boxes, or other containers.

6. Variations in title. The current or most recent title is used but significant variations are shown with dates for which each was used.

7. Change of agency. Occasionally a record is discontinued as a county record and kept by some other agency.

8. Description. A statement of the nature and purpose of the record and of what the record shows. As the contents of a record may vary, over time the description may differ somewhat from the record at any one period. Wherever feasible, changes in content are shown with dates. In map and plat entries the names of author

and publisher and the scale are omitted only when not available.

9. Arrangement. Records said to be alphabetically arranged are frequently alphabetized only as to initial letter of the surname. This is true especially where there is a secondary arrangement.

10. Indexing. Self-contained indexes are described in the entry. Separate indexes constitute separate entries with cross references to and from the record entry.

11. Nature of recording. Changes are indicated with dates.

12. Condition. No statement is made if good or excellent.

13. Number of pages. Averaged for the series.

14. Dimensions show size of volumes, maps, file boxes, or other containers and are expressed in inches in every instance. The dimensions of volumes are given in order of height, width, and thickness; of file boxes in order of height, width, and depth.

15. Location. Rooms referred to are in the county courthouse unless some other building is specified.

Title line cross references are used to complete series where a record is kept separately for a period of time or in other records for different periods of time. They are also used in all artificial entries which are made to show, under their proper office, records kept in the same volume or file with records of another office. In both instances, the description of the master entry shows the title and entry number of the record from which the cross reference is made. Dates shown in the description of the master entry are for the part or parts of the record contained therein, and are shown only when they vary from those of the master entry. Artificial entries show only title, dates, and description.

Separate third paragraph cross references from entry to entry, are used to show prior, subsequent, or related records which are not a part of the same series. If, however, both entries are under the same subject headings, no third paragraph references are made. "See also" references from subject headings refer to entries in the same department which contain records logically belonging under that heading but which have been classified under an equally appropriate heading.

Lake County is situated on Lake Erie in the extreme northeastern part of Ohio. The ancient shoreline of Lake Erie, the edge clearly marked, extends through the county passing through the village of Mentor, and about a mile south of Painesville, and, at the eastern line of the county, through Unionville. Approximately one-half of its area is in this old lake bed with its characteristic surface soils of muck and silt. South of this line the topography is that of a plateau region modified by glacial action, and, in spite of its proximity to the lake, the southern part of the county has a rolling contour and in spots even rugged scenery. The great inequalities which characterize the topography of the county, are due partly to erosion. The general surface is an almost uniformly inclined plane rising gradually from the lake to an altitude of more than 600 feet at the base of the conglomerate wherever it strikes the southern line of the county. It is estimated that 30 percent of the total area is undulating, 30 percent gently to heavily rolling, and around 40 percent hilly to very hilly.

The drainage of Lake County follows the marked surface slope around the lake. The western end of the county is in the drainage basin of the Chagrin River, but most of the area drains into the Grand River, which cuts its way between bluffs, frequently rising as high as 200 feet to the lake plains at Painesville, and thence to its mouth at Fairport Harbor. The Chagrin River at Kirtland and the Grand River at Painesville afford extensive water power.

About seven miles south of Painesville on the Geauga County line is a prominence known as Little Mountain. It is a cone of sandstone seamed with layers of white gravel and pierced with deep fissures or caverns. It had a sacred character among the Indians and as early as 1846 it was a favorite summer resort for the settlers in this region.

The lake plains extend back from the lake shore for distances varying from five to eight miles. The soil is stiff clay and the surface is much eroded. Deep ravines cutting down into the Erie shales give good surface drainage and produce conditions admirably adapted to fruit growing. In nearly all the northern part of Willoughby and Mentor Townships, the surface is covered with a fine clay loam containing sand and is dotted with a profusion of granite boulders. In the northeastern part of the county the surface generally has a loamy, gravelly clay soil which is somewhat swampy in some places. East of Painesville there is an extensive deposit of peaty material or black muck which has proved to be an excellent fertilizer.

The geological formations are of the Olentangy and Ohio shales along Lake

Erie, the width of the county, and of the Waverly and Maxville series in the southeastern part of the county. The mineral resources of the region are negligible. Considerable salt is removed for use in the chemical industries at Fairport, however. Clay and sandstone in sufficient amounts to be of commercial value occur in the county, as well as occasional deposits of limestone. In the eastern part of the county, chiefly in Madison Township, considerable quantities of bog iron ore have been found, but the coal-bearing rocks did not reach so far north.[1]

Lake County contains four enclosures, six mounds, and a village site as evidence of having been the abode of prehistoric man. The important trail of the aborigines which followed the southern shore of Lake Erie passed through this region, and while the existing evidences of prehistoric settlement are relatively few, they are sufficient to attach to this territory considerable archaeological and anthropological interest. Of particular importance is the enclosure occupying the point of land at the juncture of Painesville Creek and Grand River. It is irregular in form, occupies a strong position, and is of the so-called defensive type of structure.[2]

The Eries were the earliest of the historic tribes to settle in this region. However, they were vanquished about 1650 by the Iroquois, and northeastern Ohio became the home of many tribes, among them the Senecas, Wyandots, Ottawas, Chippewas, Cayugas, Tonawandas, Iroquois, and Delawares. The Massasaquas, a tribe of the Delawares, were the most numerous Indian inhabitants in the region of Lake County.[3] In 1726 at Albany the Iroquois ceded to the white man all territory east of Lake Erie and a strip 60 miles in width along Lakes Ontario and Erie to the Cuyahoga River. The western tribes did not recognize the validity of their action, however, and it was not until several other treaties had been concluded that the Indian claims to northern Ohio were cleared. The treaty at Fort Industry in 1805 completely relinquished the Indian title to the Western Reserve.[4] At no time were the Indians a serious menace to the settlers of Lake County. They were present in great numbers in the vicinity of the Grand River, but they became friendly with the whites and even participated in their religious gatherings. Chief Seneca was the most noted of the leaders of these Indians.[5]

---

1. *Report of the Geological Survey of Ohio*, ser. ii (Columbus, 1873), I, pt. I, 510-519; Williams Brothers, pub. *History of Geauga and Lake Counties Ohio* (Philadelphia, 1878), 16.

2. William C. Mills, *Archaeological Atlas of Ohio* (Columbus, 1914), 43.

3. Williams, *op. cit.,* 17-18.

4. Williams, *op. cit.,* 11.

5. L. B. Hillis, *Lake County Illustrated* (Painesville, Ohio, 1912), 3.

As late as 1797 Indians still remained on the eastern side of the river opposite Willoughby.[6] When rumors of the approaching war with England reached this region in 1811, the scanty Indian population disappeared from Lake County and moved farther west.[7]

Except for explorers who may have passed through the region on the lake shore path, Lake County remained untouched by the whites until comparatively late in history. In November 1760 Major Robert Rogers and a band of rangers camped on the banks of the Grand River where Fairport is now situated and negotiated with Chief Pontiac for the purchase of lands in this vicinity. The result of this effort seems not to have been recorded, but apparently it was unsuccessful since more than 30 years elapsed before steps toward settlement were taken.[8]

Four states, New York, Virginia, Massachusetts, and Connecticut had claims on the Northwest, but, with certain reservations, these lands were eventually ceded to the United States. Connecticut reserved ownership and jurisdiction over a strip south of Lake Erie north of the 41st parallel, and extending 120 miles westward from the Pennsylvania line. In 1792 Connecticut granted half a million acres of the western end of the Western Reserve to those inhabitants of certain Connecticut towns whose property had been destroyed by Tory raids during the Revolution. This region of the Reserve became known as the "Fire Lands." In May 1795 practically all the rest of the Reserve was offered for sale, and a few months later the land was sold without survey for $1,200,000 to a group of 48 men who organized as the Connecticut Land Company. In 1796 Moses Cleaveland led a party which included surveyors into the region.[9] From 1795 to 1800 the Reserve was without formal government, but in the latter year the United States was given jurisdiction and the entire Reserve was made into one county named in honor of Governor Trumbull of Connecticut.[10]

The directors of the Connecticut Land Company selected, to offer for sale to actual settlers only, six townships in which the first improvements were to be made. Three of these were in the area included in present-day Lake County; namely, Madison, Mentor, and Willoughby Townships. The remainder of the Reserve east

---

6. Harvey Rice, *Pioneers of the Western Reserve* (Boston and New York, 1898), 286.
7. C. B. Crary, *Pioneer and Personal Reminiscences* (Marshalltown, Iowa, 1893), 4
8. Hillis, *op. cit.,* 3.
9. Eugene Holloway Roseboom and Francis Phelps Weisenburger, *A History of Ohio* (New York, 1934), 71, 94.
10. Williams, *op. cit.,* 21-22.

of the Cuyahoga River was divided in a complicated manner. The four best townships in the eastern part of the Reserve were selected and surveyed into lots, an average of 100 lots to the town to the township. As there were 400 shares of stock in the company the four townships would yield one lot for each share. Perry Township in Lake County was one of these four townships. Then the directors selected as equalizing townships certain other tracts which were considered next in value to the four already selected. These included Concord, Painesville, and Kirtland Townships in Lake County.[11] As was the case throughout the Reserve, the land was surveyed into townships five miles square, but because of the irregularity of the lake shore the townships bordering upon it are fractional.[12]

The first permanent settler in Lake County was John Walworth, who established himself near Mentor in 1799. Charles Parker, an early surveyor, built a cabin in the county in about 1796, but remained only temporarily.[13] Within a short time settlement had been undertaken in each of the townships of the county: Mentor in 1798 by Charles Parker, Jared Ward, and Moses Park; Willoughby in 1798 by David Abbott; Painesville in 1800 by John Walworth; Madison in 1802 by John Harper; Concord in 1802 by William Jordan; LeRoy in 1802 by Colonel Amasa Clapp; Perry in 1808 by Ezra Beebee; and Kirtland in 1810 by John Moore, Jr.[14] Willoughby was originally called Chagrin but in 1834 the name was changed in honor of Professor Willoughby of Herkimer County, New York.[15]

One of the largest stockholders in the Connecticut Land Company was Henry Champion, who, in 1805, surveyed the site of a town which for a time was called Champion. This village later took the name of Painesville from Edward Paine, an officer of the Revolution, who had settled in this region in 1799 or 1800.[16] Another prominent figure and pioneer, Samuel Huntington, was one of several men who, in 1803, erected a warehouse at the mouth of the Grand River. However, a pioneer named Joseph Rider had settled here as early as 1803. In 1825 the harbor

---

11. Williams, *op. cit.,* 12-13; H. B. Stranahan and G. C. Corey, *Atlas of Lake County Ohio* (Cleveland, 1898), 8-9.

12. Simeon D. Fess, ed., *Ohio Reference Library* (Chicago and New York, 1937), III, 163.

13. Hillis, *op. cit.,* 3.

14. Williams, *op. cit.,* 20.

15. Henry Howe, comp., *Historical Collections of Ohio* (Norwalk, 1896), II, 34.

16. *Ibid.,* 42; William Stowell Mills, "Lake County and its Founder," *Ohio State Archeological and Historical Quarterly,* X (1902), 361-371

became so important that the United States built a lighthouse there, and in the years following made improvements on the harbor. Its most prosperous period was between 1842 and 1852 when it was the outlet for much of northern Ohio, but after the advent of railroads the village declined in importance as a business center. In 1847 it exported $462,028 in merchandise, of which cheese and cereals were highest in value.[17] About a mile above Fairport, Thomas Richmond established the village of Richmond in 1832, which for a time promised to be the most important shipping center in the county, but after 1835 it gradually declined.[18] The pioneer physician in the county was John H. Mathews, who came to Painesville in 1808.[19]

The War of 1812 caused a temporary cessation of settlement in the county, the pioneers were discouraged from settling in this region by the surrender of Detroit by General Hull in 1812. There was a call for all capable of bearing arms to assemble at Sandusky in order to make a stand against the expected invaders. However, after the British and Indians had failed to take Fort Meigs and Fort Stevenson, the volunteers returned to their homes and no further fears were felt concerning settling in the region. At the close of the war a wave of immigrants began to arrive.[20]

In the 1830s Kirtland Township was invaded by a large group of Mormons whose religious principles aroused much controversy. Sidney Rigdon was an ardent Campbellite minister at Kirtland, but became a Mormon convert and in 1830 many of his congregation adopted this faith. In the spring of 1831 many Mormons from Palmyra, New York, came to Kirtland, among them being Joseph Smith, the prophet, and Brigham Young. In 1834 a large temple costing about $40,000 was erected and the settlement began to assume large proportions. Between 2,000 and 3, 000 Mormons settled in the vicinity of Kirtland and a bank, a printing press, stores, and other enterprises were established and appeared to prosper. At Kirtland the Latter-day Saints perfected the fundamentals of their religious organization, including their doctrine of faith and their policies for regulating both the temple and spiritual activities of their members. Polygamy however, was not officially proclaimed until long after the church had moved from Ohio.

---

17. Williams, *op. cit.,* 219; Howe, *op. cpt.,* II, 43.
18. Warren Jenkins, Ohio Gazetter and Travelers' Guide; . . . (Columbus, 1837), 348; Fess, *op. cit.,* III, 164.
19. Williams *op. cit.,* 31.
20. Crary, *op. cit.,* 4-10.

The Mormons were bound together by ties of economic as well as religious interests and prospered to a remarkable degree.

Their prosperity, however, proved to be short-lived. Their bank was unable to redeem the script that it had issued, judgments were rendered by the courts against the property of the Mormon leaders, and religious prejudice rose so high against the sect in neighboring communities that Rigdon and Smith were tarred and feathered. In 1838 the majority of the group moved to Missouri, leaving only a small number of the sect in Kirtland. The family of a Mr. and Mrs. Stratton held the key of the temple and claim to have a title to it, but in 1880 a court decision returned the temple to the Mormons and it became the center of this religion in Ohio. In 1873 a group which called itself the Reformed Church of Latter-day Saints came to Kirtland and it became the leading Mormon group there.[21] The temple remains standing today and may be viewed by the public.

Despite the loss of its Mormon population, Lake County steadily grew, and in March 1840, was organized as a separate county, taking seven of its townships from Geauga County, and Willoughby Township from Cuyahoga County.[22] As the eight townships did not embrace sufficient territory to meet the conditional requirements for a county, the deficiency was supplied by including the waters of the lake in the northern boundary.[23] The county is bounded on the north and northwest by the lake, on the east by Ashtabula County, on the south by Geauga County, and on the west and southwest by Cuyahoga County. It is the smallest county in the state, containing only 215 square miles.[24] No changes have ever been made to its boundaries.[25] Without serious controversy Painesville was made the county seat, and the courthouse, begun in 1840, was eventually completed in 1852, though occupied some years earlier.[26]

---

21. Emilius O. Randall and Daniel J. Ryan, *History of Ohio* (New York, 1912), III, 403-429; Harold E. Davis, "Religion in the Western Reserve," *Ohio State Archaeological and Historical Quarterly*, XXXVIII (1929), 495-496; Williams, *op. cit.*, 247-248; Crary, *op. cit.*, 33-35; Fess; *op. cit.*, III, 166; Howe, *op. cit.*, II, 34-41.
22. *Laws of Ohio*, XXXVIII, 171.
23. Williams, *op. cit.*, 24.
24. Hillis, *op. cit.*, 3.
25. Randolph Chandler Downes, "Evolution of Ohio County Boundaries," *Ohio State Archaeological and Historical Quarterly*, XXXVI, (1927), 463.
26. Williams, *op. cit.*, 24.

Since most of the early settlers of the county came from New England, the region naturally became a center for the activities of the Underground Railroad in the pre-Civil War period. Madison was one of the most important stations, and George Harris, of *Uncle Tom's Cabin* fame, was once arrested there.[27] However, the industrial and agricultural opportunities attracted settlers from many sections to this region, not the least famous being James A. Garfield whose home in Mentor has recently been acquired by the Western Reserve Historical Society as a museum. In 1840 the population of the county was 13,719; in 1860, 15,576; in 1880, 16,326; and in 1900 , 21,680.[28] Among the unusual settlers who came into Lake County were the Finns who settled at Fairport Harbor and vicinity about 1880. About 2,500 persons of this nationality came to the county and proved to be most industrious and desirable citizens.[29] By 1930 the population of the county had grown to 41,674 inhabitants of whom 83.7 percent were native-born whites.[30] Of the 6,173 foreign-born whites, the largest numbers came from Finland, Hungry, Italy, England, Germany, and Czechoslovakia.[31]

In 1930 Painesville, with a population of 10,944, was the only city in the county. There were, however, 13 incorporated villages; Kirtland Hills, Waite Hill, Mentor-on-the-Lake, North Perry, Lakeline, Willowick, Willoughby, Madison, Mentor, Fairport Harbor, Richmond, Perry, and Wickliffe. The first six of these villages were incorporated in recent years chiefly because of the progressive urbanization of the western part of the county as the area became a region of suburban homes in the Cleveland metropolitan district.[32]

Like most Ohio counties, Lake was predominantly agricultural in the early years of settlement. This tendency was aided by favorable conditions, the average temperature of the county being about 48 degrees, the rainfall 40 inches, and the growing season from 150 to 178 days.[33]

---

27. Charles B. Galbreath, *History of Ohio* (Chicago and New York, 1925), I, 374; Hillis, *op cit.,* 25.

28. U.S. Bureau of the Census, *Twelfth Census of the United States, 1900, Population,* I, 35.

29. Eugene Van Cleef, "The Finns in Ohio," *Ohio State Archives and Historical Quarterly,* XLIII (1934), 454-456.

30. U.S. Bureau of the Census, *Fifteenth Census of the United States, 1930, Population,* III, pt. ii, 481.

31. *Ibid.,* 500-501.

32. Fess, *op. cit.,* III, 169.

33. Roderick Peattie, *Geography of Ohio, Geological Survey of Ohio,* series iv, Bulletin XXVII (Columbus, 1923), 15-21.

The pioneers soon learned that the conditions of soil and climate were particularly favorable for the cultivation of fruit as well as of the cereals and grasses.[34] For some years the county led Ohio in the production of pears, grapes, and onions, and was noted for its dairy products, especially cheese.[35] In 1854, a nursery was established at Painesville, which proved so successful that several others were opened in the county. This industry has become nationally famous, maple sugar was produced in large quantities in the early period and fine cattle were bred.

In 1930 there were 1,059 farms occupying 44 percent of the area of the county, and of these farms 52.4 percent were in crop lands, 17.4 percent in woodlands, and 27.1 percent in pastures.[37] The land and buildings were valued at $26,749,690,[38] and produced products valued at $1,692,299 of which dairy products were the largest item.[39] The grand tax duplicate for the county in 1933, was more than $85,000,000;[40] it is apparent therefore, that agricultural wealth constituted no less than one-third of the taxable property in the county. In 1930 the county exceeded the state average in value and production of fruit, and raised more grapes than any other county. The average income from farms in 1935 was $1,487, as compared with $1,112 for the state.[41] In 1930 only 9.3 percent of the farms were operated by tenants,[42] but in 1935 this had increased to 15.3 percent. This figure, however, was still considerably lower than that of the state as a whole.[43] In 1930 over 44 percent of the farms of the county were mortgaged,[44] but despite this handicap, the relief cost for the county in 1934 were only $4.72, in contrast with the state average of $9.22 per capita.[45]

---

34. Hillis *op. cit.,* 4.
35. Fess, *op. cit.,* III, 166.
36. Williams *op. cit.,* 213, 214. *et passim.*
37. U.S. Bureau of the Census, *Fifteenth Census of the United States, 1930, Agriculture,* II, pt. i, 405.
38. *Ibid.,* 418.
39. *Ibid.,* III, pt. i, 299.
40. Ohio State Auditor, *Annual Report, 1934,* 481.
41. Ohio Study of Local School Units, *A study of Public Schools of Lake County, with Recommendations for the Future Organization* (mimeographed, Columbus, 1937), 5. Hereafter sited, *Lake School Survey.*
42. U.S. Bureau of the Census, *Fifteenth Census of the United States, 1930, Agriculture,* II, pt. i, 470.
43. *Lake School Survey,* 7.
44. U.S. Bureau of the Census, *Fifteenth Census of the United States, 1930, Agriculture,* II, pt. i, 470.
45. *Lake School Survey,* 9.

Of the total number of workers gainfully employed in the county, 17.8 percent were in agriculture in 1930,[46] and the population is about equally divided between urban and rural residence.[47]

The earliest industrial developments in Lake County were based upon the primary products of wood and grain. In 1807 Joel Scott constructed a damn across the Grand River and erected a grist mill and a sawmill. This example was followed by many similar enterprises in the county.[48] Because of easy availability of bog iron, iron furnaces were opened at Mentor in 1821; in 1822 a forge was in operation; and in 1825 an iron works in Painesville made stoves, castings, and hollow ware. In 1830 there were four furnaces in operation at Painesville and vicinity. However, the lack of coal made this industry economically impracticable when strong competition began to arise.[49] Numerous other enterprises were undertaken at Painesville; in 1819 a distillery, in 1850 a plow works, in 1853 a mill machinery plant, in 1855 a planing mill, in 1859 a steam engine and a mill machinery factory, in 1864 a fence material plant, in 1865 a boot and shoe factory, and in 1868 of a carriage factory. Plants for the production of cheese and of cider products were also built at an early period. In 1869 Charles Ruggles of Huron opened a commercial fishery at Fairport Harbor which soon developed into a large industry.[50]

At present many products are manufactured in the county. The most important are: veneer cutting machinery, washing powder, phenol, lye, soda ash, barium products, baskets, coke, metallic carpet trimmings, brass and rubber goods, fabricated steel, cranes, tools, and lamp shades. Other products include dairy products, wine, and fish.[51] In 1930 there were 48 industrial establishments in Lake County, employing 3,537 workers, and manufacturing products worth $29,639,210.[52]

---

46. U.S. Bureau of the Census, *Fifteenth Census of the United States, 1930, population,* III, pt. ii, 510.
47. *Ibid.,* 481.
48. Williams, *op. cit.,* 217, *et passim.*
49. Williams, *op. cit.,* 217, 251; Wilbur Stout, "Early Forges in Ohio," *Ohio State Archaeological Archives Historical Quarterly.* XLVI (1937), 27, 35-37; John Kilbourne, *The Ohio Gazetteer . . .* (Columbus, 1831), 233.
50. Crary, *op. cit.,* 23; Williams, *op. cit.,* 213, 214, 235, *et passim;* D.J. Lake, *Atlas of Lake and Geauga Counties Ohio* (Philadelphia, 1874), 12-13.
51. N.W. Ayer and Son's, *Directory of Newspapers and Periodicals* (Philadelphia, 1937), 715-734, *passum.*
52. U.S. Bureau of the Census, *Fifteenth Census of the United States, 1930, Manufacturers,* III, 398.

In that year, 748 workers were unemployed and 211 temporarily laid off in the county, which represents a higher percentage than in purely agricultural counties.[53]

The rapid development of Lake County was due in part to the fact that three of the oldest roads in northeastern Ohio passed through this area. The natural highway leading through the county was the ancient lake-shore route. Under the direction of the Connecticut Land Company a road was surveyed in 1798 by Thomas Sheldon, which followed, in the main, this old trail from the Pennsylvania line toward the Cuyahoga River. This was known as the "Gridled Road." A road called the Old State Road extended northwest from Warren and entered Lake County in Concord Township where it turned north and continued on to Fairport. The third historic highway was known as the Chillicothe Road which led south to Kirtland and thence to its terminus at the old capital of Ohio.

A great volume of produce from the back country came down to the shores of Lake Erie through Lake County to be loaded upon the sailing vessels, and, after 1817 the steamboats, which called at Fairport Harbor. In 1845 a line of stages ran from Wellsville on the Ohio River to Fairport, using the Painesville and Warren plank road, one of the old toll roads of the county. A crude railroad with wooden rails protected by strap iron was completed in 1837 from Fairport to Painesville. It required two years to construct these three miles of track, over which horses drew the cars. This was probably the first railroad in Ohio. The first steam railroad in the county was the Cleveland, Painesville, and Ashtabula on which work was begun in 1849. It was open from Cleveland to the Pennsylvania line in 1852, and later became part of the New York Central system. Fairport's dream of becoming a railroad terminus was not realized until 1872 with the completion of a railroad running south to Chardon. It was extended on to Youngstown in 1874. The Baltimore and Ohio, which acquired this line, developed the old village of Richmond with elevators, warehouses, and shops. The docks and northern connection at Fairport had made that harbor an important place for the shipment of coal, iron ore, and other commodities. The first electric traction line was opened between East Cleveland and Painesville in 1896.[54] There are four railroads in the county at present of which the New York Central, the Baltimore and Ohio, and the Nickel Plate are the most important.[55]

---

53. *Ibid., Unemployment*, I, 799.
54. Fess, *op. cit.*, III, 165; Hillis *op. cit.*, 4.
55. Ohio Tax Commission, *Annual Report, 1934*, 72.

In addition, 561 miles of highway have been constructed.[56]

The first bank in the county was the Bank of Geauga, established at Painesville in 1829. This bank merged with the First National Bank of Painesville in 1864. In 1854 a private bank was established there, and in 1860 the Lake County bank was opened. The exchange bank was organized at Madison in 1875, and by 1912 the county had four banks, two of which were branches of the Cleveland Trust Company.[57]

The settlers of Lake County carried with them the New England appreciation of education, and in the early years of settlement many schools were opened. Abraham Tappan held school in a log hut near Painesville in 1804-1805, and his work was later taken over by Hugh MacDougall, Franklin Paine, and Flavis J. Huntington who taught at Painesville from 1816 to 1849.[58] The Huntington Private School was the first to be incorporated in the county.[59] Grammar schools were also soon opened in other townships: in 1811 in Mentor, in 1814 in Leroy and Kirtland, in 1815 in Concord and Perry, and in the other townships soon after.[60] These schools were of the tuition type and the teachers were poorly paid. Lovina Hulbert taught at Leroy for the salary of 75 cents a week and her board.[61]

In 1823 George Thompson open a classical school, which was succeeded in 1831, by an academy operated by the Painesville Education Society. The school continued until about 1850 and at one time, had an enrollment of 300 students. In 1838 Painesville and contiguous territory were divided into three school districts and the schoolhouse was erected. The Akron Plan of school organization was adopted in 1851 and the Education Society transferred its property to the union school district.[62]

Several other academies and colleges were founded in Lake County though some of them were short-lived. From 1833 to 1846 a medical college was located in Willoughby, but because of rumors of body snatching, it was obliged to move.

---

56. *Lake School Survey*, 10.

57. Williams, *op. cit.*, 216, 235; Hillis, *op. cit.*, 69.

58. Williams, *op. cit.*, 36.

59. W.W. Boyd, "Secondary Education in Ohio Previous to the Year 1840," *Ohio State Archaeological and Historical Quarterly*, XXV (1916), 123.

60. Williams, op. cit., 246, 250 *et passim*.

61. *Ibid.*, 230.

62. Williams, op. cit., 36-37.

Western Reserve teachers' seminary open at Kirtland in 1839 in the old Mormon Temple under Reverend Slater, and remained in operation until about 1853. This was one of the earliest normal schools in Ohio. The Lake Erie Female Seminary was established in the old medical college building at Willoughby in 1847, but after a fire in 1856, the school was re-established at Painesville as the Lake Erie Seminary. This institution was an outgrowth of Mount Holyoke Seminary in Massachusetts and many of its faculty were graduates of that school. It was re-organized in 1898 as the Lake Erie College and Seminary and its curriculum was broadened to get full college training. This college has retained its vigor and popularity to the present time. From 1845 until 1884 a seminary was operated at Madison, but in 1888 the buildings and grounds were donated to the National Women's Relief Corps and later made into a home for Ohio's soldiers and sailors. The Andrews School for Girls was another academy established by the wealth of one of the earliest families of Willoughby.[63]

Madison Township in Lake County was the second school district in Ohio to start a movement for the consolidation of schools, and by 1934 there were no one-room schools in the county.[64] At present there are 7,067 children enrolled in the schools of the county.[65] While the percentage of the illiteracy for the entire population is 2.5 percent,[66] the large element of foreign population may account for this comparatively high figure.

Churches were also established at an early date. In 1810 the first church of Painesville was organized by Reverend Nathan B. Darrow of the Connecticut Missionary Society and was a union of Presbyterians and Congregationalists.[67] The Methodists were organized in Painesville in 1820.[68] In other townships also churches were organized; in Leroy there was a Presbyterian mission in 1811 and a Baptist organization in 1826; in Madison there was a Congregational Church in 1814; in Concord, a Methodist Church in 1818 and a Congregational Church in

---

63. *Ibid.,* 36-40; Fess, *op. cit.,* III, 169; Edward A. Miller, "The History of Educational Legislation in Ohio from 1803 to 1850," *Ohio State Archaeological and Historical Quarterly,* XXVII, (1918), 100-117.
64. *Lake School Survey,* 3.
65. *Ibid.,* 22.
66. U.S. Bureau of the Census, *Fifteenth Census of the United States, 1930, Population,* III, pt. ii, 481.
67. Williams, *op. cit.,* 215.
68. I.F. King, "Introduction of Methodism in Ohio," *Ohio State Archaeological and Historical Quarterly,* X, (1902), 187.

1834; in Perry, Methodist meetings were held in 1815; in Kirtland, a Presbyterian Church in 1818 and a Methodist Church in 1820; in Mentor, Reverend Ira Eddy organized a Methodist Church in 1816, and the same year this sect established a church at Willoughby.[69] In 1926 there were 15,041 church members in the county of whom 4,916 were Roman Catholics, 2,830 Methodist, 1,350 Disciples of Christ, and 1,131 Congregationalist. Smaller numbers belonged to several other denominations.[70]

The oldest new newspaper in the county is the Painesville *Telegraph* established in 1822 by Eber D. Howe. Several other papers were published in this city but did not long survive. Among these were the *Republican*, issued by Horace Steele from 1836 to 1841; the *Grand River Record*, issued in 1852; the *Advertiser*, issued in 1855; and the *Northern Ohio*, issued in 1871. The latter paper espoused the Greenback idea, a scheme which gained considerable popularity in this region.[71] At present there are four papers published in Lake County; the Painesville *Telegraph*, a daily paper with Republican editorial policies; the *Lake County News-Herald*, a weekly independent paper, published at Willoughby since 1892; the Madison *Press*, a weekly newspaper, published since 1933 and non-partisan in its political views; and the *Amerikan Sanomat*, a weekly newspaper, issued at Fairport Harbor by the Finns. It is an independent Republican paper and has been printed since 1897.

---

69. Williams, *op. cit.,* 229+255, *passim.*

70. U.S. Bureau of the Census, *Religious Bodies; 1926,* I, 656, 658, 660.

71. Williams, *op. cit.,* 29-30.

The county as a political institution and as a subdivision of the state for purposes of political and judicial administration is of ancient origin.[1] In a form substantially similar in all general features and functions it has existed in England since early times, and in America since its settlement. As the tide of migration moved westward, following the American Revolution, the institutions of the seaboard states were transferred to the newer west, undergoing such alterations as best suited frontier conditions.[2]

The earliest provision for the organization of counties in what is now the state of Ohio was contained in the Ordinance of 1787, by which the governor of the Northwest Territory was directed to "lay out the parts of the district in which the indian [sic] titles shall have been extinguished into counties and townships subject however to such alterations as may therefore be made by the legislature".[3] The organization of county government, therefore, began before the organization of the state and before the adoption of a state constitution. Prior to statehood nine counties were organized. The first county lines were drawn in 1788.[4] The last county lines were altered in 1888, exactly 100 years later.[5]

The establishment of local government in the Northwest Territory was one of the first concerns of Governor St. Clair. The ordinance of 1787 furnished the framework, but details of institutions had to be constructed. All county officials, under the provisions of the ordinance, were made appointive by the governor.

---

1. Edward Channing, *A History of the United States* (New York, 1905), I, 512-519.
2. Beverly W. Bond, Jr., *The Civilization of the Old Northwest: A Study of Political, Social, and Economic Development, 1788-1812* (New York, 1934), 58-59.
3. Clarence Edwin Carter, ed. and comp., *The Territorial Papers of the United States* (Washington, 1934), II, 44.
4. *Ibid.,* III, 279.
5. *Laws of Ohio,* LXXXV, 418; Randolph Chandler Downes, "Evolution of Ohio County Boundaries," *Ohio State Archaeological and Historical Quarterly,* XXXVI, (1927), 449.

St. Clair, a former resident of Pennsylvania, in providing for local administration depended in a large part upon the Pennsylvania Code, which in some instances, was altered to meet the needs of the pioneer communities.[6]

The provisions for local administration were, for the most part, simple and effective. In each county the court of general quarter sessions of the peace, composed of three or more justices of the peace, served as the fiscal and administrative board of the county, estimating county expenditures, appointing tax commissioners, and providing for highway and bridge construction.[7] By the end of the decade the court was authorized to enter into contracts for building or repairing the county jail and the courthouse.[8] Other county officials appointed during the territorial period included a sheriff, a coroner, a recorder, a treasurer, a license commission, and justices and clerks of the various courts.[9]

Officers having been appointed, the next step in the organization of government was the establishment of a system of local courts. Evidence seems to indicate that the judicial system for the county had been carefully planned. The court of common pleas, composed of not less than three nor more than five appointive judges, was an inferior court having limited civil jurisdiction.[10] The court of general quarter sessions, of the peace, besides serving as a fiscal and administrative board of the county, had jurisdiction in lesser criminal cases.[11] A probate court, composed of a single judge, was given jurisdiction in probate and testamentary matters.[11]

---

6. The governor and judges were given power to "adopt and publish in the district such laws of the original states" as they thought necessary and these laws were to remain in force unless disapproved by congress. In many cases the governor and judges had not adopted laws of the original states, as the Ordinance stipulated, but had passed measures that conformed in spirit. Since there was some question of the legality of these laws St. Clair, in 1795, after the lower house of congress disapproved of the laws passed at the legislative session of 1792, called a legislative session to revise the territorial code. The commission, after sitting for three months, completed Maxwell's Code, named in honor of the printer, W. Maxwell. Few changes were made in the Maxwell Code by the territorial assembly which was elected in 1798. Carter, *op. cit.*, II, 43. The minutes of the legislative assembly were reproduced in the *Ohio State Archaeological and Historical Quarterly*, XXX (1921), 13-53.

7. Theodore Calvin Pease, comp., *The Laws of the Northwest Territory, 1788-1880 (Illinois State Bar Association Law Series*, Springfield, 1925, I), 4, 36, 337; 69-70; 467-478; 74, 77, 453, 456, 485.

8. *Ibid.,* 485.

9. *Ibid.,* 8, 24-25, 61, 68-69, 197.

10. *Ibid.,* 7.

11. *Ibid.,* 4-7.

A probate court, composed of a single judge, was given jurisdiction in probate and testamentary matters.[12] In 1795 following St. Clair's revision of the territorial code, circuit courts were established and orphans' courts were instituted.[13]

In the meantime the local government was further developed by the organization of civil townships. The governor and judges adopted a law from the Pennsylvania Code requiring the justice of the court of quarter sessions to divide each county into townships and appoint in each township a constable to serve specifically in his township and in the county, a clerk, and one or more overseers of the poor.[14]

The territory entered the second stage of administration when, in 1798, the population having reached the requisite 5,000 the governor ordered the election of a representative assembly.[15] The system of local government continued as established by the governor and judges, and the transition was achieved without a disturbance of local administration.

The admission of Ohio as a state did not, in the main, materially affect county organization and administration. The system of local government having been organized by the governor and judges and the legislature of the Northwest Territory, the basic offices were continued. Except for the provision for the election of a county sheriff and the county coroner in each county, two officials of upmost importance in pioneer communities, the constitution was silent on such matters as titles, number, and duties of officials.[16]

It developed, therefore, upon the legislature to confer powers upon the county. In 1804 the legislature made provision for a board of county commissioners, composed of three members elected for a three-year term.[17]

---

12. *Ibid.,* 9.
13. *Ibid.,* 157, 181-188.
14. *Ibid.,* 37-41, 338. The system a local governmental administration was the result of sectional compromise, since it combined the county system of the southern and middle states with the elements of the New England town. Dwight G. McCarty, *The Territorial Governors of the Old Northwest: A Study in Territorial Administration* (Iowa City, 1910), 53-54.
15. Carter *op. cit.,* III, 514-515.
16. *Ohio Const., 1802*, Art. VI, sec. 1.
17. *Laws of Ohio,* II, 150.

The board of county commissioners, supplanting the court of quarter sessions, became the administrative and fiscal board of the county. In 1803 the legislature, recognizing the need for a more adequate system of land records, provided for a recorder to be appointed by the court of common pleas for a seven-year term and for a surveyor to be appointed by the court of common pleas.[18] Another act authorized the appointment of a county treasurer by the associate judges, a later one provided for the appointment by the county commissioners.[19]

The legislature also provided during its first session for a prosecuting attorney to be appointed by the supreme court to prosecute cases on behalf of the state.[20] In 1805 the appointing power was transferred to the court of common pleas.[21]

The new office was created in 1820, that of county auditor. The auditor, first appointed by the legislature, had as his duty the preparation of the tax duplicate.[22] The county board of revision, the purpose of which was to correct some of the inequities of assessments, was established in 1825. The first board of revision or equalization, as it was sometimes called, was composed of the county commissioners, the auditor, and the assessors.[23]

The judicial power of the state in matters of law and equity was vested in the supreme court, the court of common pleas, and the justices' courts. The articles of the constitution provided for a court of common pleas to be composed of a president and associate justice. The members of the court, appointed by a joint ballot of both houses of the general assembly, were to hold court in three judicial circuits into which the state was to be divided by the legislature.[24] The court was assigned common law and chancery jurisdiction in all cases as provided by law.[25]

---

18. *Ibid.,* I, 136, 90-93.
19. *Ibid.,* I, 97-98; II, 154.
20. *Ibid.,* I, 50.
21. *Ibid.,* III, 47.
22. *Ibid.,* XVIII, 70.
23. *Ibid.,* XXIII, 68-69.
24. *Ohio Const., 1802,* Art. III, secs. 3, 8.
25. *Ohio Const., 1802,* Art. III, sec. 3.

To the court was assigned jurisdiction in probate and testamentary matters and in the appointment of guardians, functions performed during the territorial period by the probate court.[26] Finally, the court was authorized to appoint a clerk.[27]

The county offices graded by the legislature were designed to transact the business of a state as yet unaffected by transformations wrought by industrialism and the problems presented by large urban areas. Aside from the maintenance county poorhouses, the county had no functions in the administration of public welfare.

As the wave of democratic philosophy swept across the county in the eighteen twenties and thirties there arose a demand not only for an extension of the franchise but also for the election of public officials. Accordingly the auditor became an elective official in 1821, the treasurer in 1827, the recorder in 1829, and the prosecuting attorney in 1833.[28]

While the legislature responded to the general demand for the election of county officials, there arose a further demand for a revision of the constitution which failed to meet the needs of the expanding state. This movement came as result of dissatisfaction with the judicial system which placed the burden of judicial administration upon four judges who had the task of holding court each year in all the counties.[29] Then, too, there arose a demand for the election of all public officials, for the prohibition of charters that granted special privileges, and for a limitation on the power of the legislature to create a state debt. In February 1850 the legislature, following a favorable popular vote on the proposition, called for the election of delegates to meet in convention in May. The constitution drafted by the delegates, was approved by special election on June 17, 1851. The constitution of 1851, like the constitution of 1802, failed to provide a definite form of county government and administration.

---

26. *Ibid.,* Art. III, sec. 5; Pease, *op. cit.,* 9.

27. *Ibid.,* Art. III, sec. 9.

28. *Laws of Ohio,* XIX, 116; XXV, 25-32; XXVII, 65; XXXI, 13-14.

29. J.V. Smith, rep., *Official Reports of the Debates and Proceedings of the Ohio State Convention . . . held at Columbus Commencing May 6, 1850, and at Cincinnati, Commencing December, 1850* (Columbus, 1851), 597 *et seq.* (Jacob) Burnet, *Notes on the Early Settlement of the north-Western Territory,* (Cincinnati, 1897), 356. *See also the Ohio State Journal,* December 11, 1840

Aside from the constitutional provision for the election of a county treasurer, sheriff, and clerk of courts and re-creating the probate court which had existed during the territorial period, the organic instrument was silent on the administration duties of the county.[30] Again all matters pertaining to county government were entrusted to the legislature. While the legislature conferred certain powers upon the county, it was limited by constitutional provision which required all laws of a general nature to be uniform throughout the state.[31]

The present of administrative organization of Ohio county government presents a picture of extraordinary complexity. Each county quadrennially elects, besides the board of county commissioners, nine administrative officials; the recorder, the clerk of courts, the probate judges, the prosecuting attorney, the coroner, the sheriff, the treasurer, the auditor, and the county engineer. While these officials conduct a major portion of the county's business, there are a variety of appointive officers and boards, as well as of ex-officio commissioners. For convenience the work of county government may be classified under the following general heads: administration, judicial system, law enforcement, finance and taxation, elections, health, public welfare, and public works.

Administration

The board of county commissioners is the central feature of the present structure of county government. The functions of this board touch either directly or indirectly every other branch and department. The board is the agency in whose name actions for and against the county are brought. This board is empowered to determine certain matters of policy for the conduct of county affairs such as adoption of the budget, establishment of services left optional by law, and the authorization of improvement.[32] Thus, in a limited sense it constitutes the legislative branch of the county. The commissioners, however, have no ordinance-making powers.

---

30. *Ohio Const.,* 1851, Art. X sec. 3; Art. IV, sec. 16; Art. IV, sec. 7.
31. *Ibid.,* Art. II sec. 26.
32. *General ode,* sec. 2421.

The board also functions as a central administrative body although much of the administration, centered in other elective offices, is beyond its immediate control. The county auditor was originally made secretary of the board and still functions as such in a majority of the counties. Later provisions of the law permit the board to appoint its own clerk, thus removing this duty from the auditor.[33]

Judicial System

The constitution of 1851 made significant changes in the composition of the court of common pleas. The judges, heretofore appointed by the legislature, were made elective for a term not to exceed five years. For the purpose of electing judges the state was divided into nine districts. Each district was divided into three parts, in each of which one common pleas judge was to be elected. Court was to be held in every district or county with such jurisdictions as should be provided by law.[34] The legislature provided for the districts but left the jurisdiction of the court much as it had been in the earlier years of its existence.[35] The constitutional amendment of 1912 abolished the divisions and subdivisions provided by the constitution of 1851, and authorized the election of one or more common pleas judges in each county.[36]

The judicial system was extended in 1851 by the creation of district courts composed of one supreme court justice and several common pleas judges in each district.[37] For administrative purposes the nine common pleas districts were apportioned into five judicial circuits.[38] The courts were assigned original jurisdiction in the same manner as the supreme court and such appellate jurisdiction as might be provided by law.[39] The district courts, abolished by the constitutional amendment of 1883, were superseded by the circuit courts which were given the same jurisdiction as their predecessors.

---

33. *Laws of Ohio*, XIX, 147; G.C. sec. 2566.
34. *Ohio Const., 1851*, Art. IV, secs. 3, 4, 10.
35. Willis A. Estrich, *et al*, eds., *Ohio Jurisprudence*, XI, 827-839.
36. *Ohio Const., 1851*, (Amendment), Art. IV, sec. 3.
37. *Ohio Const., 1851*, Art. IV, sec. 5.
38. *Laws of Ohio*, L, 69.
39. *Ohio Const., 1851*, Art. IV, sec. 6.

The state was divided into seven circuits. In each district three judges were to be elected.[40] The judicial system was again altered in 1912 when, by constitutional amendment, the circuits were renamed courts of appeals.[41] The state is divided into nine appellate districts. There are three judges in each district elected by the people of the districts for a six-year term.[42]

The constitution of 1851 re-created the probate court, which, existing during the territorial period, was abolished by the first amendment, its authority and jurisdictions being then vested in the courts of common pleas. Each county has one probate judge elected by the people for a four-year term.[43] By constitutional provision, the probate judge has original jurisdiction in probate and testimentary matters, the appointment of guardians, the settlement of the accounts of executors, administrators, and guardians,[44] and the issuance of marriage licenses. An amendment to the constitution of 1912 authorized the common pleas judge, when petitions by 10 percent of the voters in counties having a population of less than sixty thousand, to submit to the voters at any general election the question of combining the probate and common pleas courts.[45] This combination exists in Adams, Henry, and Wyandot Counties.

Due to an increased amount of juvenile delinquencies, the legislature, in 1904, authorized the judges of the court of common pleas, the probate court, and the superior and insolvency courts where established, to appoint one of their members as juvenile judge to hear cases involving neglected, dependent, and delinquent children. In counties which have a court of domestic relations the judge of that court serves in this capacity. This is not the case in Lake County, which has no court of domestic relations. Here juvenile cases are brought before the probate judge.[46]

---

40. *Ibid.,* Art. IV, sec. 6; *Laws of Ohio,* LXXXI, 168.
41. *Ohio Const., 1851,* Art. IV, sec. 6 (Amendment, 1912).
42. G.C. sec. 1514.
43. *Laws of Ohio,* CXIV, 320; *Ohio Const., 1851,* Art. IV, sec. 7.
44. *Ohio Const., 1851,* Art. IV, sec. 8.
45. *Ibid.,* Art IV, sec. 7 (Amendment, 1912).
46. *Laws of Ohio,* XCVII, 561-562; G.C. sec. 1532.

Law Enforcement

Closely related to the courts are the agencies of law enforcement in the county. Law enforcement is conducted by four officials: sheriff, prosecuting attorney, coroner, and dog warden. These officials are concerned primarily with the enforcement of state laws, and leave the enforcement of municipal ordinances, and, in some instances, the state statutes in urban centers to municipal law-enforcement agencies.

The county sheriff whose duties have been materially curbed by municipal law-enforcement agencies and the state highway patrol, has as his duty the enforcement of state laws.[47] He serves as custodian of the county jail,[48] and as an executive agent of the courts.[49] It has been estimated that approximately one-half of the sheriff's time is devoted to duties connected with the courts. The sheriff is restricted by lack of scientific equipment which has become essential to law enforcement.[50]

The county prosecuting attorney, the most important agent and the enforcement of criminal law, is directed by law to "inquire into the commission" of crime within his county, and to prosecute on behalf of the state all complaints, suits, and controversies to which the state is a party.[51] In conjunction with the state attorney general, he prosecutes in the supreme court cases arising in his county.[52] He acts also in a civil capacity as legal counsel for the commissioners and other county officials.[53]

---

47. G.C. sec. 2833. The sheriff's authority extends to all parts of the county, although for obvious practical reasons he rarely makes an arrest in incorporated areas.

48. G.C. sec. 3157.

49. G.C. sec. 2834.

50. *The Reorganization of County Government in Ohio:* Report of the *Governor's Commission on County Government* (n.p., December 1934), 102 *et seq.* The sheriffs' system worked admirably in rural communities. From the standpoint of police administration, it is unsatisfactory in areas of dense population. In such areas there is need for a force of officers whose duty it is not merely to apprehend law violators but to prevent the infraction of the law by patrolling the territory. For an interesting discussion of some of the newer problems confronting law enforcement agencies see Donald C. Stone. "The Police Attack Crime," *Nat. Mun. Review,* XXIV, (1935), 39-41.

51. G.C. sec. 2916.

52. G.C. sec. 2916.

53. G.C. sec. 2917.

The prosecuting attorney may institute proceedings against an individual, but as a rule charges must be filed against the offender before action is taken. The prosecuting attorney has certain administrative duties such as serving as a member of the county budget commission and of the board of sinking fund trustees.[54]

The county coroner has the ancient duty of determining the cause of death where death occurs under suspicious circumstances or by unlawful means.[55] The proper distribution of property found on or about the deceased,[56] and the management of the county morgue.[57] It has been suggested by authorities on county administration that the office be abolished and the duties transferred to a medical examiner appointed by the prosecuting attorney.[58]

Another law-enforcement agent existing within the county is the dog warden. This official is appointed by and is responsible to the county commissioners. No special qualifications are required for the office. The dog warden has as his duty the enforcement of the sections of the General Code "relative to the licensing of dogs, the impounding and destruction of unlicensed dogs, and the payment of compensation for damages to livestock inflicted by dogs." The dog warden and his deputies, in the performance of their legal duties, have the same "police powers" as those conferred by statute upon sheriffs and police.[59] Prior to 1927 the duties now performed by the dog warden were performed by the county sheriff.[60]

---

54. *Laws of Ohio,* CXII, 399-400; CVIII, pt. i, 700-702.
55. G.C. sec. 2856.
56. G.C. secs. 2863, 2864.
57. G.C. sec. 2851-1.
58. W.F. Willoughby, *Principles of Judicial Administration* (Washington, 1929), 165-173. According to a recent act, effective June 8, 1937, only a licensed physician or a person who shall have previously served as coroner is eligible to fill the office. G.C. sec. 2856-3.
59. *Laws of Ohio,* CVIII, pt. i, 535; CXII, 348; G.C. sec. 5652-7.
60. *Laws of Ohio,* CVIII, pt. i, 535.

Law enforcement in the county is defective and two respects: first, there is little or no co-ordination between the four agencies of law enforcement, and second, there is little or no responsibility for neglect of duty. Evidence seems to indicate that the present inefficient and antiquated system could be corrected by consolidating all law-enforcement agencies into a county department of law enforcement under the immediate supervision of the county prosecuting attorney.[61]

The administration of criminal justice in the county has grown up in more or less hit-or-miss fashion and is for the most part unsatisfactory and extremely cumbersome. Arrests are made by the sheriff, or other police officers, who is theoretically an officer of the state, but who is under little or no supervision. The accused person is brought before a legal magistrate for a preliminary hearing. In the event the accused is committed, it is necessary, in most cases, to receive an indictment before a grand jury.[62]

Finance and Taxation

There are three types of financial functions performed by county officers: tax administration, handling of the physical affairs of the county, and the trustee ship of individuals in court procedure. The principal financial authorities are the board of county commissioners, the auditor, and the treasurer. The commissioners levy taxes, appropriate funds, and authorize payments.[63] The auditor's primary duties are the keeping of accounts, the issuance of warrants, the valuation of real estate, and the preparation of the tax list.[64] The treasurer collects taxes, receives and has custody of the county money, and disperses it upon warrant from the auditor.[65] Other functions relating to county finance are performed by the board of revision, budget commissioners, and board of sinking fund trustees.

---

61. *Reorganization of County Government,* 117-122.
62. For a criticism of the administration of criminal justice, see, Edwin H. Sutherland, *Principles of Criminology* (Chicago, 1934), chap. xiv: Willoughby, *op. cit.,* chaps. xi, xxxvi.
63. G.C. secs. 5630, 5637, 7419.
64. G.C. secs. 2568-2570, 2573, 2583-2589.
65. G.C. secs. 2649, 2649-1, 2656, 2674.

During the early years of Ohio history, the principal sources of state and county revenue were the general property tax, the poll tax, and fees received from licenses and permits to engage in certain kinds of business.[66]

A tax law enacted by first territorial legislature (1799) designated certain types of property as taxable for county purposes. All houses and towns, town lots, out- lots, all water and wind mills, ferries, cattle and horses, were put on the county tax duplicate. A tax on land, subsequently used for county purposes, was originally devoted exclusively to the needs of the territorial government. County officials were to assist in the administration of this tax as well as that of the county levy.[67]

In the course of time many editions were made to the original list of taxables. Taxable property came to include capital employed in merchandising (1826), and by exchange brokers (1825), pleasure carriages (1825), money loaned at interest (1831), and stock in steamboats.[68] In the latter year dividends of bank, insurance, and bridge companies were also made taxable.[69] The first act of a general nature directing the taxation of railroads was passed in 1851.[70] In 1862 a tax on the gross receipts of express and telegraph companies was enacted.[71] A levy on the capital stock of freight lines was authorized in 1896.[72] Subsequent enactments brought into the category of "general property" the possessions of public utilities in general. By such accumulations "property," by the end of the nineteenth century had become a much more inclusive term than it had been one hundred years earlier.

---

66. An act of 1825 levied a tax on the income of attorneys, physicians, and surgeons for state purposes. Amount of tax was determined by the court of common pleas. Salmon P. Chase, comp. *The Statutes of Ohio and of the North-western Territory, 1788-1833* (Cincinnati, 1833), 1471. This act was repealed in 1852. Maskell E. Curwen, comp., *Public Statutes at Large of the State of Ohio* (Cincinnati, 1853), 1755. The poll tax was perpetually abolished by constitutional authority and 1802. *Ohio Const., 1802,* Art. VIII, sec. 23.
67. Chase, *op. cit.,* 267-279. Previous acts of 1792 and 1795 were temporary in nature.
68. Chase, *op. cit.,* III, 1517; 1476; *Laws of Ohio,* XXIX, 272-280.
69. *Laws of Ohio,* XXIX, 302-303.
70. Curwen, *op. cit.,* 1647.
71. J.R. Saylor, comp., *The Statutes of the State of Ohio* (Cincinnati, 1876), 301.
72. *Laws of Ohio,* XCII, 89-93.

County agencies became even more useful with the discovery of new tax sources. When, at the turn into the twentieth century the general property tax lost its importance as a revenue source for the state, taxes on inheritance and cigarettes, then, later, on gasoline, liquid fuel, liquor, retail sales, malt, and the like, took its place.[73] County officials continued to administer the general property tax, which was devoted henceforth to the uses of local governments, but they assisted in the administration of a number of those newer taxes as well.

The assistance rendered by county officials has been equally extensive in the system of issuing licenses and permits. The issuance of marriage licenses began during the territorial period (1788).[74] An act to license merchants, traders, and tavern keepers was passed in 1792.[75] Ferry licenses were authorized in 1799.[76] With the passage of time, one license after another had been required until unlicensed businesses have become something of an exception rather than the rule. Even with the increasing assumption of license authority by the state, county officials have continued to issue certain licenses assigned to their jurisdiction long ago.[77]

The early laws (1792) county commissioners, appointed to annual terms by the courts of common pleas, were to list the male inhabitants above the age of 18, stocks of cattle, yearly value of improved land, and other property. Valuation of this property was made by township and village assessors, appointed annually by the court of common pleas.[78] These local assessors, who became elective in 1795, were again appointed in 1799.[79] In 1825 property valuation was assigned to a new official, the county assessor, also appointed by the court of common pleas.[80] This official, became elective in 1827, was succeeded in turn, in 1841, by township assessors to be elected annually.[81]

---

73. Ohio Tax Commission, *Financing State and Local Government in Ohio, 1900-1932* (mimeographed, Columbus, 1934), 2.

74. Chase, *op. cit.,* I, 101.

75. Chase, *op. cit.,* I, 114-115.

76. Chase, *op. cit.,* I, 219.

77. *See* p. XXXIV.

78. *Laws of the Territory of the United States Northwest of the River Ohio* (Philadelphia and Cincinnati, 1792-1796), II, 17-18.

79. Chase, *op. cit.,* 169, 273.

80. Chase, *op. cit.,* 1477.

81. Curwen, *op. cit.,* 775-779.

In conjunction with these administrators a system of real estate reappraisal was initiated. In 1846 county commissioners were directed to divide their counties into suitable districts and to appoint an assessor for each whose chief function should be to revise the valuation of real property.[82] An act of 1863 made these officers elective and provided for reappraisal every tenth year.[83] This was subsequently changed (1868) to every fifth year and in 1878 returned to the 10-year interval.[84]

In 1913 the assistance of county officers in tax administration was temporarily dispensed with and their duties were given to state officials. The county was again made an entire assessment district but district (or county) was directed to supervise and direct the assessment of real and personal property.[85] This attempt at unification of authority in the state was partially abandoned, however, in 1915 when assessment was returned to the county auditor and to elected township, village, and ward assessors.[86] In 1925 the latter officers were discontinued and the duties of assessment devolved upon the county auditor alone.[87]

The advent of the state tax commission brought no great alteration in the process of assessment. The county remains the basic unit and the county auditor continues to serve as an agent of the state. Though the state commission now assesses certain forms of property, certification is made to the county auditor. For example, public utilities are now assessed by the commission and proportional shares of the revenue are apportioned to the counties which contains such property.[88] Financial institutions report directly to the commission which certifies to each county auditor the assessment of each taxable deposit.[89]

---

82. Curwen, *op. cit.*, 1269.

83. Sayler, *op. cit.*, 413.

84. Sayler, *op. cit.*, 1641; *Laws of Ohio*, LXXV, 459.

85. *Laws of Ohio*, CIII, 786-787.

86. *Ibid.*, CVI, 246 *et seq.*

87. *Ibid.*, CXI, 486-487. Revaluation of real estate was required in 1925 and every sixth year thereafter.

88. G.C. sec. 5430.

89. G.C. secs. 5411, 5412, 5412-1.

Intangible property (defined in 1931) owned by individuals and corporations, not otherwise excepted, is listed and valued by the county auditor. Returns showing more than $500 in taxable income are forwarded to the commission for appraisal and certified by it back to the county auditor.[90] From these certifications of the commission, the personal property list returned to him by individuals, and the real estate assessment for which he is personally responsible, the auditor makes up the grand duplicate of real and personal property taxes.

The county continues to be the basic unit also in the matter of budgeting and levying of taxes on property. In 1792 the courts of general quarter sessions were directed to estimate the sums needed to defray the cost of county government, specifying as nearly as possible the purposes for which such sums were necessary. This earliest of budgets was to be laid before the governor and judges and approved by the legislature. Special commissioners were to apportion or levy the tax.[91] In 1799 it became the duty of these commissioners to ascertain the probable expenses of the county as well as levy the tax – a duty which continued until refinements in administration were made necessary because of the increasing number of taxing authorities.[92]

In order to achieve some systematic arrangement in the county fiscal system, the function of estimating expenses, or budgeting, was consolidated in recent years in the hands of a county budget commission. Since the Ohio legislature, in 1911, estimated a tax rate limitation, it was necessary to establish a commission vested with the authority to reduce the amounts set up in the annual tax budgets when the overlapping districts required more than the aggregate maximum tax rate permits.[93] The county budget commission organized in 1911 was composed, for a time, of the auditor, the mayor of the largest municipality, and the prosecuting attorney. The taxing authorities in the county were directed to submit their budgets to this body through the agency of the auditor.[94]

---

90. *Report of the Governor's Commission,* 75; G.C. secs. 5372-3, 5376, 5377.

91. Chase, *op. cit.,* I, 118-119.

92. Chase, *op. cit.,* I, 276-272.

93. G.C. sec. 5625-3. Since 1934 there has been a limitation of 10 mills on the dollar. G.C. sec. 5625-2.

94. *Laws of Ohio,* CIII, 270-272.

The board was authorized to make adjustments in the budgets, alterations which the taxing authority might appeal to the tax commission. The budget commission, directed in 1911 to certify its action to the auditor, was subsequently instructed by law to make such certification to the various taxing units which should themselves authorize the necessary tax levies and certify them to the auditor.[95] In 1927 the composition of this board was altered when the county treasurer replaced the mayor.[96]

Early appeals against unjust assessments (1792), were heard by judges of the general territorial court, judges of the common pleas court, or justices of the general quarter sessions court.[97] After 1795 petitions for redress were directed to the county commissioners.[98] This appeal agency was superseded in 1825 by the board of equalization, composed of commissioners, assessors, and auditor.[99] This agency continued to function through the following years though occasionally changes in personnel were made.[100]

With the reorganization of property administration in 1913 the function of tax revision was taken away from the county officers. In each district (county) the tax commission was directed to appoint three persons for the term of 3 years to form a district board of complaints.[101] An act of 1915 abolished this plan however, and returned the function of revision to the care of county officials. A board composed of the treasurer, prosecuting attorney, probate judge, and president of the board of county commissioners, was directed to appoint a county board of equalization.[102]

---

95. G.C. sec. 5625-25.
96. *Laws of Ohio,* CXII, 399.
97. *Laws of the Territory of the United States Northwest of the Ohio River,* II, 20-21.
98. Chase, *op. cit.,* I, 171.
99. Chase, *op. cit.,* II, 1476-1492.
100. The county surveyor became a member at times, in 1868, for example. Sayler, *op. cit.,* 1642.
101. *Laws of Ohio,* CIII, 790-791.
102. *Ibid.,* CVI, 254-255.

This plan, too, was soon dispensed with. An act of 1917 constituted county treasurer, auditor, and president of the board of commissioners as a county board of revision.[103]

The history of tax collection is equally intricate. The fiscal duties of the county treasurer, who now collects the property tax, comprised, in the very early period, only the receipt and custody of revenue funds. The actual collection was performed by other agencies. Due to the fact that in earlier years, there were two district tax levies – one on land for territory and later the state, and one on property for county purposes – tax collections involved a double operation and duplicate officials.

The collectors of the county levy assessed in 1792 were appointed by the judges of the court of common pleas who were empowered to designate the sheriff, constable, or any other suitable person to perform this function.[104] By an act of 1795 township collectors were appointed by the commissioners and assessors.[105] From 1799 to 1805 taxes for county purposes were collected by county collectors.[106] An act of 1805 designated the township listers as collectors of the county levy but, in 1806, the commissioners were permitted to appoint a county collector instead if they believed such a course to be expedient. This arrangement remained in force until 1825.[107]

The first statute of a general nature providing for a tax on land for territorial purposes was enacted in 1799. From 1799 to 1803 the collectors of the county tax were to collect the territorial tax also.[108]

---

103. *Ibid.,* CVII, 40; G.C. secs. 5580, 5596. *See also* p. 175. Highest appellate jurisdiction, held originally by the general court and later (1805) by the associate judges of common pleas, was given, in 1825, to the state board of equalization composed of the state auditor and one member from each congressional district. Later these boards were composed of the state auditor and a member from each state senatorial district. With the establishment of the state tax commission that agency was made the body of final appeal. *Laws of Ohio,* III, 111; Chase, *op. cit.,* II, 1481; Curwen, *op. cit.,* 1784; G.C. sec. 5625-28.
104. Chase, *op. cit.,* I, 119.
105. Chase, *op. cit.,* I, 171.
106. Chase, *op. cit.,* I, 277.
107. Chase, *op. cit.,* I, 471, 5277; II, 771, 1384-5.
108. Chase, *op. cit.,* I, 270.

In 1804, however, the county sheriff was specifically designated as collector of the state tax.[109] From 1806 to 1816 the county commissioners were again permitted to use their own discretion as to whether a county or township collector should be appointed.[110] The county collector of the land tax mentioned in the statutes from 1816 to 1825 was, in all probability, the same official who collected the county tax, though due to a lack of definite terminology it is impossible to be certain.[111.]

In 1825 the arrangement for a separate tax duplicate for state and county purposes was abolished and levies for both were made on the same property. In 1827 the office of county collector, who had performed that function in the intervening two years, was abolished and the treasurer, henceforth to be an elective officer, was given the duty of tax collection.[112]

The collection of certain taxes other than that on general property is performed by county agency. Thus, for example, inheritance taxes, authorized by the legislature in 1894, are computed by the county auditor, adjusted by the probate court, collected by the county treasurer, and distributed to the proper agency by the county auditor.[113] County auditors certify to the tax commission lists of persons licensed to engage in the business of selling cigarettes. County treasurers are the agents of the state treasurer for the sale of cigarette tax stamps.[114] The tax on wines, cordials, and beer is collected by means of the sale of stamps by county treasurers in a manner similar to that employed in collecting the cigarette tax.[115] The tax on brewers' wort and malt is collected in an identical manner.[116]

The dispersal of administrative functions among county agencies is demonstrated more effectively, perhaps, in the issuance of licenses and permits which furnish a source of revenue of both the state and the county. The county auditor has issued, collected, and accounted for dog licenses from 1917 to the present.[117]

---

109. Chase, *op. cit.,* I, 415.
110. Chase, *op. cit.,* I, 537, 727; II, 973.
111. Chase, *op. cit.,* II, 973, 1370-71.
112. *Laws of Ohio,* XXV, 25.
113. G.C. secs. 5330, 5341, 5345, 5348-11.
114 G.C. sec. 5894-1 *et seq.*
115. G.C. sec. 6064-42.
116. G.C. sec. 5545 *et seq.*
117. *Laws of Ohio,* CVII, 534.

He has issued and the treasurer has collected the fees from cigarettes (1893—),[118] malt (1933—),[119] peddlers' (1862—)[120] and show licenses (1827—).[121] Hunting and fishing licenses have been issued by the clerk of courts since 1904 and 1919 respectively.[122] In addition, the clerk has issued for the court of common pleas ferry licenses (1805—),[123] auctioneers' licenses (1818—), [124] and peddlers' licenses (1810-1862).[125] Marriage licenses issued from 1803 to 1851 by the clerk of courts, since the latter date, have been in the jurisdiction of the probate court.[126]

The establishment of a board of trustees of the sinking fund (1919) was a logical development in county fiscal administration. This board, composed of the auditor, treasurer, and prosecuting attorney, has as its principal function the payment of bonds issued by the county and the investment in bonds of moneys credited to the sinking fund. Bonds issued in the process of county borrowing must be recorded in the office of the sinking fund trustees and signed by the auditor, as secretary of the board. The trustees certified to the board of commissioners the rate of tax necessary to provide a sinking fund for the payment of the principal and interest of the bonded and indebtedness. The trustees are required to keep a full and complete record of transactions and a complete record of the funded debt of the county.[127]

---

118. Jay F. Laning, comp., *Revised Statutes of the State of Ohio* (Norwalk, 1905), 1513.

119. G.C. sec. 5545-5 *et seq.*

120. Sayler, *op. cit.,* 273; *Laws of Ohio, LIX,* 67-68; G.C. sec. 6347.

121. Chase, *op. cit.,* III, 1582; G.C. secs. 6374, 6375.

122. *Laws of Ohio, XCVII,* 474; G.C. (Page and Adams) sec. 1430.

123. *Laws of Ohio,* III, 96; VIII, 107; XXIX, 447. Ferry licenses were issued by the associate judges 1803-1805. *Ibid.,* I, 94.

124. Chase, *op. cit.,* II, 1040; G.C. secs. 5868, 5869.

125. Chase, *op. cit.,* I, 670.

126. Chase, *op. cit.,* I, 354; *Ohio Const., 1851,* Art, IV, sec. 8.

127. G.C. sec. 2976-18 *et seq.*

Elections

During the first nine decades of Ohio history the county sheriff was charged with the duty of announcing the time and place of holding elections, providing ballot boxes, ballots, and other supplies, and the township trustees were directed by law to serve as judges of the elections.[128] This system continued, with slight alterations designed to facilitate the conduct of elections in municipal centers until 1892. At that time there were created the offices of state supervisor of elections and deputy state supervisors of elections with duties prescribed for the conduct and supervision of all elections in the state.[129] The secretary of state, designated as a state supervisor of elections, was authorized and instructed to appoint four deputy supervisors for each county, who, in turn, appointed in all precincts four judges and two clerks of elections.[130]

Under the present election laws, provision is made for a chief election officer, a board of elections in each county, and judges and clerks in each precinct. The board of elections in each county consists of four qualified electors in the county, the members of which are appointed by the secretary of state, two of such members being appointed on the first day of March in the even-numbered years to serve a four-year term.[131] In making appointments to the membership of the board, equal representation is given to the political party polling the highest and the next highest number of votes for the office of governor in the last preceding state election. In this connection provision is made for party recommendations of persons for such appointments.[132]

---

128. *Laws of Ohio,* I, 76-77; III, 331-332; VII, 113; XXIX, 44; L, 312.
129. *Ibid.,* LXXXIX, 455. This act, however, did not apply to the election of school directors.
130. *Laws of Ohio,* LXXXIX, 455. In 1870 each township, exclusive of the territory embraced within the limits of a municipal corporation which was divided into wards, composed an election precinct. *See Ibid.,* LXVII, 47. An act of 1891 provided for the division of precincts in which 500 or more votes had been polled. *Ibid.,* LXXXVIII, 464.
131. G.C. secs. 4785-6, 4785-8. *See also* p. 137.
132. G.C. sec. 4785-9. Under the Ohio election law, it is the duty of the secretary of state to appoint persons so recommended, unless he has reason to believe that such a person would not be a competent member of the board.

Under the early election laws the canvassing board was composed of the clerk of the court of common pleas and two justices of the peace called by him to his assistance.[133] This practice continued until 1892 when the board of state supervisors of elections succeeded to the duties formally performed by the clerk of the court of common pleas and the county sheriff. The sheriff, however, continued to announce the time and place of holding elections in the county until January 1, 1930 when the board of elections assumed this historic duty.[134] The duty of canvassing the returns, under the present statutes, is performed by the board of elections. The board in each county is required, within five days after each general or special election, to canvas the returns, and to prepare abstracts of the votes cast.[135] A certified copy of the abstract is to be transmitted to the secretary of state, and another copy filed in the office of the board.[136] The board is required also to prepare and transmit to the president of the senate a separate abstract of the returns of election of governor, lieutenant governor, secretary of state, auditor of state, and attorney general.[137]

Health

Prior to 1919 the county had few responsibilities regarding health administration. With the development of urban centers with congested areas the problem of health administration was brought to the attention of the legislature. Prior to the enactment of the present health code in 1919, jurisdiction in matters of health was vested in the cities, villages, and townships. Under the act of 1919 all villages and townships in the county were combined into a general health district under the supervision of a board appointed by the advisory council composed of the mayors of villages, and chairman of township trustees. Each city in the district is organized as a separate health district.

---

133. *Laws of Ohio,* I, 83; III, 336-337; VII, 119-120; XXIX, 49; L, 316; LXI, 68; LXXXII, 30.
134. G.C. sec. 4785-5; *Laws of Ohio,* LXXXIX, 455; CXIII, 307. The election laws of Ohio were revised and re codified by an act of the general assembly, passed April 5, 1929. *Laws of Ohio,* CXIII, 307-413.
135. G.C. secs. 4785-152, 4785-153.
136. G.C. sec. 4785-153.
137. *Ohio Const. 1851,* Art. III sec. 3; G.C. sec. 4785-154.

Two general health districts or a general health district and a city health district located within such a district may combine.[138] All physicians are required to report communicable diseases to the district health commissioners who impose quarantines.[139]

The legislature has placed on the county the burden of responsibility in the treatment of tuberculosis. Any county, regardless of its size, may employ nurses, operate clinics, and care for patients in private, municipal, or county sanatoriums. Any county having a population of 50,000 or more inhabitants may, with the consent of the state department of health, erect and operate sanatoriums, and two or more counties may form districts for the same purpose. The sanatoriums are operated by the county commissioners for special boards appointed by the county commissioners.[140]

Besides establishing sanatoriums for the treatment of tubercular patients, counties are authorized to operate general hospitals. The county hospital is operated by a board appointed by the county commissioners.[141] Evidence seems to indicate that the county is a proper unit for hospital administration.

Public Welfare

The administration of public welfare is one of the most complex and one of the most expensive functions of county government. The administration of institutional and outdoor relief is delegated to eight boards and commissions operating independently and with little regard for efficiency.

The administration of the county home is vested in the county commissioners and a superintendent appointed from a list of names of persons eligible under civil service regulations. Employees are appointed by the superintendent.[142]

---

138. *Laws of Ohio,* CVIII, pt. i, 238; CVIII, pt. ii, 1085-86.
139. *Laws of Ohio,* CVIII, pt. ii, 1088-89.
140. G.C. secs. 3148-1 - 3148-3.
141. G.C. secs. 3127 - 3138-4.
142. G.C. secs. 2522, 2523.

Although provision was made for the institutional care of the county's indigent as early as 1816, it was not until after the conclusion of the War between the States when hundreds of Ohio children were left homeless, that the legislature enacted measures for the care of dependent children.[143] Prior to the act of 1865, the trustees of the poorhouse were authorized to apprentice dependent children. The administration of the children's home is vested in the board of trustees, appointed by the county commissioners, and a superintendent appointed by the board of trustees.[144]

The board of county visitors, and agency for the examination of county institutions, was created by the general assembly in 1882. Until 1906 the board was appointed by the court of common pleas and after that date by the probate judge.[145] The board consists of six persons appointed for terms of three years.

In 1886 counties were required by law to provide relief for indigent soldiers and sailors and their indigent wives, children, and parents.[146] Soldiers' relief is administered by a commission consisting of three persons appointed by the court of common pleas for terms of 3 years. This commission, in turn, selects township and ward committees.[147]

In 1884 the legislature made provision for a soldiers' burial commission in each county.[148] The administration of soldiers' burials is vested in a commission consisting of two persons in each township and ward appointed by the county commissioners.[149]

Counties maintain a system of pensions for the needy blind. Prior to 1936 blind relief was administered in the county by the probate judge (1904-1908), by a blind relief commission appointed by the probate judge (1908-1913), and by the county commissioners (1913-1936).[150]

---

143. *Laws of Ohio,* III, 276; VIII, 223-224.
144. G.C. secs. 3081, 3084.
145. *Laws of Ohio,* LXXIX, 107; XCVIII, 28; G.C. sec. 2971.
146. *Laws of Ohio,* LXXXIII, 232-234.
147. G.C. secs. 2930, 2933.
148. *Laws of Ohio,* LXXXI, 146-147.
149. G.C. sec. 2950.
150. *Laws of Ohio,* XCVII, 392-394; CXVI, pt. ii, 86-88, 216-221; G.C. sec. 1359-2.

The present system originated in 1936 when the legislature accepted the provisions of the Federal Social Security Act. Blind relief is financed by Federal, state, and local funds and is administered in the state by the Ohio commission for the blind and in the county by the county commissioners, whose decisions are subject to review by the Ohio commission for the blind.[151]

Prior to 1932 the county confined its relief activities to the institutional care of the indigent. Outdoor relief, except for those persons lacking a legal settlement, was provided and administered by the townships and cities. With the coming of the economic depression the resources of the municipalities and townships proved inadequate for financing relief activities. Accordingly, in 1932, the legislature conferred on all counties the authority to care for the poor in their own homes. Funds for such purposes were provided by the issuance of bonds and by a diversion of gasoline taxes for financing such services. While the state relief commission, created for administering state relief, is required to pass upon local relief budgets, the county relief offices, administered by the county commissioners, provide relief services in the county.

Today old age pensions are relieving the counties of the increased burdens of institutional relief. This system, originating in 1933, provides for persons 65 or more years of age. No persons may be granted a pension if the net value of his property is in excess of $3,000 or his annual income is in excess of $480.[152] The old age pension system is financed by state and federal funds and is administered by a division of the department of public welfare through county boards of aid for the aged.[153] Under the provision of the initial act the county commissioners serve as ex-officio members of the board of aid for the aged in the county. Since May 1, 1937, the chief of the division has been required by law to appoint an advisory board in each county consisting of five members. This board, appointed for a two-year term, succeeded to the duties formally performed by the county commissioners.[154]

_____

151. *Ibid.,* CXVI, pt. ii, 195-200.
152. *Ibid.,* CXV, pt. ii, 431-439; CXVI, pt. ii, 86-88, 216-221; G.C. sec. 1359-2.
153. *Ibid.,* CXV, pt. ii, 431-439.
154. G.C. sec. 1359-12. *See also* p. 166.

Aid to dependent children, although provided by the legislature in 1913 and the form of mothers' pensions, assumed a new significance, when, in 1936, the legislature accepted the provisions of the Federal Social Security Act. Aid to dependent children is financed by Federal, state, and local funds. The administration of the act in the state is delegated to the department of public welfare in Lake County to the judge of the juvenile court.[155]

Public Works

The responsibility for the administration of public works in the county rests with the board of county commissioners, county engineer, and sanitary engineer. The county commissioners, since the inauguration of county government, have had the responsibility for the authorization and financing of public works. With the immense development of highway improvement, occasion by the introduction of automobiles and trucks as means of transportation, public works became one of the most important functions of the county commissioners and consequently the county engineer, who, during the first 120 years of his office, had as his principal duty the surveying of lands, received new duties responsibilities with respect to the construction of roads, culverts, ditches, and in most cases bridges.[156] Within the last two decades the township roads, under the joint authority of the county and township trustees, have been gradually absorbed by the county-state system of highways.[157]

---

155. *Laws of Ohio,* CXVI, pt. ii, 188-196.
156. *Laws of Ohio,* XCVIII, 245-247; CVIII, pt. i, 497.
157. The centralization of highway construction was guaranteed under the road law of 1915. The township trustees, at one time one of the most important agencies in local highway construction, have become a local improvement board with powers to authorize but not to supervise road construction. *Laws of Ohio,* CVI, 589-594.

The Ohio counties were formed to meet the needs of rural pioneer communities with a population spread relatively uniformly over the entire state. Recent decades have brought remarkable changes. Many sections of the state have become thoroughly industrialized, and, as a result of the change, have been forced to deal with such problems as housing, health, sanitation, police administration, scientific transportation, and sewage disposal. These problems with which the county organization has been unable to cope are rapidly taking the form of city problems.

When it is considered that in 1930, of the 1,201,455 persons in Cuyahoga County 900,429 were in Cleveland, that of the 361,455 people in Franklin County 290,564 were in Columbus that of the 589,356 people in Hamilton County 541,160 were in Cincinnati, and that of the 347,700 people in Lucas County 290,719 were in Toledo, it is not strange that demands were made for a reorganization of county government to eliminate the waste and confusion occasion by overlapping jurisdiction of county and municipal functions.[158]

In view of the growth of large cities and the confusion occasion by the conflict of county and municipal powers, there has been an attempt to work out a more satisfactory relationship between the two organs of local government. This took the form of a constitutional amendment, which, defeated in 1919, was placed on the ballot in 1933 by initiative petition and adopted by the electorate. The amendment provides:

"The general assembly shall provide by general law for the organization and government of counties, and may provide by general law alternative form of county government. No alternative form shall become operative in any county until submitted to the electors therefore and approved by a majority of those voting thereon under regulations provided by law. Municipalities and townships shall have authority, with the consent of the county, to transfer to the county any other powers or to revoke the transfer of any such power, under regulations provided by general law, but the rights of initiative and referendum shall be secured to . . . every measure . . . giving or withdrawing such consent."[159]

---

158. U.S. Bureau of the census, *Fifteenth Census of the United States, 1930, Population,* III, pt. ii, 518, 520, 521, 525. C.A. Dykstra, "Cleveland's effort for City-County Consolidation," *Nat. Mun. Review,* VIII (1919), 551-556.

159. *Ohio Const., 1851,* (Amendment, adopted November 7, 1933), Art. X, sec. 1.

The constitutional amendment of 1933 altered the status of the county. Where the status of the county was formerly fixed by statute, it is now subject to local determination in the same manner as municipalities.

The arguments advanced in favor of the system fall under three heads:

1.   It makes possible a different form of government for urban centers where political, social, and economic conditions differ from those rural counties.

2.   It promotes efficiency and economy by the elimination of duplicate officers and employees.

3.   It promotes efficiency by the centralization of power and responsibility.[160]

A commission on county government was appointed by Governor White in 1933 to formulate optional plans of county government for submission to the legislature.[161] Accordingly, in 1935, the commission submitted to the legislature 10 bills embodying its recommendations as to matters of county reorganization. The major bills authorized three optional forms of county government, subject to adoption by the local electorate (1) a county manager plan, (2) the elective plan, (3) the appointive executive plan.[162] Of the 10 bills presented, two became laws. One of these authorized the transfer to the county of any local governmental activity by voluntary agreement between the county and a local subdivision within the county. This measure, of course, opens the way for the consolidation as such activities as welfare, police, and sewer construction which need unification in counties having a large urban population.[163] The other act authorized the charter county to take over health administration, noninstitutional relief, and park construction.[164]

---

160. *Ohio State Journal.* October 9, 1933; Dykstra, *loc. cit.*
161. R.C. Atkinson, "County Home Rural Developments in Ohio," *Nat. Mun. Review,* XXIII, (1934), 235.
162. R.C. Atkinson, "Ohio– Optional County Legislation," *Nat. Mun. Review,* XXIV, (1935), 228.
163. *Laws of Ohio,* CXVI, 102-104.
164. *Ibid.,* CXVI, 132-135.

While the amendment offers an opportunity for the improvement of local government in counties in which large municipalities have developed, no use has been made of the provision.[165] At present Franklin County with a population of 361,055 has essentially the same type of county government as Vinton County with a population of 10,287.[166]

While unsuccessful attempts have been made to correct some of the defects of county administration in areas containing large urban populations, little consideration has been given to rural counties where, due to a constant decline in population, the old governmental organization has become unduly expensive and ill-suited to the needs of the population. This is particularly true in the counties located in the southeastern and northwestern portions of the state where the population has steadily declined since 1880. There is a question as to whether the services of modern government in such counties can continue to be maintained without the consolidation of continuous territory for purposes of administration. The Ohio Constitution, from its beginning in 1802, has contained a restriction upon the legislature regarding the minimum area of counties. None could be formed with less than 400 square miles or reduced below to that size.[167] With the development of modern means of transportation and communication this area is ridiculously small. The combination for administrative purposes of sparsely populated counties, having social and economic interests would eliminate waste, overhead, and duplication of personnel.

Governmental service is constantly requiring the employment of better trained officials. Evidence seems to indicate that only by enlarging the size of the administrative area to make possible the specialization in work can the requisite degree of training and skill be secured in the performance of public service.[168]

---

165. Home rule charters were submitted to the voters in Hamilton, Cuyahoga, Lucas, and Franklin counties. Advocates of home rule attributed to the defeat of those measures to politicians who saw in the scheme the destruction of the spoils system. *See* R.C. Atkinson, "Ohio– County Charter Elections," *Nat. Mun. Review,* XXIV, (1935), 702-703.

166. U.S. Bureau of the Census, *Fifteenth Census of the United States, 1930, Population,* III, pt. ii, 520, 531.

167. *Ohio Const., 1802,* Art. VII, sec. 3; *Ohio Const., 1851,* Art. II, sec. 30.

168. Cf. H. Eliot Kaplan, "A Personnel Program of County Service," *Nat. Mun. Review,* XXV (1936), 596-600.

The relation of the county to the state is also a matter of importance. As a result of radical changes in economic life, matters which were at one time a purely local interest and concern have become of state-wide importance. During recent years the old type of county organization has proved inadequate to meet the needs of modern civilization. Recognition of this fact is found in the steady growth of state control of such matters as public accounting, health and welfare administration, and law enforcement.

At the same time the county has definitely supplanted the township as the administrative unit. This is particularly noticeable in the substitution of the general health district for the township district, and the transfer of tax assessment from the township assessor to the county auditor. The county state administration of highway maintenance and public welfare has been affected. Although many deplore the passing of the little red schoolhouse, the substitution of the county school district for the township area has resulted in better educational advantages for children residing in rural areas.

It is significant that modern invention has removed the necessity for the rural administrative units of such small proportions. The transfer of power from the smaller to the larger unit has arisen out of the desire for better service and economy. Little remains to justify the retention of the township.

Records Systems

It has been the duty of most officials since the beginning of county government to keep a record of the business of their offices. Differences in population between counties however, forced a wide reference and the recording as evidenced by the fact that several types of records were kept in the same book in some counties, and in others were kept in separate books. As indicated in detail in the office essays, preceding the records of each office, the legislature eventually prescribed not only what records were to be kept but also the content. In this field there was a remarkable advance following the adoption of the constitution of 1851. Such legislation assured some uniformity in the county records system.

There are three clerical officers whose work consists mainly in the preparation and custody of records; the recorder, the clerk of courts, and the judge of the probate court. All three have some part in the recording of documents and instruments affecting the title of property and of other documents presented for record. The last two have as their principal duty the keeping of court records; the clerk of courts serves as clerk of both the court of common pleas and the courts of appeals, and the probate court keeps its own records.

It is the duty of the county recorder to copy, index, and file documents authorized to be recorded in his office. The system of recording is prescribed in detail by law. In most counties recording is done by typewriter with considerable use of printed forms. The photographic method of copying is in use in Clark, Hamilton, Lucas, Montgomery, and Summit Counties. Deeds, mortgages, plats, and leases must be copied into separate books, and indexed by direct and reverse indexes.[169] The recorder is required, also, to prepare daily an alphabetical index to such instruments.[170]

The principal records of the clerk of courts are prescribed by statute. They include an appearance docket, trial docket, execution docket, journal, and complete record of proceedings, a system of indexes, and a file of original papers.[171] The clerk is responsible for a variety of non-judicial records work of which the filing and indexing of automobile bills of sales was a major item. The bill of sale law was repealed by an act effective January 1, 1938, requiring the clerks to issue certificates of title to motor vehicles in triplicate and to file a duplicate of the certificate.[172] At present the clerk of courts may act as an agent of the state for the sale of hunting, trapping, and fishing licenses.[173] He also issues auctioneers' and ferry licenses.[174]

The office of the probate court performs the following clerical services: the recording of miscellaneous instruments, including marriage licenses[175] and certificates of physicians, surgeons, and nurses which authorize them to practice their professions in the state.[176]

---

169. G.C. secs. 2757, 2764.
170. G.C. secs. 2764, 2766.
171. G.C. secs. 2878, 2884, 2885.
172. G.C. secs. 6290-6.
173. G.C. secs. 1430, 1432.
174. G.C. secs. 5868-5869, 5947-5950.
175. *Ohio Const., 1851,* Art. IV, sec. 8.
176. *Laws of Ohio,* XCII, 45-47; XCIX, 499; CVI, 192.

The court record system of the office originating in 1853 and continued by the probate code of 1931, is prescribed by statute and involves a proper keeping of papers in each case and copying materials in appropriate record books.[177]

Few records are prescribed for the law-enforcement agencies. The county sheriff is required by law to keep at least three books: a foreign execution docket,[178] cashbook,[179] and jail register.[180] Indexes, direct reverse, to the foreign execution docket were prescribed in 1925.[181] The system of recording is prescribed by statute. The county coroner's records consist of two: a report of findings in cases of unlawful death,[182] an inventory of articles found on or about the body of the deceased.[183] Search records are required by law and the contents of the records minutely prescribed.

The number and type of records kept by prosecuting attorneys in the different counties of the state vary widely. In some counties the records of the prosecuting attorney are kept on standard forms and include such records as a grand jury docket, grand jury testimony record, and criminal court docket. In Lake County the grand jury records are kept by the clerk of courts. The prosecuting attorney keeps a criminal docket and files criminal records under four classifications: pending, disposed, and active, and liquor cases. The civil records are classified as pending cases, disposed cases, foreclosures of tax liens, tax claims, opinions on schools, and letter relative to county bank deposits. However in many counties of the state no records or files are kept and individual memoranda are disposed of by the incumbent. Since the prosecuting attorney is vested with large discretionary powers, there is need of special records and files. Such records according to authorities on judicial administration should include, among others, a permanent record of the names and addresses of witnesses, the deputy or division handling the case, and the reason for failure to prosecute, and the reason for which a *nollo prosequi* was asked and granted.

---

177. *Laws of Ohio,* CXIV, 321-322.
178. G.C. sec. 2837.
179. G.C. sec. 2839.
180. *Laws of Ohio,* XLI, 74; G.C. sec. 3158.
181. *Laws of Ohio,* CXI, 31.
182. G.C. sec. 2857.
183. G.C. sec. 2859.

Although records were kept in the earlier years, it was not until 1902 that the manner of keeping and the content of such records attracted the attention of the legislature. It was evident that accounts had not only been poorly kept but there had been little uniformity among the counties of the state. Accordingly, in 1902, the legislature enacted the most important and far-reaching laws on the subject. This act provided for a uniform system of accounting, auditing, and reporting, under the supervision of a newly created bureau of inspection located in the office of the auditor of state. The act further provided for the annual examination of the finances of all public offices.[184]

The governor's commission on the reorganization of county government, after studying the county records system and noting the illogical combination of administrating, judicial, and financial functions, made the following recommendations:[185]

1. County charters and the optional form of government should provide for a department of records and court service to take over the functions of the recorder and clerk of courts, the non-judicial record work of the probate court, and the functions of the sheriff as a court officer.

2. The issuance of licenses should be transferred from the clerk of courts to the department of finance.

3. Wider use should be made of the photographic process of recording in large counties.

4. Legislation should be adopted permitting the destruction of chattel mortgages and automobile bills of sale after they have ceased to have effect.

5. The requirement of three systems of indexes of cases in the clerk's office should be eliminated from the code and only the index of pending suits and living judgments should be required.

6. Provisions should be made in the rules of common pleas court for service of process by mail and that method should be brought into general use.

---

184. *Laws of Ohio,* XCV, 511-515.
185. *Report of Governor's Commission,* 186-187. *See also* R.E. Heiges, *The Office of Sheriff in the Rural Counties of Ohio* (Findlay, 1933). 55-56, 60-61.

Concurrently with the development of a record system, steps were taken to assure the proper restoration of damaged or dilapidated records treating of lands and surveys. The county engineer, when directed by the county commissioners, is required by law to transcribe any and all dilapidated maps and the records of plats and field notes of surveys on the records of the court of common pleas, auditor, recorder, or other officer in the state where they may be procured.[186] Similarly, the county recorder, being authorized by the county commissioners, is required to transcribe for the records of the counties all deeds, mortgages, powers of attorney, and other instruments of writing, for the sale, conveyance, or encumbrance of lands, tenements, or hereditaments, situated within his county.[187]

The large accumulation of county records occasioned by increasing governmental services, presents a serious problem. It is important, on the one hand, that valuable space in county courthouses and other county depositories be not cluttered up with vast quantities of useless materials. On the other hand, it is important that every precaution be taken to prevent public officials from destroying valuable public records in order to make space for current business.

Within recent years photography has become an increasingly important aid in archival administration. The Ohio legislature, following the modern trends in recording, has enacted measures looking forward to the conservation of space in the county courthouses by permitting county officials to destroy records which have been reproduced photographically. Under this act, passed in 1937, any county official charged with keeping public records may, when space requires it, have such records copied or reproduced by any photographic process and destroy the original papers. The original records, however, must be preserved until the time for filing legal proceedings based upon the documents shall have elapsed.[188]

While the legislature has attempted to enact legislation looking forward to conservation of much needed space in county courthouses, a significant trend is to be observed in the increasing interest which is being displayed for a department a county archives where all noncurrent records maybe properly housed, classified, listed, and made more readily accessible to those interested and consulting them.

---

186. G.C. sec. 2804.
187. G.C. sec. 2763.
188. G.C. sec. 32-1.

The arguments advanced in favor of such a system are: (1) preservation of county records should be viewed as a distinct function of county government, (2) administration of county archives should be under the direction of those qualified to serve efficiently and effectively both the needs of the administration and historians, (3) construction of county archive buildings for non-current records would make available more space for current business, which, at present, is seriously entailed.

In the field of archival administration the state, rather than the county, has been the experimental laboratory and the results have been eminently successful.[189]

---

189. For an interesting and informative article on the administration of state archives, see Charles M. Gates, "The Administration of State Archives." *The Pacific Northwest Quarterly,* XXIX, (January 1938), No. 1; also in *The American Archivist,* I (July 1938), 130-141.

In 1840 Lake County was created by an act of the Ohio Assembly, combining seven townships of Geauga County with Willoughby, originally a part of Cuyahoga County.[1] The first meeting of its commissioners took place June 1, 1840,[2] and the building of the first courthouse on the site of old Geauga County courthouse was undertaken and the same year out of funds raised by private subscription. The structure was occupied as early as 1842, though it was not completed until some years later.[3] A substantial red brick building of typical New England village style, topped with a cupola, it is practically unchanged today, and is used as Painesville's city hall.

The present courthouse was begun in 1907 and finished the following year. The contract was let together with that for the jail, at a total cost of $800,000 for both.[4] It is a large, substantial, and imposing three-story brick building, approached by a wide flight of shallow steps, and adorned with tall stone pillars over life size carved stone statues representing the Biblical character Cain and Abel, on either side of the steps. On the top of the copper dome of the building is perched a large bronze eagle with wings outspread. The spacious second floor corridor is embellished with fine murals depicting historical scenes of the old Boyce Mill at Willoughby, the ore docks at Fairport, a scene along the Ashtabula-Lake County Line Road, and the B. & O. Railroad at Painesville. In the corners between the murals are portraits of James A. Garfield, Samuel Huntington, a member of the constitutional convention of 1802, Thomas Harvey, a prominent Lake County educator, and Edward Paine, for whom Painesville was named.

The entire building is built in a substantial, permanent, and adequate manner eminently suited to the purpose for which it is designed. It is almost entirely fireproof, with solid concrete foundations, steel frames, brick walls, bronze window and door frames, and fireproof tile partitions. The floors are concrete with linoleum covering, excepting the corridors, which are floored and wainscoted to 10 feet with Vermont marble. Stairs, stairway walls, and counter fronts are made of the same marble, and the balustrades are of bronze with solid oak handrails. Only doors which are of solid oak, some paneling and wainscoting, and some of the furniture are of wood.

---

1. *Laws of Ohio,* XXXVIII, 102.
2. Commissioners' Record A (1840-1871), 1.
3. Harriett Taylor Upton, *History of the Western Reserve,* I, 278.
4. Commissioners' Record G (1906-1913), 40-41.

The building affords more than adequate space and facilities for storing records in airy, well ventilated offices and storage rooms, vaults, and the like. The offices are themselves spacious and well lighted and ventilated, and are supplied with the best equipment for arranging and preserving all kinds of documents and records. Even the attic store rooms are large, clean, well lighted, and well ventilated. All records are stored in extremely neat and orderly fashion throughout the building.

County Commissioners. The offices of the county commissioners of Lake County consist of a suite and three rooms on the west side of the third floor of the courthouse. The private meeting room of the commissioners, in the southwest corner of the courthouse is used only for the conduct of business of the office, and contains no records. The center room is the stenographer's office. This room and the commissioners' clerk's office, constitute the main record storage space of the commissioners' office. Steel files and steel shelving of a modern type are used for the storage of records, which consist of 49 volumes, 30 file boxes, 7 bundles, 9 maps, and 6 photographs. A few records are housed in the auditor's main office, aid to dependent children's office, courthouse attic, and relief administration office.

Recorder. The recorder's office consists of two rooms on the east side of the first floor of the courthouse. The business office is in the southwest corner of the building, with a file room adjoining it on the north. Both of these offices are equipped with steel shelving and steel filing cases for the accommodation of the records, which number 501 volumes, 80 file boxes, 24 bundles, and 1 map. While the office has been provided storage space in the attic, it has been found necessary to store very few records there to date.

Clerk of Courts. The clerk of courts office is on the east side of the second floor of the courthouse, and consists of the main office, designed primarily for the use of the public, but also used to accommodate the office personnel and as a repository for a part of the records, and the file room, adjoining it on the north. Most of the records consisting of 1182 volumes, 214 file boxes, 30 bundles, 16 file envelopes, 10 letter files, 5 pamphlets, and 7 folders, are filed in these two offices. Such records as those of the supreme court, the circuit court, and a few other records which are seldom used, are filed in the attic space allotted to this office.

Court of Common Pleas. The court of common pleas occupies the central portion of the north end of the second floor of the courthouse, with the jury room and judges chambers adjoining it on the east and west respectively. The records of this court, consisting of 315 volumes, 383 file boxes, 2 letter files, and 12,867 jackets, are kept by the clerk of courts. A few of the older records are kept in the attic storeroom assigned to the clerk of courts.

Assignment Commissioner. The work of this office is conducted from the court of common pleas on the second floor of the courthouse. Its records are to be found with the clerk of courts.

Supreme Court. The supreme court is no longer held in the county, but its records, consisting of 8 volumes, are stored in the attic of the clerk of courts.

Court of Appeals. The court of appeals is in the southwest corner of the second floor of the courthouse. The transcripts of the court journal and the records of the defunct district and circuit courts, are in custody of the clerk of courts, and are kept in the attic storeroom. Other records are kept in the court of appeals. Total records consist of 19 volumes, 3 file boxes, and 400 bundles.

Probate Court. The probate court occupies four offices on the west side of the first floor of the courthouse. The juvenile court file officer occupies an office in this suite of rooms, since the judge of the probate court also serves as judge of the juvenile court. Chambers of the court are in the southwest corner, opening into the probate court office to the north. The probate court vault, which is directly east of the judge's chambers, also opens into this office. The probate courtroom opens from the north side of this office. Records of the probate court include 484 volumes, 829 file boxes, 2 bundles, and 1 file jacket, stored in the clerk's office and the vault, with the exception of a few very old records, which will be found in the attic storeroom.

Juvenile Court. Juvenile court is held in the probate court. Seven volumes of records are kept in the probate court vault and 5 volumes and 27 file boxes in the office of the juvenile officer. Two volumes are kept in the aid to dependent children's office.

Aid to Dependent Children. This office opens off the first floor corridor about halfway down on the west side. Its records, consisting of 4 file boxes, are kept there.

Jury Commissioners. Records of the proceedings of the jury commission, which does not have an assigned office, are kept in the clerk of courts office. They are contained in 2 file drawers.

Grand Jury. Reports of proceedings of the grand jury are kept in the clerk of courts office. The grand jury has no separate office and keeps no separate records.

Petit Jury. Petit jury lists are kept in 3 file boxes in the clerk of courts' office. No jury records are kept in the jury room, which is used for deliberative purposes only.

Prosecuting Attorney. The suite of rooms occupied by the prosecuting attorney and his assistant is on the third floor of the courthouse in the northeast corner. The business office is in the center. It opens into the private office of the prosecutor on the north side, and into the file rooms and the assistant's office on the south. Records of the office, which are contained in 13 file boxes, are kept in the file room.

Coroner. Permanent records of the coroner are filed with the clerk of courts in 1 volume and 16 file boxes. Some old discontinued records are to be found in 1 file jacket in the probate court. The coroner has no office except his own private business office, in which he keeps only current records.

Sheriff. The office of the sheriff is on the first floor of the county jail. The records, consisting of 43 volumes, 1 file box, and 2 file drawers, are kept there on steel shelves, and in a steel cabinet, except for 5 volumes which have been stored in the attic. The jail is of the same fireproof construction as the courthouse.

Dog Warden. The records of the dog warden, who has no office assigned to him, are kept in 2 file boxes in the commissioner's stenographer's office and 1 bundle in the office of the clerk of the county commissioners.

Auditor. The work of the county auditor requires four offices. Three of them occupy the entire north end of the first floor of the courthouse and the fourth adjoins them on the east side. The main office is at the end of the corridor in the center of the north side, flanked on the west by the private office of the auditor and on the east by a work room which opens into a transfer room to the south. The records, which consist of 913 volumes, 250 file boxes, 8000 sheets, and 1091 bundles, are kept in all of the offices except the private office of the auditor, and in the attic storeroom. A few records are housed in the prosecuting attorney's stenographer's room.

Treasurer. The treasurer's main office adjoins the private office of the auditor, and is on the west corridor of the first floor of the courthouse. A work room opens off it to the south. The main office has entrances into both the auditor's main and private office. The bound volumes, consisting of 485 units, are kept on steel roller shelves in the treasurer's main office and in the attic store room. The tax duplicates, however, are kept in the auditor's office because inadequate space in the treasurer's first floor office for storing these 308 volumes, and a need for easy accessibility to these records preclude their being kept in the store room. Seventy file boxes and 60 bundles complete the records of the office.

Budget Commission. The records of the budget commission are kept in 2 volumes in the attic and 1 file box and 13 bundles in the auditor's office. Meetings of the commission are often informal and are held in the office of one of the members, all of whom are county officers.

Board of Revision. The board of revision has no separate office. Three volumes and 3 file boxes of the board's records are kept in the auditor's office, and 6 volumes are stored in the attic.

Board of Elections. The board of elections occupies an office in the southeast corner of the third floor of the courthouse. All records, consisting of 125 volumes and 1 bundle, are kept in this office.

Board of Education. The board of education has its office in the southwest corner of the second floor of the courthouse. Records consist of 217 bound volumes, 4 file boxes, 2 envelopes, 4 bundles, and 10 file drawers, which are housed in the board's office, with the exception of several records in the custody of the county superintendent of schools and in the attic.

Board of Health. The office of the board of health is on the west side of the second floor of the courthouse. There is no tuberculosis hospital in Lake County; hence records of tubercular patients are kept by the county board of health. The total records consist of 124 volumes, 20 file boxes, and 2 packing boxes.

Memorial Hospital. The Lake County Memorial Hospital is located on the corner of East Washington and High Streets, Painesville. Records, consisting of 5 volumes, 7 file boxes, and 20 cardboard boxes, are kept in the office of the stenographer and in the adjoining business office.

County Home. The office of the county infirmary is on the first floor of the home, on Riverside Drive, Route 84, Painesville, Ohio. The records, which consist of 11 volumes and t3 file folders, are kept in the infirmary office.

Child Welfare Board. The child welfare board is on the west side of the third floor in the courthouse. The records, which consist of 3 volumes, 1 file box, 1 file drawer, and 1 one bundle, are kept in that office.

Board of County Visitors. The board of county visitors has no permanent headquarters. The only records of the board are in the form of reports to the probate court, which are filed in 1 box in the probate court vault.

Soldiers' Relief Commission. Records of the soldiers' relief commission are kept in 2 volumes in the home of the incumbent secretary of the commission, since the commission has no permanent office.

Soldiers' Burial Commission. This commission has no separate office and has kept separate records only for 1900 to 1922. These 2 volumes are in the attic storeroom. Reports of the soldiers' burial commission are entered in the Commissioners' Record, entry 1.

Blind Relief Commission. The blind relief commission was abolished in 1913. Its records consist of 1 volume, kept in the commissioner's clerk's office. Since 1913 blind relief has been administered by the county commissioners. The records, consisting of 1 file box, are kept in the auditor's main office. Since 1936 aid for the blind has been administered under the social security act and its records consist of 1 volume in the commissioner's clerk's office, and 1 file box in the aid to dependent children's office.

Division of Aid for the Aged. The office of aid for the aged is on the west side of the third floor. Records consist of 2 volumes and 4 file boxes, all kept in that office.

County Engineer. The offices of the engineer are on the east side of the ground floor. They consist of the engineer's private office, entered through an outer office which is used as a stenographer's room. These rooms open on the north into the drafting room and beyond this into the blueprint room. Records consist of 288 volumes, 7 file boxes, 9 file drawers, and 400 maps, most of which are on shelves and filing cabinets in the drafting room and stenographer's room.

Sanitary Engineer. The office of the sanitary engineer is the first large office on the east side of the ground floor corridor. Records consist of 54 volumes, 82 file drawers, 31 file boxes, and 2 maps, all kept in the sanitary engineer's office.

Planning Commission. The records of the planning commission, dissolved in 1931, are contained in 1 volume which is kept in the office of the clerk of the county commissioners.

Agricultural Society. The records of the Lake County Agricultural Society, comprising 3 volumes, are kept in the office of the Society at the fair grounds, at the corner of Fair Grounds Road and Mentor Avenue, Painesville, Ohio, and in the courthouse attic.

Agricultural Extension Agency. The office of the agricultural extension agency is in the post office building, Painesville, Ohio. The records consist of 38 volumes, 51 file drawers, 16 file boxes, 1 bundle, and 675 pamphlets, all of which are kept in that office.

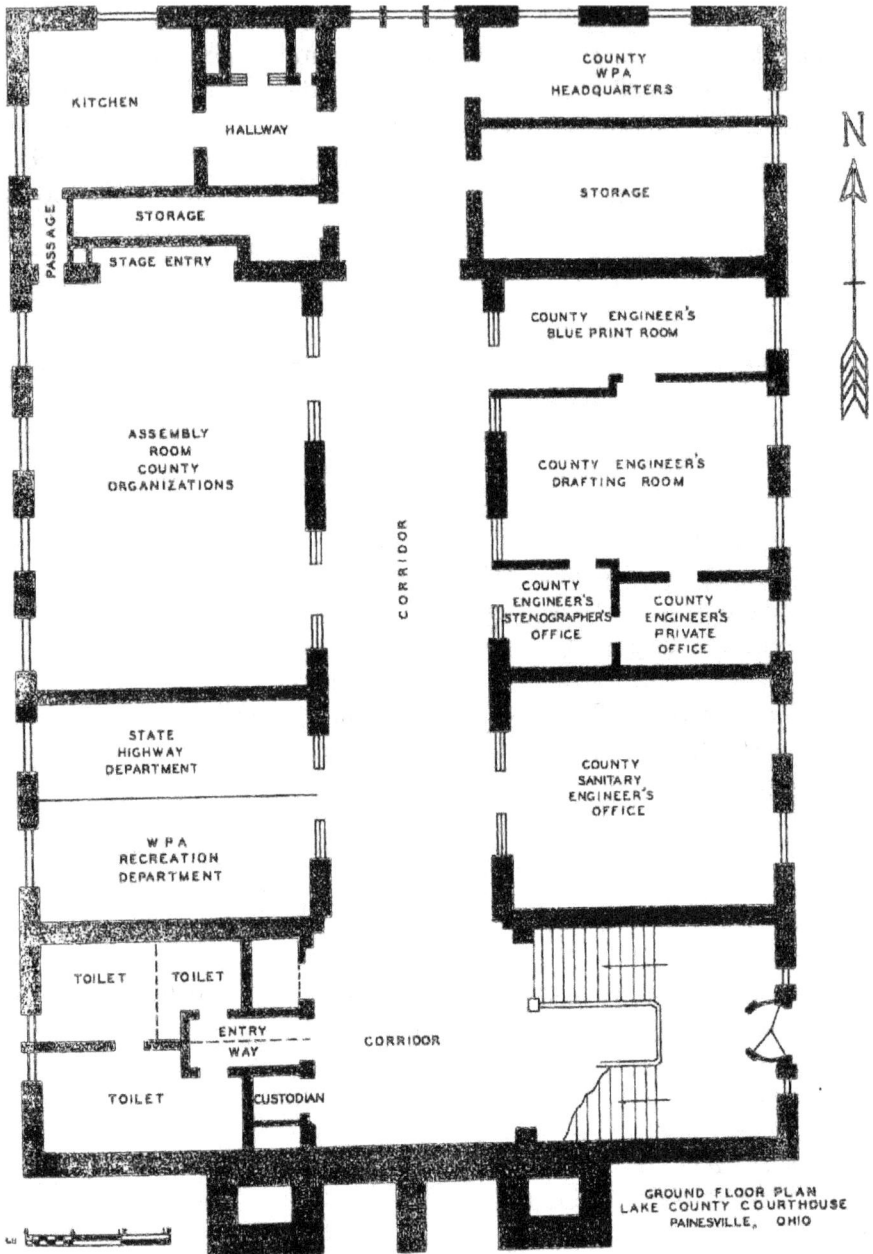

KITCHEN

HALLWAY

COUNTY
WPA
HEADQUARTERS

PASSAGE

STORAGE

STAGE ENTRY

STORAGE

COUNTY ENGINEER'S
BLUE PRINT ROOM

ASSEMBLY
ROOM
COUNTY
ORGANIZATIONS

CORRIDOR

COUNTY ENGINEER'S
DRAFTING ROOM

COUNTY
ENGINEER'S
STENOGRAPHER'S
OFFICE

COUNTY
ENGINEER'S
PRIVATE
OFFICE

STATE
HIGHWAY
DEPARTMENT

COUNTY
SANITARY
ENGINEER'S
OFFICE

WPA
RECREATION
DEPARTMENT

TOILET   TOILET

ENTRY
WAY

CORRIDOR

TOILET   CUSTODIAN

N

GROUND FLOOR PLAN
LAKE COUNTY COURTHOUSE
PAINESVILLE, OHIO

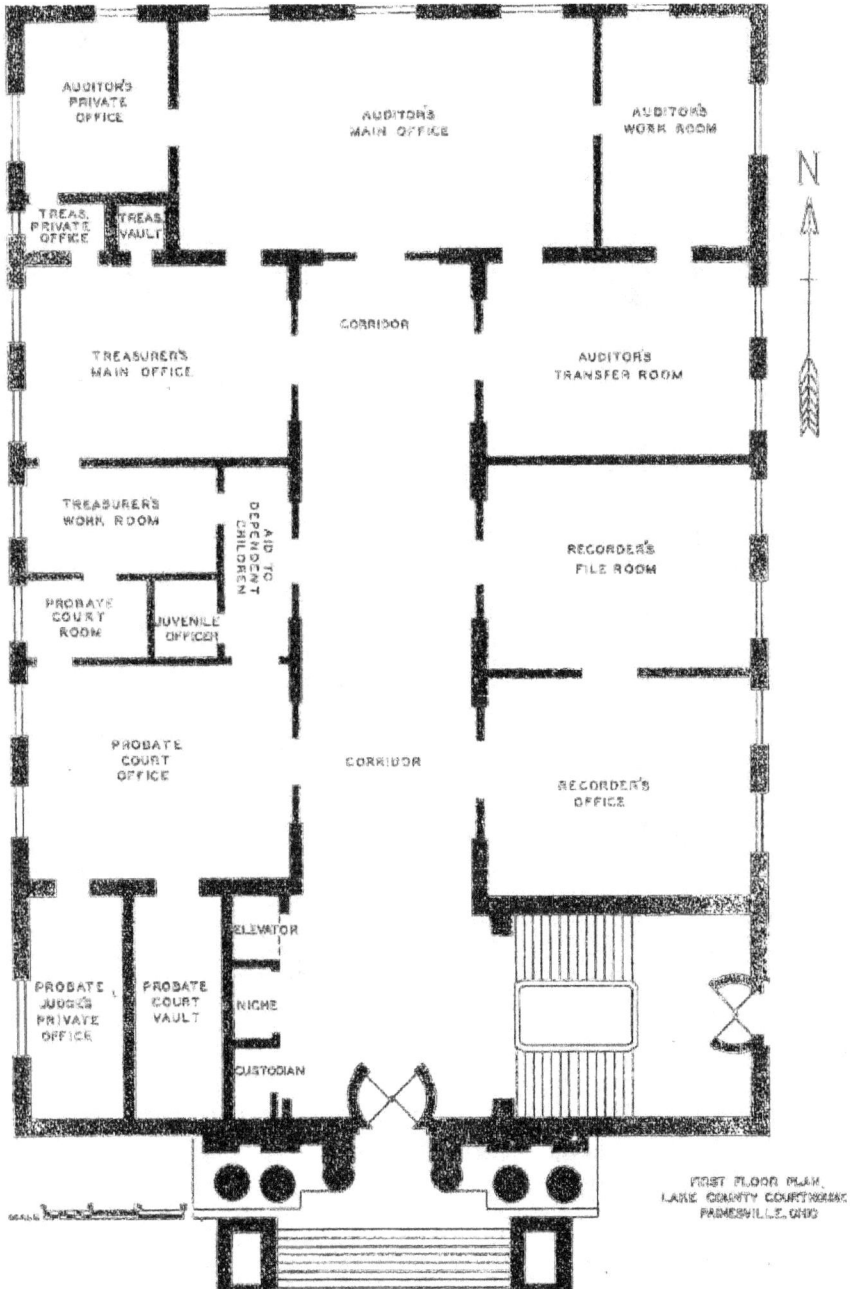

N

AUDITOR'S
PRIVATE
OFFICE

AUDITOR'S
MAIN OFFICE

AUDITOR'S
WORK ROOM

TREAS.
PRIVATE
OFFICE

TREAS.
VAULT

CORRIDOR

AUDITOR'S
TRANSFER ROOM

TREASURER'S
MAIN OFFICE

TREASURER'S
WORK ROOM

AID TO
DEPENDENT
CHILDREN

RECORDER'S
FILE ROOM

PROBATE
COURT
ROOM

JUVENILE
OFFICER

PROBATE
COURT
OFFICE

CORRIDOR

RECORDER'S
OFFICE

ELEVATOR

PROBATE
JUDGE'S
PRIVATE
OFFICE

PROBATE
COURT
VAULT

NICHE

CUSTODIAN

FIRST FLOOR PLAN
LAKE COUNTY COURTHOUSE
PAINESVILLE, OHIO

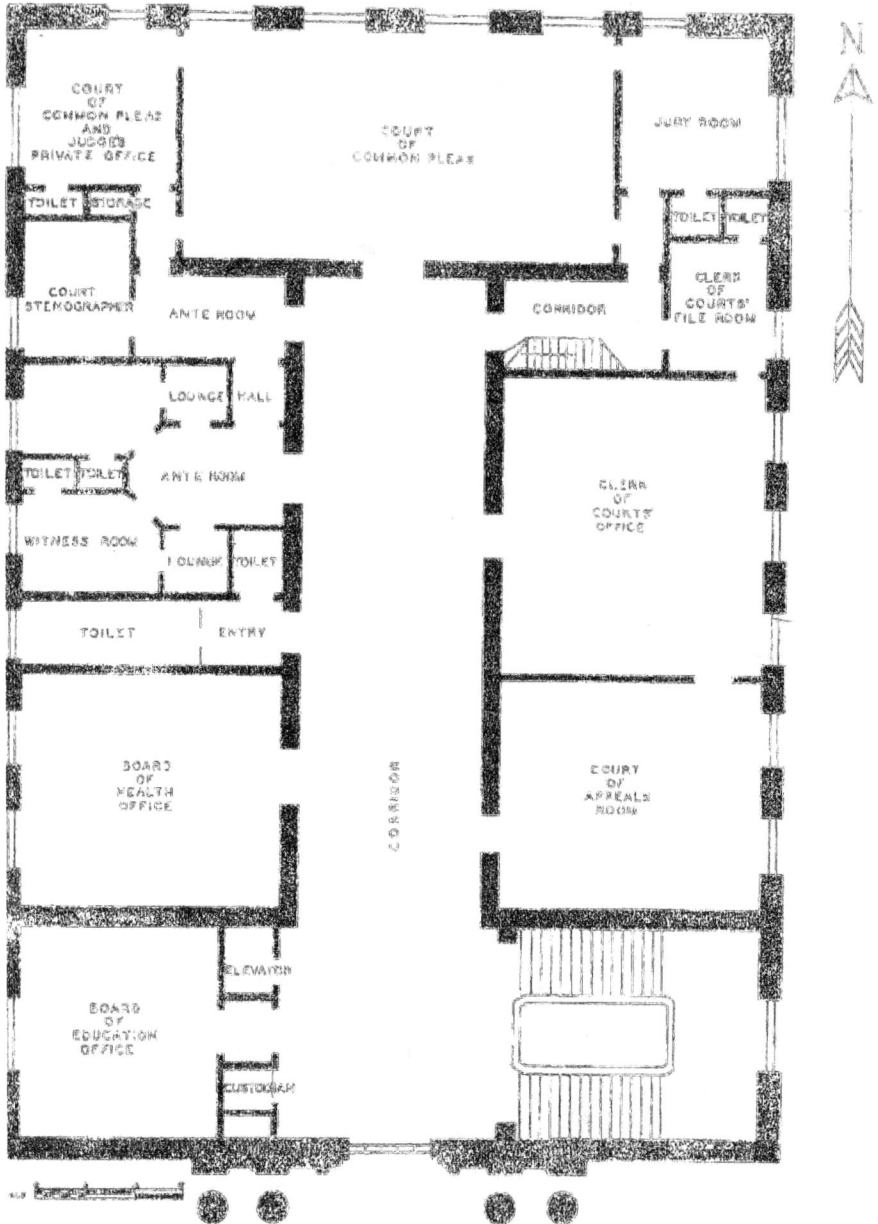

N

COURT
OF
COMMON PLEAS
AND
JUDGES
PRIVATE OFFICE

COURT
OF
COMMON PLEAS

JURY ROOM

TOILET STORAGE

TOILET TOILET

CLERK
OF
COURTS'
FILE ROOM

COURT
STENOGRAPHER

ANTE ROOM

CORRIDOR

LOUNGE HALL

TOILET TOILET

ANTE ROOM

CLERK
OF
COURTS
OFFICE

WITNESS ROOM

LOUNGE TOILET

TOILET

ENTRY

BOARD
OF
HEALTH
OFFICE

CORRIDOR

COURT
OF
APPEALS
ROOM

ELEVATOR

BOARD
OF
EDUCATION
OFFICE

CUSTODIAN

SECOND FLOOR PLAN
LAKE COUNTY COURTHOUSE
PAINESVILLE, OHIO

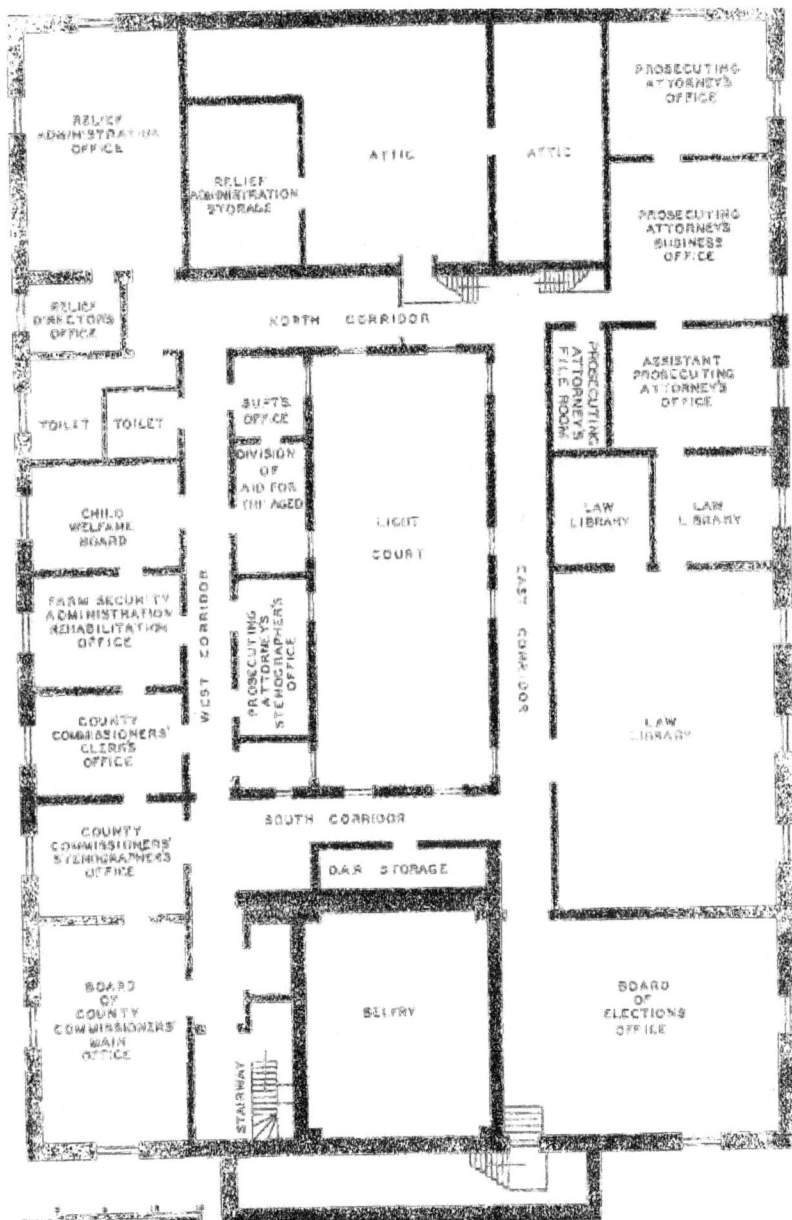

RELIEF ADMINISTRATION OFFICE

RELIEF ADMINISTRATION STORAGE

ATTIC

ATTIC

PROSECUTING ATTORNEY'S OFFICE

PROSECUTING ATTORNEY'S BUSINESS OFFICE

RELIEF DIRECTOR'S OFFICE

NORTH CORRIDOR

PROSECUTING ATTORNEY'S FILE ROOM

ASSISTANT PROSECUTING ATTORNEY'S OFFICE

TOILET TOILET

SUPT'S. OFFICE

DIVISION OF AID FOR THE AGED

LIGHT COURT

LAW LIBRARY

LAW LIBRARY

CHILD WELFARE BOARD

WEST CORRIDOR

EAST CORRIDOR

FARM SECURITY ADMINISTRATION REHABILITATION OFFICE

PROSECUTING ATTORNEY'S STENOGRAPHER'S OFFICE

LAW LIBRARY

COUNTY COMMISSIONERS' CLERK'S OFFICE

COUNTY COMMISSIONERS' STENOGRAPHERS' OFFICE

SOUTH CORRIDOR

D.A.R. STORAGE

BOARD OF COUNTY COMMISSIONERS' MAIN OFFICE

BELFRY

BOARD OF ELECTIONS OFFICE

STAIRWAY

THIRD FLOOR PLAN
LAKE COUNTY COURTHOUSE
PAINESVILLE OHIO

The office of county commissioners dates back to the system of government provided for the Northwest Territory in 1792. Upon the organization of the State of Ohio, the legislature, by its act in 1804, authorized the election of three county commissioners in each county for a three-year term.[1] In 1910 the term was changed to two years,[2] and so continued until 1920, when it was extended to four years.[3] While the duties and prerogatives of the office were a matter of growth through the succeeding years, the major functions were well established during the first decade of the state's existence. Lake County was erected in 1840, and the first commissioners were elected the same year.[4] Vacancies in the office due to health, resignation, or other causes, are filled by appointment by the probate judge, auditor, and recorder, jointly, pending the next succeeding election.[5]

The powers and duties of the commissioners include the appointment and determination of the compensation of county employees not subject to election;[6] setting bond and sureties of county officials;[7] removal of the auditor and treasurer, for cause;[8] filling vacancies in elective offices;[9] levying property taxes;[10] adopting a budget for the county;[11] designating depositories for county funds;[12] issuing bonds for various proposals;[13] constructing and maintaining necessary public buildings;[14] maintaining county roads;[15] and erecting townships or altering the boundaries of existing townships.[16]

---

1. *Laws of Ohio,* II, 150.
2. G.C. sec. 2395.
3. G.C. sec. 839; *Laws of Ohio,* XCVIII, 172; CVIII, pt. ii, 1300.
4. Commissioners' Record, A [1840-1871], 1, *see* entry 1.
5. G.C. secs. 2396, 2397.
6. G.C. secs. 1165-3, 1359-16, 2409, 2410, 2411, 2413, 2423, 2950, 2968, 3081, 3092, 3112, 3136, 3141-2, 3149-3, 3177, 5652-7, 6602-1, 7643-2, 14849-4.
7. G.C. secs. 2559, 2633, 2635, 2751, 2784, 2824, 2825, 2868, 2911, 12192-12195.
8. G.C. secs. 2580, 2581, 2713.
9. G.C. secs. 2562, 2636, 2755, 2785, 2828, 2829, 2870.
10. G.C. secs. 5625-5.
11. G.C. secs. 5625-20.
12. G.C. secs. 2715.
13. G.C. secs. 2293-2, 2293-3, 2293-10.
14. G.C. secs. 2419, 2433.
15. G.C. secs. 6860.
16. G.C. secs. 3246, 3248.

Lake County's first courthouse, begun in 1840 and completed in 1852, was built with funds collected by private subscription.[17] It occupied the site of the original courthouse of the old Geauga County, a part of which was taken to form Lake County when the latter was set up. It was converted to use as the Painesville city hall upon the completion in 1908 of the new courthouse. At the same time the present jail was erected just north of the courthouse and contracts for the two buildings were let together in 1907 for $800,000.[18] The commissioners are responsible for proper administration of the courthouse and jail, and may order desirable changes in the management.

Control of the county's finances is the conspicuous function of this office. Not only does the board levy a property tax to provide a general operating fund for the county, but it also passes upon the annual budget in collaboration with the budget commission;[19] fixes the compensation of its own employees;[20] limits the aggregate amount to be expended for personal services in the offices of the probate court, auditor, treasurer, recorder, clerk of courts, engineer, and sheriff;[21] authorizes payment of county expenditures by the treasurer upon the warrant of the county auditor;[22] has the power to borrow on short term notes in anticipation of the collection of current revenues;[23] and issues bonds to acquire or create any permanent improvement.[24]

The commissioners are active also in county welfare work. They appoint a superintendent for the county infirmary, keeps the buildings in repair, and authorize the construction of new buildings when necessary. They undertake the construction, maintenance, and supervision of the various homes and institutions for the unfortunate and needy. The first Lake County Infirmary was established in 1832 at a cost of $4,000.[25] The present home was built in 1878 at the cost of $30,000. The farm contains 190 acres.[26]

---

17. *Laws of Ohio*, XXXVIII, 102; Williams, *History of Geauga and Lake Counties, Ohio*, 24.
18. Commissioners' Record, G [1906-1913], 40-41, *see* entry 1.
19. G.C. sec. 5625-20.
20. G.C. sec. 2413.
21. G.C. sec. 2981.
22. G.C. sec. 2460.
23. G.C. sec. 2293-4.
24. G.C. secs. 2293-2, 2293-9, 2293-10.
25. Commissioners' Record, A [1840-1871], 142-143, *see* entry 1.
26. *Ibid.*, B, [1871-1876], 106.

Since January 1913, the commissioners have served as a board of directors for the home.[27] The commissioners appoint a board of five trustees to govern the Lake County Memorial Hospital, organized in 1902 as the Painesville Hospital Association, and now occupying a building constructed in 1922-1924 at a cost of $200,000.[28] Relief since 1936 has been administered by a director, appointed by the commissioners. Not only is the power of appointment of clerks, boards, and superintendents of county welfare agencies lodged with the commissioners, but they are charged also with the duty of visiting the various welfare agencies once each six months.[29]

Lake County commissioners maintain a county highway system of more than 90 miles of improved roads.[30] Gasoline and automobile license taxes are the sources of the money required to maintain them, which in 1940 amounted to $171,415.76[31]

Lake County is predominantly an agricultural community. In Lake, as in other counties, the commissioners foster organizations and activities which assist in the development of the husbandry, and have sponsored both the agricultural society and the agricultural extension agency. The society was organized in 1850,[32] but succumbed to financial difficulties during the panic of 1894.[33] In 1911 the commissioners proposed a bond issue, which was approved by a vote of electorate, providing $40,000 for the purchase of land and buildings for a fairground.[34] Since that time the society has functioned successfully. The agricultural extension service, as in other counties throughout the country, is recognized as a valuable community asset, and is given full financial support by the commissioners.

Upon petition of a majority of the householders, commissioners may alter the boundaries of townships and adjust disputed boundaries.[35]

---

27. *Laws of Ohio,* CII, 433.
28. Commissioners' Record, P [1922-1923], 571.
29. G.C. secs. 2498, 2499.
30. Information obtained from office county engineer.
31. Receipts Journal, 1940, *see* entry 279.
32. [Record Book], I [1851-1894], *see* entry 455.
33. [Record Book], I, 209; Painesville *Telegraph,* December 19, 1894.
34. Commissioners' Record, I [1910-1912], 180.
35. G.C. secs. 3246, 3248.

The townships which composed Lake County were well organized at the time they were made a part of the county, and only one change in township lines have been found desirable. In 1857 an area of about 1300 acres in Leroy Township was included within the boundaries of Concord Township.[36]

Minutes

1. COMMISSIONERS' RECORD
1840—. 28 volumes. (A-Z, AA-AB).

Minutes of county commissioners, showing date of meeting, names of members present, and business transacted; including proceedings and contracts for roads, turnpikes, sewers, water lines, bridges, and ditches; bills and salaries, showing date, name of vendor or claimant, amount, purpose, date, and amount approved; appropriations and resolutions approved or rejected; annexation proceedings, and approval of steam and electric railroad rights of way; proceedings regarding infirmary, 1851—, and reports of infirmary directors, 1871-1903, showing number of inmates received during year, number discharge, number died, amount spent for the care during year, amount spent for wages and other items, total receipts, and total expenses; list of boundary certificates, 1871-1886, showing name of payee and amount paid; reports of county officials, 1850—, showing names of officials and office, amounts of fees and fines, court cost, office expense, date of report, and date filed; monthly financial reports of auditor, 1904—, showing money received from various sources, amount expended, and balance; reports of soldiers' burial commission, 1884—, showing names of deceased and the soldier or sailor, rank, company, and regiment or ship, claim for burial fees, date, and amount approved by county commissioners; reports of soldiers' relief commission, 1886—, showing name and address of person needing relief, amount to be paid each month, relationship to soldier, sailor, or marine and date approved or rejected; sheep claims, 1871—, showing name and address of claimant, number of animals, grade, quality, and value, nature of injury, amount of damage claimed, and 1927—, dog warden's estimate of damage done, date, and amount approved; applications and approvals for parole from county jail, 1871-1933, showing name, age, and personal description of prisoner, term of parole, court notifications concerning case, and signature of prosecuting attorney, sheriff, commissioners, and judge on case;

---

36. Commissioners' Record, A [1840-1871], 196.

blind relief, 1914-1935, showing name of applicant, address, date of application, whether applicant is resident or nonresident, date case was heard, date of approval or action taken, amount of grant, and amount of payment; bids for county funds, 1894—, showing name of bank, date of report, amount of interest on active and inactive funds, and date filed; and appointments including first dog warden, August 15, 1927. Also contains; Commissioners' Journal, Infirmary, 1851-1903, entry 3; Annual Report of County Officers, 1850—, entry 7; Parole Record, 1871-1932, entry 22. Arranged chronologically by dates of meetings. For index 1840-1926, see entry2; 1895—, indexed alphabetically by subjects. 1840-1903, handwritten; 1804—, typed. Average 475 pages. 16 x 10 x 2.5. Commissioner's clerk's office.

2. INDEX TO COMMISSIONERS' RECORD
1840-1926. 4 volumes (1-4). Discontinued.

Index to Commissioners' Record, entry 1, showing date of entry, names of principals, subject covered, and volume and page number of record. Arranged alphabetically by subjects. Handwritten. Average 400 pages. 18.5 x 12 x 2.5. 3 volumes, 1840-1922 attic; 1 volume, 1923-1926, Commissioner's clerk's office.

3. COMMISSIONER JOURNAL, INFIRMARY
1904—. 3 volumes. Title varies : Infirmary Directors' Journal, 1904-1917,
1 volume 1851-1903 in Commissioners' Record, entry 1.

Minutes of infirmary directors 1904-1912, and of county commissioners as board of directors, 1913—, in matters pertaining to maintenance of county home, including resolutions passed, applications for admission to infirmary, action taken, and bills heard and approved; also includes semiannual reports of infirmary director, 1904-1912, and annual reports of infirmary superintendent 1913—, to commissioners, showing statement of all receipts and expenditures with date, amount, name of payee, and purpose of each item; also statistics on inmates and county home properties. Arranged chronologically by dates of meetings and dates of reports. Indexed alphabetically by names of principles and subjects. 1904-1912, handwritten; 1913—, typed. Average 475 pages. 16.5 x 11 x 2.5. Commissioner's clerk's office.

For original reports, 1908-1919, see entry 6.

Reports

4. SOLDIERS' RELIEF
1866—. 1 bundle, 1 file box.
Original reports and suggestions of soldiers relief commission to the commissioners and auditor, showing date of report, name of soldier, name of beneficiary, relationship of dependent to soldier, amount allowed by county commissioners, recommendations for increase or decrease of amount, and change of address (if any). Arranged chronologically by dates of reports. No index. Handwritten and typed, some on printed forms. Bundle, 8 x 11 x 3; file box, 10 x 4.5 x 13.5. 1 bundle, 1866-1905, attic; 1 file box, 1906—, Auditor's main office.

5. SOLDIERS' BURIAL REPORTS
1900-1922 . 2 volumes (1-2).
Copies of reports of soldiers' burial commission to commissioners, showing date of report, name of township, name and military history of deceased, date and cause of death, name of undertaker, and an itemized statement of expenses of burial. Arranged chronologically by dates of reports. Indexed alphabetically by names of deceased. Handwritten on printed forms. Average 300 pages. 14 x 9 x 1.5. Attic.

6. COUNTY INFIRMARY REPORT
1908-1919. 1 file box.
Original annual reports of the superintendent of county infirmary to commissioners, showing date of report, for what period, itemized account of funds received, itemized account of expenditures, number of inmates cared for, number admitted since last report, number discharged, number died, and number registered at time of report; includes applications for admission to county infirmary, 1913; also original inventory of equipment and institution furnishings, showing itemized list and estimated value of each item. Arranged chronologically by dates of reports. No index. Handwritten on printed forms. 10 x 4.5 x 13.5. Auditor's main office.
For copies of report, 1904—, see entry 3.

7. ANNUAL REPORT OF COUNTY OFFICERS
1884—. 2 volumes (1, 2). 1850—, also in Commissioners' Record, entry 1.
Annual reports to commissioners by prosecuting attorney, clerk of courts, sheriff, and treasurer: prosecuting attorneys, showing date of report, criminal prosecution,

name of accused, fine assessed, recognizance forfeited, and amount collected; clerk of courts', showing fines assessed, name of accused, amount assessed, amount collected, sources of fund paid into treasury, and amount paid in; sheriff's (criminal cases), showing date of report, name of defendant, amount collected, date and amount paid to clerk of courts; and treasurer's report, showing date of report, source of fees, and amount of each item. Arranged alphabetically by names of offices and chronologically thereunder by dates of annual reports. No index. Handwritten on printed forms. Average 380 pages. 16 x 11.5 x 2. 1 volume, 1884-1913, attic; 1 volume, 1914—, Auditor's main office.

8. GENERAL [Weekly Report of County Dog Warden]
1936—. 2 file boxes, 1 bundle.
Copies of weekly reports of dog warden to the board of commissioners of all dogs seized, impounded, redeemed, or destroyed, showing date, name and address of owner, keeper, or harbor (if known), sex, breed, color, and other description of dog, amount of fees and cost collected, final disposition (whether redeemed or destroyed), and date monies paid into treasury; also includes copies of weekly reports of dog warden to the board of commissioners of investigation of claims for damage to livestock inflicted by dogs, showing date of report, name and address of claimant, number, kind, grade, quality, value, nature of injury to animals, amount claimed for such injuries less deduction for carcasses or pelts sold or used, net damage claim, and warden's estimate of net damage of injury. Arranged chronologically by dates of reports. No index. Handwritten on printed forms. File boxes, 11 x 16 x 24; bundle, 16 x 9 x 2. 2 file boxes, 1936-1937, commissioners' stenographers office; 1 bundle, 1937—, Commissioner's clerk's office.

Improvements

9. INDEX TO FILES
1917—. 1 file box.
Card index to Road Files, 1917—, entry 10, and bridge, culvert, and ditch, entry 11, showing assigned folio number, location of road, bridge, culvert, and ditch, and name of township or district. Arranged alphabetically by names of roads, bridges, culverts, or ditches. Handwritten. 5 x 7 x 18. Commissioners' stenographer's office.

10. ROAD FILE
1919—. 4 file boxes. (labeled by contained folio numbers).

Original papers in connection with legal procedure in building and repairing of county roads and bridges, including petitions, claims for damages, appointments and reports of committees and appraisers, surveys, village and city ordinances, transcripts of council's and commissioners proceedings, copies of bids or bonds, proposals and agreements, contracts, bonds, copies of specifications, and contracts with bonds attached, all showing date of entry, names of principles, name of road, and assigned folio number. Arranged numerically by assigned folio numbers. For index, see entry 9. Handwritten; specifications printed. 11 x 15 x 24. Commissioners' stenographer's office.

11. BRIDGE, CULVERT, AND DITCH
1917—. 1 file box.

Original correspondence and documents pertaining to building and repairing of bridges, culverts, and ditches in the county, showing notice to bidders, estimates of county engineer, amount of bids, specifications, contracts, and assigned folio number. Arranged numerically by assigned folio numbers. For index see entry 9. Handwritten on printed forms. 11 x 16 x 24. Commissioners' stenographer's office.

12. SEWER AND WATER RECORD
1923—. 6 volumes (1-6).

Record of applications to commissioners to construct sewer and water lines, including resolutions passed, procedure in the issuing of contracts, and list of expenditure by commissioners, showing location of proposed project, names of contractors, date of entry, and amount of contract. Arranged chronologically by dates of entries. Indexed alphabetically by subjects. Typed. Average 550 pages. 16 x 11 x 2.5. Commissioners' stenographer's office.

13. SPECIAL APPLICATIONS AND CONTRACTS
1927—. 4 file boxes.

Original papers, carbon copies, and duplicate copies of specifications and contracts for construction and repair of bridges, roads, culverts, and ditches, showing date, name of township or district, name of contractor, and cost of project. Arranged alphabetically by names of townships or districts. No index. Handwritten on printed forms. 11 x 16 x 24. Commissioners' stenographer's office.

Fiscal Accounts

14. REQUISITIONS, ALL DEPARTMENTS
1929—. 5 bundles, 1 file box.
Cancelled requisitions for materials and supplies for various county departments, showing requisition number, date of requisition, list of supplies wanted, cost, and name of department. Arranged alphabetically by names of departments and chronologically thereunder by dates of requisitions. No index. Handwritten on printed forms. Bundles, 9 x 9 x 7; file box, 11 x 16 x 24. Commissioners' stenographer's office.

15. PURCHASE ORDERS
1933—. 3 file boxes.
Purchase orders for material and supplies for county use, showing purchase order number, date of orders, amount, purpose, and signatures of county commissioners. Arranged numerically by ordered numbers. No index. Handwritten on printed forms. 11 x 16 x 24. Commissioners' stenographer's office.

16. NEW COURTHOUSE AND JAIL LEDGER [Purchase Records, All Departments]
1904-1913. 1 volume.
Commissioners' daily record of equipment and furnishings purchased for the various county offices, showing item, name of vendor, for what, amount charged, and date paid; also includes record of purchase orders for all departments. Arranged chronologically by dates of payments. Indexed alphabetically by names of vendors. Handwritten on printed forms. 188 pages. 16.5 x 12 x 1. Attic.

Miscellaneous

17. CENSUS LAKE COUNTY
1860. 1 volume.
Census of inhabitants of Lake County, showing number of freeholders in county and each township; number of dwellings; number of persons and family; name of each person, age, sex, color, value of real and personal property, and place of birth; number of persons married during that year; foreign born; number of illiterates under 20 years of age, number of deaf, blind, dumb, insane, idiotic, paupers, and convicts; also recapitulation with total number of each class in county, and each

township and municipality. No index. Handwritten. 419 pages. 18.5 x 14 x 1.5. Commissioners' clerk's office.

18. ANNEXATIONS, ABSTRACTS OF VOTES, RECEIPTS FOR CHECKS
1898-1922, 1 file box.

Original petitions of taxpayers to county commissioners to annex certain territory, showing declaration of incorporation, proceedings of councils authorizing annexation with description of territory to be annexed; map of survey and plat of territory, showing name of survey, tract and lot numbers, location and names of roads, streets, and watercourses, lot and property boundary lines, property owners names, footage, and acreage owned by each; signatures of petitioners and attorneys, and date of filing; also includes minutes and proceedings of county commissioners pertaining to the annexation of territory, showing date of meeting, members present, title of resolution, description of territory to be annexed, result of vote on resolution and auditor's certificate of transcript; remonstrances of residence and taxpayers to county commissioners, showing reason for remonstrances signatures of president, and date of filing; abstract of votes, with certificate to the auditor by judges of election in special elections held in connection with issuing bonds for various improvements, 1899-1911, showing title of document, name of auditor, place of election, total number of votes cast, number for and against proposal, signatures of judges and clerks of elections, and date of filing; receipts given by auditor for certified checks deposited by bidders submitting bids for materials and furnishings of county jail and courthouse, 1907-1911, showing name and address of bidder, amount of bid, date of receipt, acknowledgment of receipt of check from county auditor, and signature of bidder; and inventory of jail furniture, 1901, showing name of sheriff, item, and quantity. All papers of each subject are filed together in a jacket showing name of subdivision. Arranged alphabetically by names of subdivisions and alphabetically thereunder by subjects. No index. Handwritten and typed, some on printed forms. 10 x 4.5 x 13.5. Auditor's main office.

19. SURVEY BILLS– PAINESVILLE AND EAST
1872-1929. 338 papers in 2 file boxes.

Miscellaneous records including original documents, carbon copies, and engineer's pencil memo of preliminary drawings of surveys of lands, showing date of survey, description of tract surveyed, calculations, and name of owner of tract; plat sketches of surveyed tract, showing boundary lines, length of each boundary line, area of tract, streams, roads, and locations of landmarks; ink tracings and blueprints of surveyed lands; auditor's certification of the correctness of figures and survey; affidavits of vacation of property, showing name and address of owner, location of property, and date vacated; plat sketches filed for corrections and amounts of acreage, boundary lines, correction of acreage for authority to drop from Auditor's Tax List, entry 246, and corrections for transfer of property. All papers of each township are filed together in a jacket, showing name of township. Prepared by county engineer's office. Arranged alphabetically by name of townships. No index. Handwritten and typed, some on printed forms; plats hand drawn and blueprint; sketches, traced with ink. 10 x 4.5 x 13.5. Auditor's main office.

20. COUNTY DEEDS
1911—. 1 file box.

Original deeds to real estate transferred to Lake County commissioners, showing names of grantors, date of deed, date of filing, date of recording, and type of instrument, as warranty, quit claim, or trustees' deeds, easements for highway purposes, and land options. No obvious arrangement. No index. Handwritten on printed forms. 10 x 4.5 x 13.5. Auditor's main office.

21. ANNUAL INVENTORY COUNTY PROPERTY BOARD OF COUNTY COMMISSIONERS, LAKE COUNTY
1928—. 1 volume.

Inventory of all property belonging to Lake County, showing dates, name of the department or office, location, description, quantity and value of each item and total value. Arranged alphabetically by names of departments or offices. No index. Typed. 25 pages. 15 x 12 x 1. Commissioners' clerk's office.

22. PAROLE RECORD
1933—. 1 volume. 1871-1932 in Commissioners' Record, entry 1.

Record of parole of prisoners from county jail, showing date of parole, description of prisoner, name, last address, term of parole, fines, and court costs and the case;

also record of payments to be made on fine by prisoner on parole, and signatures of prosecuting attorney, sheriff, commissioners, and committing magistrate. Arranged alphabetically by names of prisoners and chronologically thereunder by dates of paroles. No index. Typed on printed forms. 500 pages. 18.5 x 13 x 3.5. Commissioners' clerk's office.

23. GENERAL FILE
1927—. 7 file boxes. (labeled by contained file numbers).
Miscellaneous correspondence regarding general county business, including letters sent to and received from individuals, companies, and institutions, showing date of correspondence, name of correspondent, subject matter, and file numbers. Arranged alphabetically by subjects and chronologically thereunder by filed numbers. For index see entry 24. Handwritten and typed. 11 x 16 x 24. Commissioners' stenographer's office.

24. GENERAL FILE [Index]
1927—. 1 file box.
Card index to all subject matters in General File, entry 23, showing subject and file numbers of each letter. Arranged alphabetically by subjects. Typed. 5 x 7 x 18. Commissioners' stenographer's office.

Maps and Photographs

25. ROAD MAPS OF LAKE COUNTY TOWNSHIPS
1937. 8 maps.
Communications maps of roads and county by townships, showing name or number of road, route number, name of township, and names and locations of towns, bridges, and railroad crossings. Prepared by county engineer. Blueprint. Scale, 4 inches equals 1 mile. 50 x 28. Commissioners' clerk's office.

26. MAP OF Kirtland
n.d. 1 map.
Land tenure map of Kirtland Township, Lake County, showing names of roads, boundary lines of properties abutting on road, and names of owners. Prepared by M.E. Kale. Blueprint. Scale, 6 inches equals 6000 feet. Commissioners' clerk's office.

27. [ARIEL PHOTOGRAPHS]
n.d. 6 photographs.
Ariel photographs of parts of Lake County: two photographs show different views of Fairport Harbor and docks in limited sectors of surrounding land; the other four are photographs of unidentified private estates. Published by Ariel Survey Inc. East 40th Street, Cleveland, Ohio. Photographs. Scale for photographs. 4 photographs, 1 inch equals 600 feet; 2 photographs, 1 inch equals 300 feet. 4 photographs 22 x 18; 2 photographs 17 x 13. Commissioners' clerk's office.

Aid For The Blind

28. REPORT OF BLIND COMMISSION
1908—. 1 file box.
Original applications to blind commission and county commissioners for relief of needy blind, showing date, name and address of applicant, marital status, date and place of birth, citizenship, when naturalized, term of residence in county, and in United States, name, address, age, marital status of each person in direct family connection, general health of applicant, how long blind, at what age blindness occurred, occupation, other physical defects, amount of education, name of physician, by whom supported, total income, total expenditures, applicants oath, and names of witnesses; also includes evidence in blind cases, showing date of hearing, physician's name and address, name of applicant, and affidavit of physician and applicant; action on claims by county commissioners, showing date, name of applicant, statement of claim, names of attesting physician, amount allowed, and method of payment; copies of certificates of award from the blind commission to the auditor, showing date, name of person, findings of the board of county commissioners, amount allowed, order to auditor to pay, post office address of recipient, and signatures of commissioners; copies of certificates of award for medical care from the blind relief commission to the auditor, showing date, name of applicant, findings of the board of county commissioners, amount entitled to for medical care, kind of treatment, order to auditor to pay, how to pay, and signatures of applicant and county commissioners; copies of resolutions adopted by county commissioners in blind relief cases, showing date of meeting, members present, title of resolution, amount awarded, and record of votes on resolution; relief of blind affidavits for mailing, showing date, name and address of recipient, request to mail warrant, affidavit of identification, signature of recipient, and oath; copies of notices of changing of the status of needy blind from county commissioners to the

auditor, showing date, name and address of recipient, increase, decrease or discontinuance of allowance, date of meeting of county Commissioners, and reason for change; copies of county commissioners' voucher list to auditor, 1936—, showing date, period covered, names of recipients, monthly payments for each, warrant numbers, total monthly payments, and commissioners' certification of correctness. Arranged chronologically by dates of instruments. No index. Handwritten and typed, some on printed forms. 10 x 4.5 x 13.5. Auditor's main office.

29. RELIEF OF NEEDY BLIND
1936—. 1 volume.

Register of applications of needy blind persons for relief, showing name of applicant, address, date of application, consecutive number, whether applicant is resident or non-resident, whether case was heard or not; and if granted shows amount of annual grant and record of monthly vouchers; rejections show date of rejection of application and reason; appeals show date appealed, findings, commissioners' orders, and remarks. Arranged chronologically by dates of applications. No index. Handwritten on printed forms. 50 pages. 17.5 x 14.5 x 1. Commissioners' clerk's office.

30. [AID FOR THE BLIND]
1936—. 1 file box.

Applications and records of cases of needy blind, showing case number, name and address of applicant, date of application, to whom assigned for investigation, date reported to county commissioners for approval, dates of rejection, or referral, commissioners' findings, and amount of grant; also includes personal, family, and statistical information, reports of investigators, and correspondence. Arranged alphabetically by names of applicants. No index. Handwritten on printed forms. 11.5 x 16 x 24. Aid to dependent children's office.

31. [CARD INDEX, AID TO BLIND]
1936—. In [Index to Children and Blind Files], entry 221.

Cards record of aid to blind recipients, showing date of application, name and address of recipient, case number, and amount of grant.

Relief Administration

Case Records

32. [CASE RECORD]
1933—. 12 file boxes (labeled by contained letters of alphabet).
Complete case records of active and inactive cases, showing name and address of applicant and client, case number, marital status, age, nativity, number of dependents, investigator's report on the application, and itemized record of aid furnished. Arranged alphabetically by names of clients. No index. Handwritten on printed forms. 12 x 16 x 24. Relief administration office.

33. [CARD INDEX]
1933—. 3 file boxes.
Card index file of active and closed direct relief cases, showing name and address of client, case number, date of application, number of dependents, and date and kind of relief granted; also date and reason for closing. Arranged alphabetically by names of clients. Typed on printed forms. 4 x 6 x 17. Relief administration office.

34. RELIEF ORDERS
1934—. 7 file boxes.
Original itemized relief orders issued by the county relief agency and paid by county funds, showing name of retail vendor, name of client, date of order, period covered, and kind of order, as grocery, coal, rent, or clothing. Arranged by dates of orders and alphabetical thereunder by names of clients. No index. Handwritten and typed on printed forms. 12 x 16 x 24. Relief administration office.

Work Relief and C C C

35. CERTIFICATION OF ELIGIBILITY
1935—. 12 file boxes. Subtitled by status of case as Active and Inactive.
Copies of certificates of eligibility for W P A employment, showing name and address of applicant, case number, relief district, names of county and relief agency, work classifications, and all information required by W P A regulations. Also includes copies of forms terminating employment and changing work classification. Arranged numerically by case numbers. No index. Typed on printed forms. 6 x 9 x 14. Relief administration office.

36. C. C. C.
1934——. 1 file drawer.

Records of C C C enrollees, including applications, showing date and name of applicant, address, age, number and names of dependents, and name of proposed allottee; medical certificates; investigation reports on applications; and enrollment certificates, showing date of assignment and name of camp. Arranged chronologically by dates of assignments and alphabetically thereunder by applicants. No index. Typed on printed forms. 12 x 16 x 24. Relief administration office.

37. CARD INDEX TO C. C. C. FILE
1934——. 1 file box.

Card index file of C C C applicants and enrollees, showing name of applicant or enrollee, date of application, case number, date enrolled, to what camp assigned, name and address of allottee, and date discharged. Arranged alphabetically by names of applicants or enrollees. Handwritten and typed on printed forms. 4 x 6 x 17. Relief administration office.

38. APPLICATIONS FOR EMPLOYMENT
1933. 1 bundle. Discontinued.

Applications for employment by needy persons of county under C W A, showing date, name of township and municipality, name and address of applicant, personal history, and work classification. Arranged alphabetically by names of townships and municipalities and alphabetical thereunder by names of applicants. No index. Handwritten on printed forms. 11 x 8.5 x 5. Attic.

Correspondence

39. [CORRESPONDENCE]
1934——. 1 file box.

Originals and copies of inquiries and replies concerning relief cases and clients from agencies other than Lake County relief administration, date of inquiry or reply, name of correspondent, text of correspondent of filing. No index. Typed. 12 x 16 x 24. Relief administration office.

When Lake County was erected in 1840, the office of recorder was, according to the existing state law, elective for a term of three years.[1] The term was altered in 1906 to two years,[2] and again in 1933 to four years, to take effect in 1937.[3] The recorder's bond is $2000.[4] He may be removed from office on petition of 10 percent of the electors, conviction by the common pleas court of bribery, and on failure to give bond.[5] Vacancies are filled by the county commissioners until the next succeeding election.[6]

The function of the office is to record in an accessible way the transfers of real property, mortgages on all forms of property, and various liens and powers relating to the ownership and use of property. A vast amount of material is filed with the recorder, including deeds, mortgages, leases, liens, power of attorney, soldiers' discharges, and other related records. In Lake County records preserved to date number 501 volumes, 79 file boxes, and 24 bundles. The number of documents of various types filed annually indicates, in general, the activity of the office. During 1940, 2404 deeds, 4000 transfers, 55 mechanical liens, 475 leases, 25,000 chattel mortgages, and 1257 mortgages on real property were deposited with the recorder.[7] The most conspicuous change in business handled by this office during the past 20 years is the mounting number of chattel mortgages.

In 1940 the salary budget for the recorder and the staff was $5420. The office is self-supporting, since fees exceeded this sum by $4403.55.[8]

---

1. *Laws of Ohio,* XXVII, 65.
2. *Ibid.,* XCVIII, 271.
3. *Ibid.,* CXV, 191.
4. G.C. sec. 2751.
5. G.C. secs. 7, 10-1, 12824.
6. G.C. sec. 2755.
7. Record of Deeds, 1840, entry 40; Daily Register of Deeds, 1940, entry 42; Record of Mechanics Liens, 1940, entry 51; Record of Leases, 1940, entry 44; Record of Chattel Mortgages and Bills of Sale, 1940, entry 72; Record of Mortgages, 1940, entry 46.
8. Cash Book, 1940, entry 80

Real Property Transfers

Deeds

40. RECORD OF DEEDS
1840——. (A-P, R-Z; 1-166).

Copies of all deeds including warranty deeds, sheriff's, trustee's, administrator's, executor's, assignor's, assignee's, land contract, estate, patent, assignment, bank superintendent's, deeds and partition, receivership deeds, right-of-way deeds and quick claim deeds, showing name of grantor and grantee, kind and date of instrument, amount of consideration, description and location of property transferred, and date recorded. Also contains: Record of Leases, 1840-1864, entry 44; Record of Mortgages, 1840-1849, entry 46; Power of Attorney, 1840-1892, entry 76. 3 volumes, 1840-1850, arranged chronologically by dates of recording: 188 volumes,-1851——, arranged by kinds of instruments and chronologically thereunder by dates of recording. For index, see entry 41; also separate index to mortgages, 1840-1849, entry 47. 1840-1891, handwritten; 1892-1916, handwritten on printed forms; 1917——, typed on printed forms. Average 600 pages. 18 x 12 x 3. 5 volumes, 1840-1857, attic; 186 volumes, 1858——, Recorder's file room.

41. GENERAL INDEX TO DEEDS
1840——. 15 volumes (1-9, 1A; 5 volumes dated).

Direct and reverse index to Record of Deeds, entry 40, showing names of grantor and grantee, volume letter or number and page number of record, number of acres, township, tract, number of lot and sublot, amount of consideration, and remarks; Also 1915——, number of deed. Arranged alphabetically by names of grantors and grantees. 1840-1852, handwritten; 1853-1917, handwritten on printed forms; 1917——, typed or printed forms. Average 500 pages. 19 x 16 x 3. Recorder's file room.

42. DAILY REGISTER OF DEEDS
1896——. 9 volumes (1-9).

Daily record of deeds filed, showing amount of consideration, description and location of property, date filed, names of grantor and grantee, kind of instrument consecutive number, and remarks. Arranged chronologically by dates of filing. No index. Handwritten on printed forms. Average 300 pages. 18 x 17 x 1.5. Recorder's office.

43. DEEDS AND MORTGAGES [Unclaimed]

1840—. 35 file boxes (labeled a bike contained letters of alphabet).
 Original deeds and mortgages left for recording and not claimed, showing date
drawn, names of grantor and grantee, date recorded, description of property,
consideration, and terms of mortgage. Arranged alphabetically by names that
grantors. No index. Handwritten on printed forms. 10 x 4.5 x 13.5. Recorder's
office.

Leases

44. RECORD OF LEASES

1865—. 12 volumes (A-L). 1840-1864 in Record of Deeds, entry 40.
Copies of leases and lease agreements, showing date, name of lessor and lessee,
terms of lease, description and location of property, amount of lease, and date of
filing; Includes record of oil and gas leases. Arranged chronologically by dates of
filing. For index, see entry 45. 1865-1898, handwritten; 1899-1919, handwritten on
printed forms; 1919—, typed on printed forms. Average 640 pages. 18 x 12 x 3.5.
Recorder's file rooms.

45. GENERAL INDEX TO LEASES

1865—. 1 volume.
Direct and reverse index to Record of Leases, entry 44, showing date of lease,
names of lessor and lessee, volume letter and page number of record, number of
acres, range, township, tract, lot number, sublot number, amount of consideration,
and remarks. Arranged alphabetically by names of lessors and lessees. Handwritten
on printed forms. 600 pages. 18 x 12 x 3. Recorder's file room.

Mortgages

46. RECORD OF MORTGAGES

1850—. 136 volumes (A-P, R-U, W-Z; 25-136). 1840-1849 in Record of
Deeds, entry 40.
Copies of mortgages conveying condition title to real estate and security for value
received, showing names of mortgagor and mortgages, date of mortgage, number
of instrument, amount secured, condition of mortgage, description of property
covered by mortgage, names of witnesses, notarizations, and date filed and
recorded; also record of discharges of mortgages, 1850-1891. Arranged

chronologically by dates of recording. For index, see entry 47. 1850-1867, handwritten; 1868-1916, handwritten on printed forms; 1917—, typed on printed forms. 640 pages. 18.5 x 12.5 x 3. Recorder's file room.

For subsequent record of discharges, see entry 49.

47. GENERAL INDEX TO MORTGAGES

1840—. 10 volumes (1-5; 5 volumes dated).
Direct and reverse index to Record of Mortgages, entry 46, and to mortgages recorded in Record of Deeds, 1840-1849, entry 40, showing name of mortgagor and mortgagee, date of instrument, volume letter or number and page number of record, number of acres, range, township, tract, number of lot and sublot, amount, and remarks; 1913—, also shows number of mortgage. Arranged alphabetically by names of mortgagors and mortgagees. 1840-1904, handwritten; 1905—, handwritten on printed forms; Average 400 pages. 18 x 12 x 3.2. Recorder's file room.

48. DAILY REGISTER OF MORTGAGES

1896—. 9 volumes (1-9).
Daily register of mortgages filed, showing date filed, names of mortgagor and mortgagee, consecutive number, and remarks. Arranged chronologically by dates of filing. No index. Handwritten on printed forms. Average 300 pages. 18 x 17 x 1.5. Recorder's office.

49. RECORD OF CERTIFICATE OF DISCHARGE OF MORTGAGES

1891—. 11 volumes (1-11). For prior record of releases, see entry 46.
Record of discharges or partial releases of mortgages, showing names of mortgagor and mortgagee, amount of mortgage, description of property, date of mortgage, date recorded, and date of release or partial release. Arranged chronologically by dates of recording. Indexed alphabetically by names of mortgagors and mortgagees. Handwritten on printed forms. Average 640 pages. 18 x 12.5 x 3.5. Recorder's file room.

50. CERTIFICATE OF RELEASE OF MORTGAGE
1933—. 1 file box.

Copies of court certificates of release of mortgage, showing date of certificate, names of grantor and grantee, case number, volume and page numbers of Executive Docket, entry 84, and of Journal, entry 131, kind of mortgage, date, volume and page numbers of Record of Mortgages, entry 46, recorder's file number, and date of filing. Arranged chronologically by dates of filing and numerically thereunder by file numbers. No index. Handwritten on printed forms. 10 x 4.5 x 13.5. Recorder's office.

Liens

51. RECORD OF MECHANICS LIENS
1843—. 6 volumes (A-F).

Record of mechanics' liens charged against property for labor and material, including affidavits for liens, showing names of creditor and debtor, amount of lien, satisfaction and discharge of lien, itemized list of labor and material, what construction or improvement, copy of notarization of claim, and date filed and recorded. Arranged chronologically by dates are recording. Indexed alphabetically by names of creditors and debtors. 1843-1891, handwritten; 1892-1932, handwritten on printed forms; 1932—, typed on printed forms. Average 350 pages. 18 x 12.5 x 3.5. 2 volumes, 1843-1891, attic; 4 volumes, 1892—, Recorder's file room.

52. INDEX TO LIENS [Stallion Service]
1885-1892. 1 volume.

Record of liens for stallion service rendered, showing names of principals, in favor of whom, against whom, number of instrument, date of service, date of cancellation of lien, amount involved, and date of filing. Arranged alphabetically by names of principles and chronologically thereunder by dates of service. Handwritten on printed forms. 75 pages. 14 x 8.5 x .5. Attic.

53. EXCISE AND FRANCHISE TAX LIEN AND CORPORATION RECORD INDEX
1930—. 1 volume.

Record of notices of excise and franchise tax liens, showing recorders file number, name of public utility or corporation, date of filing, amount of tax penalty, total, file number of payment, date of payment, and date of filing notice of payment; also serves as an index to Corporate Record, entry 54, by showing file number and page. Arranged alphabetically by names of utilities or corporations and chronologically thereunder by dates of filing. Handwritten on printed forms. 250 pages. 17 x 16 x 1.5. Recorder's file room.

54. CORPORATION RECORD
1930—. 1 volume.

Record of notices issued by state tax commission of payment of franchise or excise tax and discharge of lien, showing date, name of taxpayer, amount of tax assessed, penalty, date and amount of payment, date of recording, and file number. Arranged numerically by filed numbers. For index, see entry 53. Typed on printed forms. 300 pages. 16 x 12 x 2.5. Recorder's office.

55. [Excise and Franchise] TAX LIENS
1930-1935. 1 file box.

Copies of tax commissioner's notices to corporations of liens for excise and franchise taxes, notices of payment, and discharge of lien, showing name of taxpayer, kind of tax, amount of tax and penalty, total amount, name and location of company, and date of filing. Arranged chronologically by dates of filing. No index. Typed or printed forms. 10 x 4.5 x 13.5. Recorder's office.

56. PERSONAL TAX LIEN
1933—. 1 file box.

County treasurer's certificates of release of delinquent personal tax liens and of partial discharges of personal property tax, showing date of certificate, name of property owner, amount of tax, recorder's file number, dates of filing and recording, years delinquent, and name of taxing district. Arranged chronologically by dates of filing and numerically thereunder by filed numbers. For index, see entry 57. Handwritten on printed forms. 10 x 4.5 x 13.5. Recorder's office.

57. INDEX TO PERSONAL TAX LIEN
1933—. 1 volume.

Record of personal tax liens, showing recorder's file number, certificate number, and name of taxpayer; also serves as an index to Personal Tax Lien, entry 56, by showing file number. Arranged alphabetically by names of taxpayers. Handwritten on printed forms. 250 pages. 14.5 x 12 x 2. Recorder's file room.

58. FEDERAL TAX [Liens]

1923—. 1 file box.

Notices to taxpayer of tax lien under internal revenue law given by federal tax collector, showing collector's serial number, dates, name and residence of delinquent taxpayer, nature of tax taxable period, amount of tax, amount of penalty assessed, recorder's file number, and date of filing. Arranged chronologically by dates of filing and numerically thereunder by file numbers. For index, see entry 59. Typed on printed forms. 10 x 4.5 x 13.5. Recorder's office.

59. FEDERAL TAX LIEN INDEX

1923—. 1 volume.

Record of notices of federal tax liens, showing name and address of taxpayer, collector's notice number, recorder's file number, date and time of filing, amount assessed, penalty, collector's serial number of certificate of discharge, and date of filing certificate of discharge. Serves as an index to Federal Tax [Liens], entry 58, by showing file number. Arranged alphabetically by names of taxpayers and chronologically thereunder by dates of filing. Handwritten on printed forms. 250 pages. 17.5 x 16 x 1.5. Recorder's file room.

60. SURETY LIENS

1929—. 1 file box.

Notices of liens given as surety to recognizances, showing file number of document, against whom issued, date of filing, amount pledged, names of sureties, and description of real estate; also includes notices of discharge of recognizance. Arranged chronologically by dates of filing and numerically thereunder by file numbers. For index, see entry 61. Handwritten and typed on printed forms. 10 x 4.5 x 13.5. Recorder's office.

61. INDEX TO NOTICES OF LIENS SURETY TO RECOGNIZANCE

1929—. 1 volume.

Record of notices of liens as surety to recognizances, showing recorders file number, date of filing, name of defendant, names of sureties, amount of recognizance, description of real estate, and file number and discharge of recognizance. Serves as an index to Surety Liens, entry 60, showing file number. Arranged alphabetically by names of sureties and chronologically thereunder by dates of filing. Handwritten on printed forms. 250 pages. 17.5 x 16.5 x 1.5. Recorder's file room.

Registered Lands

62. REGISTERED LANDS – INDEX OF OWNERS, LIENS, AND LESSER ESTATES
1913—. 1 volume.

Index to Registered Lands–Reception Book, entry 63, and Registered Lands–Register of Title, entry 64, showing owner's name, date of certificate or document, volume and page numbers of record, and dates transferred and cancelled. Arranged alphabetically by names of owners. Handwritten on printed forms. 425 pages. 10 x 19 x 3. Recorder's office.

63. REGISTERED LANDS – RECEPTION BOOK
1913—. 21 volumes (1-21).

Record of daily receipts of documents affecting registered lands, showing date and time filed, document number, kind of instrument, from or against whom, in whose favor, date of document, terms, description of lands, and certificate number. Arranged chronologically by dates of filing. For index, see entry 62. Handwritten on printed forms. Average 425 pages. 20 x 18 x 3. Recorder's office.

64. REGISTER OF LANDS – REGISTER OF TITLE
1913—. 14 volumes (1-14).

Record of certificates of title, showing from whom transferred, to whom, certificate and document numbers, date originally registered, date of filing certificate, plat of property, and date of recording; also includes record of memorials of lesser estates and liens against lands described in certificate of title, showing to whom issued, number and kind of document, in whose favor, against whom, date of recording, date of certificate, to whom assigned, date of cancellation, and number of instrument cancelled. Arranged chronologically by dates of recording. For index, see entry 62. Handwritten on printed forms. 300 pages. 20 x 18 x 2.5. Recorder's office.

Plats and Maps

65. RECORD OF PLATS [Original]
1840-1852. 1 volume.

Record of plats and surveys containing same information and transcribing in 1904 into Record of Plats, entry 66. Arranged chronologically by dates are recording. No index. Condition poor. 100 pages. 30 x 24 x 2. Recorder's file room.

66. RECORD OF PLATS
1840—. 8 volumes (A-H).

Record of surveys and plats of roads, allotments, and subdivisions, showing name of plat, boundary lines, border lines, watercourses, railroads, streets, street names, distances, bearings, footage, acreage, dates are receiving and recording, document number, amount of fee, date transferred, and in some cases, scale. Prepared by county engineer. Arranged chronologically by dates of recording. For index, see entries 67, 68. Hand drawn and lettered, and blueprint. Scale vary, 1 inch equals 50 feet, to 1 inch equals 50 rods. Average 100 pages. 30 x 24 x 2. Recorder's file room.

67. INDEX TO PLATS
1840—. 1 volume.

Index to Record of Plats, entry 66, showing date of plat (year, month, day), name of plat, name of landowner at time of recording, volume letter and page number of record, and remarks; also shows, 1914, plat number. Arranged by townships and chronologically thereunder by dates of plats. Index alphabetically by names of plats. Handwritten on printed forms. 425 pages. 18.5 x 12 x 2.5. Recorder's file room.

68. INDEX TO PLATS [Original]
1840-1825. 1 volume.

Index to Record of Plats, entry 66, which contains same information and has been transcribed into Index to Plats, entry 67. Arranged by townships and chronologically thereunder by dates of plats. Indexed alphabetically by names of plats. Condition poor. Handwritten on printed forms. 425 pages. 18.5 x 12 x 2.5. Recorder's file room.

69. PARTITION FENCE RECORD
1916-1917. 1 volume.
Copies of agreements and assignments by township trustees in matters of partition fences, assigning each landowner his share of fence to maintain, showing name of litigants, township, description of land and adjoining lands, dividing line, length of line, and dates petition filed and recorded. Arranged chronologically by dates of recording. No index. Handwritten. 300 pages. 18 x 13 x 2.5. Recorder's file room.

70. MAP OF GEAUGA AND LAKE COUNTIES
1857. 1 map
 Political map of Geauga and Lake Counties, showing political subdivisions, location of roads, rivers, lakes, and creeks; route numbers; names of townships and corporations, sections, range lines, boundary lines of land tracts, boundary lines of towns, and locations of public buildings. Printed. Published by S.H. Mathews, Philadelphia, Pennsylvania. Scale, 1.5 inch equals 1 mile. 59 x 43. Recorder's file room.

Personal Property Transfers

71. CHATTEL MORTGAGE INDEX
1878—. 17 volumes (1-17).
Index to Record of Chattel Mortgages and Bills of Sale, 1893—, entry 72, and [Chattel Mortgages and Bills of Sale], entry 73, showing names of mortgagor and mortgagee, mortgage number, date of mortgage, date recorded, amount, and date cancelled. Arranged alphabetically by names of mortgagors and mortgagees. Handwritten on printed forms. Average 600 pages. 17.5 x 16 x 3. 4 volumes, 1878-1913, attic; 13 volumes, 1914—, Recorder's office.

72. RECORD OF CHATTEL MORTGAGES AND BILLS OF SALE
1893—. 2 volumes (1, 2).
Record of chattel mortgages and bills of sale, showing mortgage number, date, names of mortgagor and mortgagee, amount of mortgage, terms, list of chattels or purchases, date of filing, description of property mortgaged, notarization, date recorded, and copy of cancellation of mortgage. Arranged chronologically by dates of recording. For index see entry 71. 1893-1910 handwritten on printed forms; 1911—, typed on printed forms. Average 475 pages. 16 x 12 x 2.5. 1 volume, 1893-1910, attic; 1 volume, 1911—, Recorder's file room.

73. [CHATTEL MORTGAGE AND BILLS OF SALE]
1878—. 14 bundles, 35 file boxes, (bundles unlabeled; file boxes labeled by contained mortgage numbers).
Originals and copies of chattel mortgages and bills of sale, showing date of mortgage, mortgage number, names of mortgagor or mortgagee, amount of mortgage, terms, and date of filing. Arranged numerically by consecutive numbers of mortgages. For index, see entry 71. Handwritten and typed on printed forms. 10 x 4.5 x 13.5. 14 bundles, 1878-1914, attic; 35 file boxes, 1915—, Recorder's office.

Corporations and Partnerships

74. [INCORPORATION OF CHURCHES, ORGANIZATIONS, SOCIETIES]
1847-1887. 1 volume. Discontinued.
Copies of certificates filed with secretary of state, of organizations and corporations of churches, partnerships, and societies, showing date of certificate, name of corporation and officers, purpose of organization, and date of recording. Arranged chronologically by dates of recording. No index. Handwritten. Condition poor. 150 pages. 12.5 x 8 x 1. Recorder's file room.

75. BANK RECORD [Partnership Record]
1845-1846. 1 volume. Discontinued.
Copies of partnership agreements and certificates of incorporation, showing title, names of partners or officers, date organized, date filed and recorded. Also contains: [Certificates of Compliance and Licenses of Insurance Agents], 1868-1872, entry 77; [Certificates of Compliance], 1868-1872, entry 78. Arranged chronologically by dates of filing. No index. Handwritten. 150 pages. 12.5 x 8 x 1. Attic.

Grants of Authority

76. POWER OF ATTORNEY
1893—. 2 volumes (1, 2). 1840-1892 in Record of Deeds, entry 40.
Record of powers of attorney, showing date of agreement, names of grantor and grantee, purpose for which given, date of expiration, signatures of grantor and witnesses, and date of filing and recording. Arranged chronologically by dates of

agreements. Indexed alphabetically by names that grantors and grantees. Handwritten. Average 450 pages. 18.5 x 12 x 3. Recorder's file room.

77. [CERTIFICATES OF COMPLIANCE AND LICENSES OF INSURANCE AGENTS]
1895——. 10 bundles, 1 file box. 1868-1872 in Bank Record [Partnership Record], entry 75.

Certified copies of insurance agents' and solicitors' licenses, showing name and address, type of insurance, employer's name and address of home office, and dates of certification and filing. Also contains [Certificate of Compliance], 1895-1935, entry 78. Arranged alphabetically by names of agents. No index. Typed on printed forms. Bundles, 4.5 x 3 x 7.5; file box, 7 x 5 x 17.5. 10 bundles, 1895-1936, attic; 1 file box, 1937——, Recorder's office.

78. CERTIFICATE OF COMPLIANCE]
1936——. 1 file box. 1868-1872 in Bank record [Partnership Record], entry 75; 1895-1935 in [Certificates of Compliance and Licenses of Insurance Agents], entry 77.

Original certificates issued by state department and insurance companies that have complied with state law regarding insurance regulations, showing name and location of company, type of insurance, amount of assets, liabilities, paid up capital, surplus, income for current year, expenditures, net assets, certificate number, date of certificate, and date filed. Arranged numerically by certificate numbers. No index. Typed on printed forms. 7 x 5 x 17. Recorder's office.

79. TAX RECORD [Authority to Pay Taxes]
1908-1934. 1 volume. Discontinued.

Copies of authority to pay taxes, showing instrument number, names of grantor and grantee, description of property, date of instrument, and date of recording. Arranged chronologically by dates of recording. Indexed alphabetically by names of grantors and grantees. Handwritten on printed forms. 250 pages. 18.5 x 12.5 x 2. Recorder's file room.

Fiscal Accounts

80. CASH BOOK
1907—. 21 volumes (1-21).
Cash book and record of fees collected, showing date of receipt, consecutive number of instrument, chattel mortgage number, by whom paid, kind of instrument and service rendered, and amount of fees collected for recording, filing, cancellations, searches, and sundries. Arranged chronologically by dates of receipts. No index. Handwritten on printed forms. Average 300 pages. 18 x 12 x 2. 17 volumes, 1907-1925, attic; 4 volumes, 1925—, Recorder's office.

Miscellaneous

81. [RECORDER'S STATEMENTS
1906—. 3 file boxes.
Copies of recorder's annual reports of conveyance statistics to secretary of state, showing date of report, number of instruments recorded and cancelled including deeds, mortgages, leases, and liens; also amount of fees collected for such services. Arranged chronologically by dates of reports. No index. Handwritten on printed forms. 4.5 x 4.5 x 9.5. Recorder's office.

82. SOLDIER'S DISCHARGE
1865—. 1 volume.
Record of discharges of soldiers and sailors from the United States Army and Navy (except World War Veterans), showing name of dischargee, rank assignment, date of enrollment, term of service, date discharged, conduct record, date and place of birth, occupation, record of payment of bounty, and date of recording. Arranged chronologically by dates of recording. Indexed alphabetically by names of dischargees. Handwritten. 325 pages. 16.5 x 11 x 2. Recorder's file room.

83. SOLDIER'S DISCHARGE RECORD [World War]
1918—. 1 volume.
Record of discharges of soldiers and sailors of World War from the United States Army and Navy, showing name of dischargee, rank, assignment, reason for discharge, description of soldier or sailor, enlistment record, date of discharge, and date of recording. Indexed alphabetically by names of soldiers or sailors. Handwritten on printed forms. 400 pages. 16.5 x 11 x 3. Recorder's file room.

The clerk of courts in Lake County, as in other counties, was first appointed for seven years by the judges of the common pleas court. His official duties have always been closely associated with the work of the court, and, as the name of office signifies, he performs the clerical work of the courts. The office became elective for three years in 1851, for two years in 1905, and for four years in 1936.[1]

The clerk is subject to removal by common pleas court for unsatisfactory performance of his duties or failure to furnish additional bond if required.[2] Vacancies are filled by county commissioners pending the next election, or in the event of their failure to do this, by the auditor.[3] In Lake County, his bond is fixed at $10,000.[4] The clerk may appoint and fix the bonds of his assistants and deputies, subject to the approval of the common pleas court.[5]

The chief duty of the clerk of courts is the recording of information concerning litigation. He files all court papers, and keeps appearance, trial, and execution dockets, court journals, records and indexes, both direct and reverse, court judgments, and records of fines and court costs collected.[6] He has served as a registrar of a considerable amount of non-court business as well, filing such varied documents as optometry certificates;[7] real estate brokers' licenses;[8] trademarks;[9] commissions of notaries public and justices of the peace;[10] hunting, trapping, and fishing licenses,[11] and bills of sale and assignment of motor vehicles.[12] Records preserved to date in Lake County comprise 1182 volumes, 214 file boxes, 30 bundles, 10 letter file boxes, and 23 loose file envelopes.

---

1. *Ohio Const., 1802,* Art. III, sec. 9; *Ohio Const., 1851,* Art. IV, sec. 16; *Laws of Ohio,* XCVIII, 273; CXVI, pt. ii, 184.
2. G.C. secs. 2883, 3036, 3049, 12196, 12851.
3. G.C. sec. 2870.
4. Record of Official Bonds, 1940, entry 306.
5. G.C. secs. 2871, 2981.
6. G.C. secs. 2878-80, 2881, 2883, 11599, 11609.
7. See entry 110.
8. See entry 113.
9. See entry 126.
10. See entry 107.
11. See entries 111, 112.
12. See entry 103.

The clerk also issues various legal orders, such as attachments, garnishments, summonses, subpoenas, executions, *replevins, writs* of *mandamus* and *habeas corpus,* injunctions, and warrants to arrest.[13]

Remuneration was made by fee basis until 1906; then the salaries have been fixed in proportion to population, which allows the clerk of Lake County to draw a salary of $2725 for the year 1941. He has on his staff eight assistants, who receive an aggregate salary of $9835.[14] Fees collected in 1940 amounted to $15,848.[15]

---

13. G.C. secs. 11820, 11761, 11279, 11501, 11673, 12052, 12290, 12167, 11883, 13432-8.
14. Payroll, 1941, entry 283.
15. Cash Book, 1940, entry 116.

Dockets and General Indexes

84. EXECUTION DOCKET
1840—. 56 volumes (A-Z; 1-30).
Record of execution proceedings in cases before Lake County courts, showing names of litigants, number and title of case, names of attorneys, term of court, date of hearing, judgment of court, volume number or letter and page numbers of journal, entry 131; Sheriff's Returns, entry 102; Cash Book, entry 116; [Civil] Record, entry 133, or Criminal Record entry 134, and dates of final entry and filing; also includes divorce records, 1844—, showing names of plaintiffs and defendants, case number, and record of hearings and petitions. Arranged numerically by case numbers. Indexed alphabetically by names of plaintiffs and defendants. 1840-1842 handwritten; 1843-1913 handwritten on printed forms; 1914—, typed on printed forms. 10 volumes, 1840-1886, attic; 46 volumes, 1887—, Clerk of court's office.

85. TRANSCRIPT FOR LIENS EXECUTION DOCKET
1927—. 1 volume.
Record of filing of transcript for liens, showing names of plaintiff and defendant, number and title of case, name of court, date of filing, volume and page number of journal, entry 131, dates of filing *praecipe* issue of execution, date of sheriff's return, cost bill, receipt for amount collected, volume and page numbers of cash book, entry 116, and [Civil] Record, entry 133, or Criminal Record, entry 134. Arranged chronologically by dates of filing. Indexed alphabetically by names of plaintiffs and defendants. Handwritten on printed forms. 600 pages. 21 x 12 x 3. Clerk of court's office.

86. JUDGMENT DOCKET
1935—. 1 volume.

Clerk of court's record of judgment lien certificates, showing name of court, case number, name of creditor and debtor on judgment, dates judgment rendered, filed and satisfied, amount involved, in terms of satisfying judgment. Arranged chronologically by dates of filing. Indexed alphabetically by names of creditors and debtors. Types on printed forms. 300 pages. 16 x 10 x 2. Clerk of courts office.

87. TRANSFER DOCKET
1897—. 15 volumes.

Transfer of common pleas civil and criminal docket finished cases to record binders, showing title and number of case, names of attorneys, kind of action, date of filing, orders of court, date of orders, and volume and page number of Journal, entry 131. Arranged chronologically by dates of filing and numerically thereunder by case numbers. No index. Handwritten on printed forms. Average 800 pages. 15 10 x 7. 11 volumes, 1897-1935, attic; 4 volumes, 1936—, Clerk of court's office.

88. PRAECIPE DOCKET
1874—. 10 volumes (1-10).

Record of orders to clerk of courts, showing names of litigants, title of case, volume letter or number and page numbers, of Execution Docket, entry 84, purpose, to whom issued, signature of attorney, kind of action, kind of *writ*, and date issued. Arranged chronologically by dates of issue. No index. Handwritten on printed forms. Average 200 pages. 14 x 10 x 2. 7 volumes, 1874-1932, attic; 3 volumes, 1933—, Clerk of court's office.

89. GENERAL INDEX
1840—. 7 volumes (A, 1-6).

General index to Lake County court records, showing surname and given name of plaintiff and defendant, court term, case number, date of judgment, amount of judgment, volume and page numbers of Execution Docket, entry 84; Appearance Docket, entry 128; [Civil] Record, entry 133; or Criminal Record, entry 134. Serves as index to Civil Case Papers, entry 135 by showing case number. Arranged alphabetically by names of plaintiffs and defendants. Handwritten on printed forms. Average 500 pages. 8 x 14.5 x 3. Clerk of court's office.

90. INDEX TO PENDING SUITS AND LIVING JUDGMENTS
    1880—. 6 volumes (1-6).
Record of pending suits, living judgments, and executions, showing names of
plaintiff and defendant, court of issuance, case number, number of Execution
Docket, entry 84, Appearance Docket, entry 128, and Criminal Appearance and
execution Docket, entry 129; also volume and page numbers of [Civil] Record entry
133. Arranged alphabetically by names of plaintiffs. Handwritten on printed forms.
Average 500 pages. 18.5 x 12.5 x 3.5. Clerk of court's office.

General Court Records

Jury and Witness Records

91. JURY BOOK
    1842-1856, 1864—. 7 volumes (1-5; 2 unnumbered). Title varies; Jury
    Record, 1842-1856, 1 volume.
List of grand and petit jurors for cases in Lake County courts, showing title of case,
term of court, names of jurors, number of days in attendance, mileage, total fees,
and date paid; also includes record of jurors, 1842-1856, in supreme and district
court cases. 1842-1856, arranged alphabetically by names of jurors; 1864—,
arranged chronologically by court terms. No index. 1842-1856 handwritten;
1864—, handwritten on printed forms. Average 150 pages. 13 x 18 x 1.5. 5
volumes, 1842-1856, 1864-1922, attic; 2 volumes, 1923—, Clerk of court's office.

92. PETIT JURY LIST
    1879-1903, 1932—. 3 file boxes.
Copies of venires to sheriff for petit jurors, showing term of court, name and
address of person called to serve, period of time to serve, number of miles covered,
date to appear, date of sheriff's return, signature of clerk of courts, deputy, judge,
and jury commission, sheriff's fees, date of filing, and volume and page number of
Journal, entry 131. Arranged chronologically by court terms. No index. 1879-1903
handwritten; 1933—, typed. 10.5 x 4.25 x 13.5. 2 file boxes, 1879-1903, attic; 1 file
box, 1932—, Clerk of court's office.

93. GRAND JURY FILES

1878——. 4 bundles, 5 file boxes (bundles unlabeled; file box 1-5).

Original *praecipes* by clerk of courts and subpoenas for witnesses to appear before the grand jury, showing term of court, name and address of person subpoenaed, date of appearance, manner served, date of service, sheriff's mileage, and date of filing. Arranged chronologically by court terms. No index. Handwritten and typed on printed forms. Bundles, 10 x 6 x 4.5; file box, 10 x 4.5 x 13.5. 4 bundles, 3 file boxes, 1878-1926, attic; 2 file boxes, 1927——, Clerk of court's office.

94. CRIMINAL WITNESS RECORD

1869——. 2 volumes (1, 2).

List of witnesses summoned in criminal cases in the court of common pleas, showing term of court, title of case, case number, names of witnesses, days of attendance, mileage, and amount of fees, including sheriff's and stenographer's; also includes record of grand jury witnesses, showing term of court, name of witness, days in attendance, mileage, and total fees. Arranged by court terms and numerically thereunder by case numbers. No index. Handwritten on printed forms. Average 475 pages. 16 x 11.5 x 2. 1 volume, 1869-1908, attic; 1 volume, 1909——, Clerk of court's office.

95. WITNESS RECORD

1841——. 8 volumes (A, B, 1, 1-5). Title varies: Witness Docket, 1885-1930, 1 volume.

List of witnesses summoned in civil cases before the court of common pleas and appeals courts, showing term of court, title of case, names of witnesses, and amount of fees. Arranged chronologically by court terms. 1 volume, 1885-1930, no index; 7 volumes, 1841——, indexed alphabetically by names of witnesses. 1841-1929, handwritten; 1930——, typed on printed forms. Average 400 pages. 16 x 11 x 2. 7 volumes, 1841-1929, attic; 1 volume, 1930——, Clerk of court's office.

Bonds

96. INJUNCTION BONDS

1857——, 7 file envelopes.

Original bonds in undertakings for orders of injunction, showing names of principles, date approved, and amount of bond approved. Arranged chronologically by dates approved. No index. Typed on printed forms. 9 x 4 x 2.5.

5 file envelopes, 1857-1930, attic; 2 file envelopes, 1930—, Clerk of court's file room.

97. RECEIVERS BONDS
1885—. 5 file envelopes.
Original bonds, showing name of receiver as principal, names of sureties, amount of bond, date signed, date approved by clerk of courts, and date filed. Arranged chronologically by dates of filing. No index. Handwritten on printed forms. 9 x 4 x 2. 3 envelopes, 1885-1925, attic; 2 file envelopes, 1926—, Clerk of court's file room.

98. BONDS [In Undertakings for Costs and Stay of Execution]
1903—. 2 letter files.
Original bonds and undertakings for cost and stay of execution, showing amount of bond, date of bond, date filed, case number, volume and page numbers of Appearance Docket, entry 128, name of court, names of litigants, and name of surety for plaintiff's cost. Arranged chronologically by dates of bonds. No index. Handwritten on printed forms. 9 x 4 x 1. 1 letter file, 1903-1930, attic; 1 letter file, 1931—, Clerk of court's office.

99. RECOGNIZANCE OF ACCUSED INDICTMENT BONDS
1920—, 7 letter files.
Original bonds signed by the accused for appearance at time specified for trial, showing name of accused, case number, amount of bond, names of sureties, charge by the court, signature of the clerk of courts, and date filed. Arranged chronologically by dates of filing. No index. Handwritten on printed forms. 9 x 4 x 1.5. 6 letter files, 1920-1930, attic; 1 letter file, 1931—, Clerk of court's office.

100. RECOGNIZANCE OF WITNESS BOND
1929—. 1 letter file.
Original witness bonds, showing case number, volume and page numbers of Appearance Docket, entry 128, name of court, amount of bond, and names of litigants, witnesses and sureties. Arranged alphabetically by names of witnesses. No index. Handwritten on printed forms. 9 x 4.5 x 2.5. Clerk of court's office.

101. APPEAL BONDS
1865-1879, 1911—. 1 bundle, 4 file envelopes.

Copies of appeal bonds, showing case number, volume letter or number and page number of Appearance Docket, entry 128, names of litigants, names of sureties to bond, date filed, amount of bond, conditions and date filed. Arranged chronologically by dates of filing. No index. Handwritten on printed forms. Bundles, 8 x 4 x 2; file envelopes, 8.25 x 3.25 x 1.5. 1 bundle, 1865-1879, 2 file envelopes, 1911-1929, attic; 2 file envelopes, 1930—, Clerk of court's office.

Sheriff's Returns

102. SHERIFF'S RETURNS
1855—. 10 volumes (A-J).

Record of sheriff's returns on executions, showing date of return, number of execution, kind of *writ*, and bill of fees. Arranged chronologically by dates of returns. Indexed alphabetically by names of plaintiffs and defendants. Handwritten and typed. Average 400 pages. 16.5 x 11 x 2.5. 2 volumes, 1855-1893, attic; 8 volumes, 1894—, Clerk of court's office.

Motor Vehicles

103. STATEMENT OF OWNERSHIP
1921-1937. 25 bundles, 180 file boxes, (labeled by contained bill of sale numbers). Discontinued; law repealed.

Copies of motor vehicle bills of sale and certificates of ownership, showing name and address of owner, bill of sale number, trade name, type, motor number, color of vehicle, year built, number of cylinders, horsepower, name and address of vendor, date of oath, and date of filing. Arranged numerically by consecutive bill of sales number and chronologically thereunder by dates of filing. For index see entry 104. Handwritten and typed on printed forms. Bundles 10 x 6 x 4.5; file boxes, 8 x 10 x 24. 25 bundles, 1921-1935, attic; 80 file boxes, 1936-1937, Clerk of court's office.

104. INDEX TO MOTOR VEHICLE SALES
1921-1937. 8 volumes.

Direct and reverse index to Statement of Ownership, entry 103, showing names of grantor and grantee, date file, bill of sale number, and description of motor vehicle.

Arranged alphabetically by names of grantors and grantees. Handwritten on printed forms. Average 500 pages. 21 x 13.5 x 5. Clerk of court's office.

105. CERTIFICATE OF TITLE
1938—. 8 file boxes. (1-8).
Copies of certificates of title to motor vehicles, showing consecutive certificate number, date of certificate, names of purchaser and vendor, new or used vehicle, make, type, motor number, date purchased, amount of lien, and fee. Arranged numerically by certificate numbers. For index, see entry 106. Typed on printed forms. 8 x 10 x 24. Clerk of court's office.

106. INDEX TO CERTIFICATE OF TITLE
1938—. 2 file boxes.
Index to Certificate of Title, entry 105, showing names of purchaser and vendor, date of certificate, certificate number, file box number, and description of motor vehicle. Arranged alphabetically by names of purchasers. Typed on printed forms. 8 x 10 x 24. Clerk of court's office.

Commissions and Licenses

107. RECORD OF NOTARIES AND JUSTICES COMMISSIONS
1858—. 6 volumes. (1-6). Title varies: Notary Public Record, 1858-1870 1 volume.
Copies of commissions issued by the state to notaries and justice of the peace, showing name and address of appointee, term of commission, date of issuance, signature and address of justice, oath of appointee, amount of fee, and volume and page numbers of Cash Book, entry 116. 1858-1922, arranged chronologically by dates of commissions; 1923—, arranged alphabetically by names of appointees. No index. Average 300 pages. 14 x 10 x 2. 5 volumes, 1858-1923, attic; 1 volume, 1924—, Clerk of court's office.

108. RECORD OF SPECIAL POLICE COMMISSIONS
1886—. 3 volumes. (one unlabeled; 1, 2).
Copies of commissions issued by state to special and railroad police, showing names of appointee and employer, term of service, date of issuance, oath of appointee, and certificate of commission. Arranged chronologically by dates of commissions. Indexed alphabetically by names of appointees. Handwritten on

printed forms. Average 200 pages. 14 x 9 x 1.5. 1 volume, 1886-1912, attic; 2 volumes, 1913—, Clerk of court's office.

109. [AUCTIONEERS' LICENSES]
1853—. In Appearance Docket, entry 128.
Record of auctioneers' licenses, showing name of licensee, license number, date issued, amount of bond, names of sureties, term of license, and amount of fee paid.

110. RECORD OF OPTOMETRY CERTIFICATES
1920-1934. 1 volume. Discontinued.
Copies of certificates issued by state board of optometry for practice of optometry, showing name of licensee, certificate of examination, volume and page numbers of Cash Book, entry 116, amount of fee, date of certificate, and date recorded. Arranged chronologically by dates of recording. No index. Handwritten on printed forms. 100 pages. 14 x 8.5 x 1. Clerk of court's office.

111. HUNTERS' LICENSE RECORD
1913—. 4 volumes. (1-4).
Current licenses issued to hunters, showing license number, date of issue, name, age, occupation, citizenship, personal description of licensee, and amount of fee; also includes non-resident hunters' licenses. Arranged chronologically by dates of issue. Indexed alphabetically by names of licensees. Handwritten on printed forms. Average 200 pages. 16.5 x 11.5 x 1.5. 3 volumes, 1913-1929, attic; 1 volume, 1930—, Clerk of court's office.

112. FISHERS' LICENSE RECORD
1925—. 1 volume.
Record of licenses to fish issued by clerk of courts, showing number of license, date of issue, name, address, occupation, citizenship, personal description of licensee, an amount of fee; also includes licenses for fishing with nets. Arranged chronologically by dates of issue. Index alphabetically by names of licensees. Handwritten on printed forms. 200 pages. 16 x 11.5 x 1.5. Clerk of court's office.

113. REGISTER OF REAL ESTATE LICENSES
1935—. 1 volume.
Record of real estate licenses filed with clerk of courts, showing date filed, license number, name and address of licensee and employer, classification, and dates of issue and cancellation. Arranged chronologically by dates of filing. Indexed alphabetically by names of licensees. Handwritten on printed forms. 100 pages. 17.5 x 14.5 x 1.5. Clerk of court's office.

Partnerships

114. [CERTIFICATES OF PARTNERSHIP]
1920—. In Marks of Ownership - Certificates of Partnerships, entry 126. Certificates of partnerships, showing names of partners, title of partnership, notarial oath, and date of filing.

Elections

115. POLL BOOK AND TALLY SHEETS
1000 volumes. Subtitled by voting districts.
List of registered voters, showing name and address of voter, voting districts, name of political party, and signature of voter. Tally sheets show total votes received by each candidate and issue in each voting district, also signatures of clerks and judges of elections. Poll books arranged alphabetically by names of electors; tally sheets, arranged by offices and issues. No index. Handwritten on printed forms. 17.5 x 10.5 x .25. Clerk of court's file room.
For board of elections copy, 1936—, see entry 357.

Fiscal Accounts

116. CASH BOOK
1873—. 22 volumes. (A, 1-21).
Record of receipts and disbursements by clerk of courts, showing date of entry, case number, title of case, total amount paid, by whom paid, to whom due, 1909—, distribution record with headings for each account, signature of payee, and volume and page numbers of Execution Docket, entry 84. Arranged chronologically by dates of entries. Indexed alphabetically by titles of cases. Handwritten on printed

forms. Average 200 pages. 21.5 x 17.5 x 1.5. 11 volumes, 1873-1928, attic; 11 volumes, 1929—, Clerk of court's office.

For record of accrued fees, 1907-1922, see entry 119.

117. ALIMONY DOCKET
1932—. 2 volumes. (1, 2).
Record of alimony payments to clerk of courts and by clerk of courts to payee, showing case number, names of payer and payee, date received by clerk, amount of alimony allowed, amount received, amount paid out, volume and page numbers of Cash Book, entry 116, and signature of payee or agent. Arranged chronologically by dates of entries. Indexed alphabetically by names of payers showing names of payees. Handwritten on printed forms. Average 225 pages. 12.5 x 9 x 2. Clerk of court's office.

118. RECORD OF UNCLAIMED COSTS
1886-1921. 2 volumes. (1,2).
Record of unclaimed costs and other money paid into the county treasury by clerk of courts, showing date, name of payee, to whom due, amount, source, and volume and page numbers of Case Book, entry 116; also shows date paid into treasury, amount, and date of certificate of recovery. Arranged chronologically by dates paid into treasury. Indexed alphabetically by names of payees. Handwritten on printed forms. Average 150 pages. 14 x 9 x 1.5. Attic.

119. RECORD OF ACCRUED FEES
1907—1922. 1 volume. Discontinued.
Clerk of courts record of accrued fees, showing date of accrual, case number, to whom charged, total fees, civil causes, criminal causes, due from county for transcripts and copies, and sundries, and date paid. Arranged chronologically by dates of accrual. No index. Handwritten on printed forms. 240 pages. 18 x 13 x 1.5. Attic.

For subsequent records, see entry 116.

120. [CIVIL COST BILL]
1841-1854, 1874-1876. 4 volumes.
Record of court costs in civil cases before common pleas court, showing case number, title of case, itemized cost bill including sheriff's costs and amounts

charged to plaintiff and defendant. Arranged numerically by case numbers. No index. Handwritten on printed forms. 200 pages. 12 x 11 x 1.25. Attic.

121. CLERK'S REFERENCE BOOK
1913-1914. 1 volume. Discontinued.
Reference record of fees received by clerk of courts for plaintiff and defendant, showing case number, date received, and amount. Arranged chronologically by dates of receipts. Indexed alphabetically by names of plaintiff and defendant. Handwritten. 200 pages. 12 x 11 x 1.25. Attic.

Judicial Statistics

122. REPORT OF JUDICIAL STATISTICS TO SECRETARY OF STATE
1927—. 5 pamphlets, 7 folders.
Copies of reports of judicial statistics by clerk of courts to secretary of state, showing year, number of cases tried, kind of case, fines, fees, number of cases at beginning of year, decided during year, and still pending, all classified under special type of action; civil and criminal jury fees; total number of crimes against persons with number under each offense and total against property with number under each offense; indictments disposed of, number of convictions, number acquitted, number nolled, numbers still pending and totals; sentences imposed, fines and imprisonments, total cases paid by county, amount of cost to county; number of offenses against public peace, public chastity, public justice, public health; number inquest held by coroner with nature and cause of death; number of cases pending in each court, number received, and number heard; classified list of the divorce cases, alimony allowed, and custody of children; list of persons nationalized; grand and petit jury fees in criminal and civil cases. Arranged chronologically by years of reports. No index. Handwritten on printed forms. Pamphlets average 20 pages. 16 x 12 x .25; folders 12 x 8 x .25. Clerk of court's office.

Coroner's Inquests

123. RECORDS OF INQUEST
1914—. 1 volume.
Record of inquest held by the coroner and justices of the peace, showing case number, name of deceased, description, cause of death, whether or not superinduced by intemperance, date of post-mortem examination, and name of physician.

Arranged numerically by case numbers. Indexed alphabetically by names of deceased. Handwritten on printed forms. 140 pages. 16 x 12 x 2. Clerk of court's file room.

124. CORONER'S INQUEST
1880—. 16 file boxes. (dated).

Original reports to clerk of courts of corner's inquest held in cases of homicidal, accidental or sudden deaths, showing date of report, name of decedent, date of inquest, date and cause of death, and description of body; also includes names of witnesses, testimony, coroner's findings, and certificate of clerk. Arranged chronological by dates of reports. No index. Handwritten and typed on printed forms. 11 x 16 x 24. 11 file boxes, 1880-1906, attic; 5 file boxes, 1907—, Clerk of court's file room.

Miscellaneous

125. RECORD OF OATHS OF OFFICE
1840-1870. 1 volume.

Record of oaths of office for county officers, showing name, title of official, duties, and date of oath. Arranged chronologically by dates of oaths. Index alphabetically by names of officers. Handwritten. 300 pages. 12.5 x 8.5 x 2. Attic.

126. MARKS OF OWNERSHIP - CERTIFICATES OF PARTNERSHIP
1920—. 1 volume.

Copies of applications for registration of trade-marks, showing name of applicant, location of business, kind of business, article manufactured, wording and design of trade-mark, date of filing, and amount of fee. Also contains [Certificates of Partnership], entry 114. Arranged chronologically by dates of filing. Indexed alphabetically by names of applicants. Handwritten. 300 pages. 11.5 x 9.5 x 2. Clerk of court's office.

The common pleas court of the old Northwest Territory served as the model for the court of the same name which was set up by the constitution of 1802 when Ohio became a state.[1] The counties were grouped in three judicial districts and a court of common pleas was authorized for each one. The constitution stipulated the appointment of a president judge and no less than two, nor more than three, associate judges for each district. Only the president judge must be a lawyer. All were appointed by joint session of both houses of the legislature for a period of seven years. Each county was visited and served by the court of the district to which it belonged.[2]

This system remained in force until the constitution of 1851 redivided the state into nine districts, because of the greatly increased population which had resulted in overcrowding the courts and clogging proceedings. Lake County became a part of judicial district number nine, along with eight other counties. The districts themselves were divided into three parts, in each of which one common pleas judge was to be elected for a term of five years.[3] The legislature then provided by special statute for the frequency of the sessions in each county, as needs of the dockets indicated.[4]

In 1912 the constitution was amended to permit elections of common pleas judges in each county,[5] a provision which became effective in Lake County in 1916.[6] Since 1917 all judges must have been admitted to the practice of law in Ohio at least six years preceding their election.[7]

The court of common pleas has original jurisdiction in all civil disputes involving state law, but not involving the exclusive jurisdiction of the federal courts,[8] and in criminal matters except minor criminal cases in which justice of peace courts have original jurisdiction.[9] It hears appeals from justice of the peace courts, except in cases in which the amount involved is less than $20, and from probate court, since 1853, when the latter was separated from common pleas.[10]

---

1. Pease, *op. cit.,* 7; *Ohio Const., 1802,* Art. III sec. 1.
2. *Ohio Const., 1802,* Art. III, sec. 3, 8, 10.
3. *Ohio Const., 1851,* Art, IV, sec, 3.
4. *Ibid.,* Art. IV, sec. 3.
5. *Ohio Const., 1851,* (Amended 1912) Art. IV, secs. 12, 15.
6. *Laws of Ohio,* CIII, 675.
7. *Ibid.,* CVII, 164.
8. Chase, *op cit.,* I, 95; G.C. sec. 11215.
9. G.C. sec. 13522-5.
10. *Laws of Ohio,* LI, 377.

It was given jurisdiction in naturalization proceedings by act of congress in 1906.[11] In 1853, also, exclusive jurisdiction in divorce matters, until that time lodged with the legislature, was transferred to the court of common pleas.[12]

The court of common pleas of Lake County consists of one judge, provided with a court reporter, one assistant, and a bailiff. The salary of the judge is paid by the state and county jointly, $3000 by the former, $1700 by the latter.[13] Judges may be excused from hearing cases of great local interest when feeling runs high. In 1940 the court terminated 456 cases, of which 54 were criminal.[14] Fifty-four declarations of intention to become a citizen were filed in 1940,[15] and 130 divorces were granted in the same period.[16]

---

11. U.S.C.A. Title VIII, sec. 357.
12. *Laws of Ohio,* LI, 377.
13. Commissioners' Journal, AA (1938-1939), 245; G.C. sec. 2251.
14. Information obtained from clerk of courts' office.
15. Record [Declaration of Intention], 1940, entry 138.
16. Report of Judicial Statistics to Secretary of State, 1940, entry 122.

Dockets

127. TRIAL DOCKET
1859-1911. 61 volumes. (four, 1859-1892, O, 7-9; fifty-seven, 1893-1911, labeled by court terms).

Record of civil cases tried before the court of common pleas, showing term of court, date of hearing, case number, title of case, names of litigants, names of attorneys, findings and judgments of court, and volume letter or number and page number of Journal, entry 131; includes court calendar, showing case number, dates, names and addresses of plaintiff and defendant, and names of attorney. 1859-1892, arranged chronologically by court terms; 1893-1911, numerically by case numbers. No index. Handwritten on printed forms. Average 250 pages. 14 x 9 x 1.5. 4 volumes, 1859-1892, attic; 57 volumes, 1893-1911, Clerk of court's office.

128. APPEARANCE DOCKET
1853—. 58 volumes. (A-Z, 1-32).

Record of civil cases tried before the court of common pleas, showing names of litigants, date and term of court, case number, title of case, names of attorneys, kind of action, dates of summons and return, sheriff's return, time of filing, court entries, volume letter or number and page number of Execution Docket, entry 84,and [Civil] Record, entry 133. Also contains: Criminal Appearance and Execution Docket, 1853-1893, entry 129; [Auctioneers' Licenses], entry 109. Arranged numerically by case numbers. Indexed alphabetically by titles of cases. Handwritten on printed forms. 6 volumes, 1853-1879, attic; 52 volumes, 1880—, Clerk of court's office.

129. CRIMINAL APPEARANCE AND EXECUTION DOCKET
1894—. 7 volumes. (1-7).

Record of criminal cases before the court of common pleas, showing case number, title of case, name of accused, names of attorneys, offense charged, proceedings of court, amount of recognizance, names of sureties to recognizance bond, date indictment return, date of plea, verdict of the court, itemized cost bill, volume and page numbers of Execution Docket, entry 84, Sheriff's Returns, entry 102, Journal, entry 131, Cash Book, entry 116, Criminal Record, entry 134, and dates of filing and final entry. Also serves as an index to Criminal Appearance Docket [Original Case Papers], entry 136, by showing case number. Arranged numerically by case numbers. Indexed alphabetically by names of defendants. 1894-1913, handwritten on printed forms; 1914—, typed on printed forms. 4 volumes, 1894-1927, attic; 3 volumes, 1928—, Clerk of court's office.

130. JUDGMENT DOCKETS
1840-1854. 1 volume. (A). Discontinued.

Record of judgments in cases before the court of common pleas, showing case number, names of judgment creditor and debtor, title of action, amount of judgment, interest date, date of decree, volume letter or number and page number of Execution Docket, entry 84, and Journal, entry 131, date of filing certificate of release, amount of fees, and officers receipts. Arranged chronologically by dates are filing. Indexed alphabetically by names of plaintiffs and defendants. 300 pages. 16 x 10 x 2. Attic.

Court Proceedings

131. JOURNAL
1840—. 48 volumes. (A-Z; 26-47).

General entries of cases filed and heard in common pleas court, showing term of court, date of hearing, case number, title of case, names of litigants, judges' decrees, and 1840-1931, amount of alimony allowed in divorce cases. Arranged chronologically by dates of hearings. Indexed alphabetically by names of plaintiffs showing names of defendants. 1840-1914, handwritten; 1915—, typed. Average 75 pages. 16.5 x 12.5 x 3. Clerk of court's office.

132. CHANCERY RECORD
1840-1952. 4 volumes. (A-D). Discontinued.
Record of proceedings in chancery cases before the common pleas court, showing date of hearing, title of case, case number, bill of complaint, names of litigants and attorneys, and date case filed; includes *writs* issued, affidavits, subpoenas, sheriff's returns, bill of fees, decrees of court, *demurrers*, answers, motions, transcripts of testimony, evidence, copies of depositions, bonds for appearance, and journal entries. Arranged chronologically by dates of hearings. Indexed alphabetically by names of plaintiffs showing names of defendants. Handwritten. Average 600 pages. 17 x 12 x 3. Attic.

133. [CIVIL] RECORD
1840—. 103 volumes. (A-Z; 1-77).
Complete record of civil cases in the court of comment pleas, showing term of court, names of litigants, title of case, names of attorneys, petitions, notice of proof of publication, motions, *demurrers*, answers, amended petitions, *praecipes,* summonses, sheriff's returns, date filed, and cost bills; also includes testamentary and guardianship matters, 1840-1852, and complete record of divorcee cases, 1844—. Arranged chronologically by dates of filing. Indexed alphabetically by names of plaintiffs and defendants. 1840-1914, handwritten; 1914—, typed. Average 500 pages. 18 x 12 x 3. 21 volumes, 1840-1881, attic; 82 volumes, 1882—, Clerk of court's office.

134. CRIMINAL RECORD
1840—. 11 volumes. (A-F; F-J).
Complete record of criminal cases before the common pleas court, showing date filed, transcript of pleas, title of case, name of defendant, case number, names of attorneys, kind of action, names of jurors, indictment, sheriff's return, verdict of jury, judgment of court, and cost bill; Also includes a record of paroles. Arranged chronologically by dates filed. Indexed alphabetically by names of defendants. 1840-1916, handwritten; 1916—, typed. Average 600 pages. 18 x 13 x 3. 9 volumes 1840-1929, attic; 2 volumes, 1930—, Clerk of court's office.

135. CIVIL CASE PAPERS
1871—. 10162 jackets, 377 file boxes. (1871-1882, 4 file boxes A-D; 1883—, labeled by contained a case numbers). Title varies: Appearance Docket, 1871-1882, 4 file boxes.

Case papers of civil cases before common pleas court, including petitions, briefs, motions, answers, *praecipes,* summonses, returns, journal entries, all court orders and *writs*, decrees, and cost bills. All paper papers of each case are filed together in a jacket, showing names of litigants, case number, date of filing, date of final entry, and volume and page numbers of Execution Docket, entry 84; Journal entry, entry 131; [Civil] Record, entry 133. Arranged numerically by case numbers. For index see entry 89. Handwritten and typed on printed forms. Jackets, 9.5 x 3.5 x 2; file boxes, 10 x 4.5 x 13.5. 138 file boxes, 10162 jackets, 1871-1930, attic; 239 file boxes, 1931—, Clerk of court's office.

136. CRIMINAL APPEARANCE DOCKET [Original Case Papers]
1883—. 2705 jackets, 4 file boxes.

Case papers filed in criminal cases before court of common pleas, including transcripts from lower courts, indictments, subpoenas, *praecipes,* journal entries, and cost bills. All papers of each case are filed together in a jacket, showing date case filed, date completed, case number, name of defendant, and 1894—, volume and page numbers of Criminal Appearance and Execution Docket, entry 129, and Criminal Record, entry 134. Arranged numerically by case numbers. 1883-1893, no index; for index, 1894—, see entry 129. Handwritten and typed on printed forms. Jackets, 9.5 x 3.5 x 2; file boxes, 10 x 4.5 x 13.5. 2705 jackets, 1883-1934, attic; 4 file boxes, 1935—, Clerk of court's office.

137. LAND APPRAISAL
1881-1914. 1 file box, 2 letter files.

Copies of land appraisals ordered by court in land sales, showing name of appraiser, date filed, case number, names of plaintiff and defendant, amount of judgment, certification of appraisement by sheriff, and date filed. Arranged chronologically by dates filed. No index. File box 10 x 4.5 x 13.5; letter filed 9 x 4 x 1.25. Attic.

Naturalization

138. RECORD [Declaration of Intention]
1907—. 14 volumes. (I-XIV).
Copies of declarations of intentions to become citizens, showing state, county court of issuance, declaration number, name, address, occupation, birth date, and birthplace of applicant, wife's name, children's names, ages, and birth places, last foreign residence, signature of applicant, and date of filing. Arranged numerically by declaration numbers. Indexed alphabetically by names of applicants. Handwritten and typed on printed forms. Average 100 pages. 11 x 9 x .5. Clerk of court's office.
For similar nationalization records, 1860-1906, see entry 195.

139. PETITION AND RECORD FOR NATURALIZATION
1907—. 8 volumes. (I-VIII).
Copies of petitions and declarations of intention to common pleas court for citizenship, showing volume and page numbers of Cash Book, entry 116, name, address, occupation and age of applicant, date and place of filing declaration of intention of petitioner, names, birth dates and birth places of wife and children, length of residence in United States, signature of petitioner, affidavits of petitioner and oath of allegiance, orders of court admitting or denying petition, and a memorandum of continuances; also includes final papers, showing name of petitioner and date of final papers. Arranged chronologically by dates of filing. Indexed alphabetically by names of petitioners. Handwritten on printed forms. Average 100 pages. 18 x 12 x 2. Clerk of court's office.
For similar nationalization records, 1860-1906, see entry 195.

Miscellaneous

140. OLD JURY LISTS [Report of Grand Jury]
1932—. 1 file box.
Reports of grand jury to judge of common pleas court, showing term of court, date of report, number of actual days in session, number of witnesses examined, number of time bills presented, report of examination of jail and sheriff's residence with statement of conditions found and recommendations, date of filing, and volume and page numbers of Journal, entry 131. Arranged chronologically by dates of reports. No index. Typed. 10.5 x 9.25 x 13.5. Clerk of court's office.

In order to eliminate irregularities in the assignment of cases for trial, the legislature, in 1913, authorized the court of common pleas to direct the members of the jury commission to serve in the capacity of assignment commissioners.[1] In 1931 the court of any county, having not more than one common pleas judge, was authorized to appoint one assignment commissioner independent of the personnel of the jury commission. A maximum salary of $1800 was set.[2]

One assignment commissioner is now serving in Lake County at an annual salary of $1320.[3]

The assignment commissioner keeps no separate records; for court calendar, see entry 127.

---

1. *Laws of Ohio,* CIII, 512; CVI, 534; CVIII pt. ii, 1114; CIX, 281.
2. G.C. sec. 3007-1; *Laws of Ohio,* CXIV, 213.
3. Information obtained from assignment commissioner.

From 1803 to 1851 the supreme court of Ohio was a court of appeals and was required by law to be held at least once a year in each county. The judges numbered three or four, depending upon the number of districts into which the state was divided, and were appointed by joint session of the legislature to serve seven-year terms.[1] This court had exclusive jurisdiction until 1843 of all cases of divorce and alimony, and concurrent jurisdiction of civil cases involving land titles, and disputes exceeding $1000. Land title disputes were settled in the county in which the land was situated. This court was an appellate court for all cases in which the common pleas court had original jurisdiction.[2] It had original cognizance in the trial of capital offenses, although persons indicted for capital crimes could elect to be tried in common pleas court.[3]

In 1831 the supreme court was directed to meet annually at Columbus for the final adjudication of all such questions of law as might have been reserved in any county for decision. This session of the court, known as the court in banc, was required to have its decisions transmitted in writing to the clerk of the supreme court in each county in which such questions were reserved. The same proceedings were to be taken as if this decisions had been made in the county.[4] The complete record of the cases handled by the supreme court in Lake County, both in circuit and in banc, is to be found in the attic of the courthouse.[5] In 1837 an act was passed providing that the final judgments in the supreme court, held within any county within the state, could be re-examined and reversed or affirmed in the court and in banco upon *writ* of error.[6]

The supreme court proved inadequate as a general court of appeals. Successive attempts to relieve overcrowding of the docket produce first the district court,[7] then circuit court,[8] and finally the court of appeals.[9]

---

1. *Ohio Const., 1802,* Art. III, secs. 2, 8, 10; *Laws of Ohio,* XXII, 50.
2. *Laws of Ohio,* I, 36-37; XIV, 310-354; XLI, 94.
3. Chase, *op. cit.,* I, 561.
4. *Laws of Ohio,* XXIX, 93-94.
5. See entries 141-147.
6. *Laws of Ohio,* XXXV, 60.
7. *Ibid.,* L, 69.
8. *Ohio Const., 1851,* Art. IV, sec. 6; *Laws of Ohio,* LXXXII, 19; LXXXI, 170.
9. *Ohio Const., 1851,* (Amendment, 1912), Art. IV, sec. 6.

The supreme court setting in Columbus at present is the reviewing court of last resort.[10]

All records are located and the attic of the courthouse.

---

10. *Ohio Const., 1851,* (Amendment, 1912), Art. IV, sec. 2.

141. GENERAL DOCKET
1841-1851. 1 volume.

Docket of cases for hearing before supreme court, showing term of court, names of litigants, case number, title of case, name of lower court of origin, number of suits, judgment of court, cost to plaintiff and defendant, and volume and page numbers of Journal, entry 144. Arranged numerically by case numbers. No index. Handwritten. 150 pages. 8 x 12 x 1.

142. JUDGMENT DOCKET
1841-1882. 1 volume.

Record of judgment of court and cases before the supreme court, 1841-1851, showing term of court, date of hearing, names of litigants and attorneys, title and number of case, volume and page numbers of Journal, entry 144 and Execution Docket, entry 84; includes copies of orders of execution, mandate and cost bills. Also [Judgment Docket, District Court], 1852-1882, entry 150. Arranged by dates of hearings. Indexed alphabetically by names of plaintiffs showing names of defendants. For index, see entry 143. Handwritten. 500 pages. 17 x 11.5 x 3.

143. GENERAL INDEX
1841-1851. 1 volume.

Reverse index to Judgment Docket, entry 142, showing names of defendant and plaintiff, and volume and page numbers of docket. Arranged alphabetically by names of defendants. Handwritten. 350 pages. 17.5 x 12 x 2.5.

144. JOURNAL
1841-1851. 1 volume.

Record of journal entries in cases heard before supreme court, showing term of court, date of hearing, number and title of case, style of action, names of litigants, finding of court, and date filed. Arranged chronologically by dates of hearings. No index. Handwritten. 350 pages. 14 x 10 x 2.5.

145. COST DOCKET
1843-1852. 1 volume.

Record costs bills in supreme court cases, showing case number, title of action, itemized bill with heading for amounts charged to plaintiff or defendant, and sheriff's bill of fees. Arranged numerically by case numbers. Indexed alphabetically by names of plaintiffs and defendants. Handwritten. 250 pages. 12 x 10 x 1.5.

146. CHANCERY RECORD
1841-1851. 1 volume.

Record of proceedings in cases in chancery heard before supreme court, showing term of court, date of hearing, title of case, case number, and style of action; includes bills of complaint, answers, exhibits, disposition, journal entries, decrees, judgments of court, and clerk's certificate of record. Arranged chronologically by dates of hearings. Indexed alphabetically by names of plaintiffs showing names of defendants. Handwritten. 600 pages. 17 x 12 x 3.

147. RECORD
1840-1851. 2 volumes. (A, B).

Complete record of proceedings in cases heard before supreme court, showing term of court, date of hearing, names of litigants, case number, title of case, and plea; includes transcripts from lower court, bills of exception, judgments of court, clerk's certificate of record, assignments, citations to sheriff, sheriff's returns, and sheriff's cost bill. Arranged chronologically by dates of hearings. Indexed alphabetically by names of plaintiffs showing names of defendants. Handwritten. Average 600 pages. 17 x 11.5 x 3.

A court of appeals has function in Ohio since the adoption of its first constitution in 1802, but under different names with slowly changing jurisdiction. In its inception its functions were discharged by members of the supreme court acting as a court of appeals and holding court in the county once a year.[1]

When a new constitution was adopted in 1851, its provisions extended the Ohio judicial system to include a district court, which was composed of a justice of the supreme court, meeting annually with several common pleas judges within each district. This court was authorized to hear cases formally taken before the supreme court in its capacity as a court of appeals.[2] From 1852 to 1884 Lake County was a part of the fourth district, made up of 18 counties comprising the eighth and ninth common pleas court districts.[3] These districts courts proved inadequate because the docket of the supreme court had become so crowded that the justice found it impossible to go on circuit to discharge their duties as presiding judges in the district courts. Accordingly, by an amendment to the state constitution in 1883, the circuit court was created to fulfill the functions of the district court, which was to continue to act until the legislature had acted upon the composition and regional jurisdiction of the newly created court, and the election of its judges.[4] Appeals from Lake County common pleas court went to circuit court of the seventh circuit[5] from this time until 1887.

Pursuant to the provisions of the amendment of 1883, the legislature in 1884 passed and act authorizing the election of three circuit judges in each of seven circuits and place Lake County in the seventh circuit.[6] In 1887 Lake County was reassigned to the seventh circuit.[7]

The name circuit court was changed to court of appeals in 1912, by constitutional amendment, and the term of the judges was fixed at six years.[8]

---

1. *Ohio Const., 1802,* Art. III, sec. 2, 10.
2. *Ohio Const., 1851,* Art. IV, sec. 6.
3. *Laws of Ohio,* L, 67.
4. *Ibid.,* LXXXI, 168; *Ohio Const., 1851,* (Amendment, 1883), Art. IV, sec. 6.
5. *Laws of Ohio,* LXXXI, 168.
6. *Ibid.,* LXXXI, 168.
7. *Ibid.,* LXXXIV, 240.
8. *Ohio Const., 1851,* (Amendment, 1912), Art. IV, sec. 6.

The jurisdiction of the court of appeals, as conferred by the constitution of 1912, is substantially the same as that of the circuit court which it replaced. The only important alteration is a provision in the amendment to the effects that no judgment of a court of common pleas, a superior court, or other court of record may be reversed except by the concurrence of all the judges of the court of appeals.[9]

Lake County was continued in the seventh district under the amendment to the constitution in 1912.[10] The court of appeals meets at least once a year in Lake County to hear appeals from adverse decisions of the court of common pleas unless the case originated in the justice or magistrate court. Litigants may take their cases originally to the court of appeals on *writs* of *quo warranto, mandamus, habeas corpus, procedendo,* and prohibition.[11] The court of appeals sitting in Lake County disposes of an average of about a dozen cases annually.[12]

---

9. *Ibid.*
10. *Ibid.*
11. *Laws of Ohio,* L, 69.
12. [Court of Appeals] Journal 1 (1913——), *see* entry 156; [Court of Appeals] Appearance Docket 1, 2 (1913——), *see* entry 154.

District and Circuit Courts

148. APPEARANCE DOCKET
1885-1912. 1 volume.
Docket of cases filed to appear before circuit court, showing names of litigants, case number, title of case, kind of action, names of attorneys, date of filing, and record of documents filed. Arranged numerically by case numbers. Indexed alphabetically by names of plaintiffs and defendants. Handwritten. 600 pages. 18 x 13 x 3. Attic.

149. DOCKET
1885-1912. 3 volumes. (1-3).
Docket of cases before circuit court, showing date of hearing, case number, title of case, names of attorneys, and a memorandum of findings and judgments of the court. Arranged chronologically by dates of hearings. No index. Handwritten. Average 350 pages. 16.5 x 11.5 x 2. Attic.

150. [JUDGMENT DOCKET, DISTRICT COURT]
1852-1882. In Judgment Docket, entry 142.

Docket of judgment cases heard in district court, showing same information as Judgment Docket, entry 142.

151. JOURNAL
1852-1912. 3 volumes. (A, 1, 2).

Record of proceedings in cases before district court, 1852-1884, and circuit court, 1885-1912, showing names of litigants, date of hearing, term of court, title of case, case number, kind of action, finding and judgment of the court. Volume 1, 1885-1899, contains copy of the rules of practice in circuit court. Arranged chronologically by dates of hearings. 1852-1884, no index; 1885-1912, indexed alphabetically by names of plaintiffs and defendants. Handwritten. Average 600 pages. 18 x 13 x 3. Attic.

152. CHANCERY RECORD
1852-1853. 1 volume. Discontinued.

Record of proceedings in chancery before district court, showing date of hearing, names of litigants, case number, title of case, and names of attorneys. Includes bills of complaints, subpoenas, sheriff's returns, bills for fees, *demurrers*, answers, replies, motions, decrees of the court, journal entries, and bonds for appearance. Arranged chronologically by dates of hearings. Indexed alphabetically by names of plaintiffs showing names of defendants. Handwritten. 600 pages. 17 x 12 x 3. Attic.

153. RECORD
1852-1912. 6 volumes. (A-C; 1-3). Title varies: Law Record, 1852-1887, 3 volumes.

Copies of documents filed in cases before district court, 1852-1884, and circuit court, 1885-1912, showing date of hearing, title of case, names of litigants, case number, kind of action, transcript of evidence, answers, and proceedings of court. Arranged chronologically by dates of hearings. 1852-1887, no index; 1885-1912, indexed alphabetically by names of plaintiffs and defendants. Handwritten. Average 600 pages. 18 x 13 x 3. Attic.

Court of Appeals

154. APPEARANCE DOCKET
1913—. 2 volumes. (1, 2).

Docket of cases filed for hearing before court of appeals, showing names of litigants, date of hearing, title of case, names of attorneys, case number, kind of action, and proceedings of court. Arranged chronologically by dates of hearings. Indexed alphabetically by names of plaintiffs and defendants. Handwritten on printed forms. Average 400 pages. 17 x 12 x 2.5. Court of appeals room.

155. APPELLATE DOCKET – PENDING SUITS
1926—. 1 volume.

Record of court orders before appellate court, showing names of litigants, title of case, common pleas court case number, appellate court case number, names of attorneys, date of filing, term of court, and volume and page numbers of Appearance Docket, entry 154. Arranged chronologically by terms of court. No index. Handwritten on printed forms. 500 pages. 15 x 10 x 3. Court of appeals room.

156. JOURNAL
1913—. 1 volume. (1).

Record of proceedings in cases before court of appeals, showing date of hearing, number and title of case, kind of action, findings and judgment of the court. Arranged chronologically by dates of hearings. No index. Handwritten on printed forms. 600 pages. 18 x 13 x 3. Court of appeals room.

157. RECORD
1913—. 1 volume.

Copies of documents filed in cases before court of appeals, showing names of litigants, date of hearing, date case assigned for hearing, date of petition, title of case, kind of action, transcript of evidence and replies, and proceedings of court. Arranged chronologically by dates of hearings. Indexed alphabetically by names of plaintiffs and defendants. Handwritten on printed forms. 600 pages. 18 x 13 x 3. Court of appeals room.

158. CASE PAPERS, COURT OF APPEALS

1928—. 3 file boxes. (1-3).

Papers of cases filed in court of appeals, including bills of exceptions, itemized cost bills, and all documents in the case, showing nature of case, names of litigants, case number, date filed, and volume and page numbers of Appearance Docket, entry 154. All papers of each case are filed together in a separate jacket, showing case number. Arranged chronologically by dates filed. No index. Handwritten and typed on printed forms. 11.5 x 5 x 16. Court of appeals room.

159. [ORIGINAL PLEADINGS AND TRANSCRIPTS OF JOURNAL ENTRIES, COURT OF APPEALS]

1922-1934. 400 bundles.

Original pleadings and transcript of journal entries filed in court of appeals, including briefs, exhibits, transcripts of testimony, bill of exceptions, and replies, showing case number of common pleas court and case number of court of appeals, title of case, dates of filing, and volume and page numbers of Appearance Docket entry 154. No obvious arrangement. No index. Handwritten and typed on printed forms. 14 x 8.5 x 5. Attic.

The probate court was originally provided for by an act of the Northwest Territory, of which Ohio was a part, by the ordinance of 1787.[1] In 1802 the constitution of Ohio vested its jurisdiction in courts of common pleas,[2] which functions has a probate court until the constitution of 1851, which created the probate court as such, and gave its original jurisdiction in probate and testimony matters, appointment of administrators and guardians, and settlement of their accounts.[3] This court also appoints and removes guardians of minors,[4] renders adoption decrees,[5] commits the insane and feebleminded to institutions,[6] and assesses inheritance taxes.[7] From 1853 until the adoption of the probate code in 1931, the probate court of Lake County had limited jurisdiction in criminal cases in which the sentence did not impose capital punishment or imprisonment.[8]

In addition a multiplicity of other functions has been gradually assigned to probate court. Marriage license, and licenses to ministers to perform marriages are granted.[9] Since 1896 it has been required to file for record certificates of doctors, and since 1916 of trained nurses.[10] In 1913 the court was vested with power to grant injunctions and in 1915 was given concurrent jurisdiction with the common pleas court to hear condemnation proceedings for roads.[11] Applications for change of name are made to the probate court.[12] Until 1906 probate court had jurisdiction, which is now lodged with the court of common pleas, over naturalization proceedings.[13] The probate judge of Lake County also serves as a judge of the juvenile court.[14]

---

1. Chase, *op. cit.,* I, 66.
2. *Ohio Const., 1802,* Art. III, secs. 3, 5.
3. *Ohio Const., 1851,* Art. IV, secs. 7, 8.
4. *Laws of Ohio,* LV, 54.
5. *Ibid.,* LVI, 82; LXVII, 14.
6. *Ibid.,* LIII, 81-86.
7. *Ibid.,* CVIII, pt.i, 561.
8. *Ibid.,* LI, 145; LIV, 97; LV, 176; CXIV, 475.
9. *Ohio Const., 1851,* Art. IV, sec. 8; *Laws of Ohio,* L, 84.
10. *Laws of Ohio,* XCII, 46; XCIX, 499; CVI, 193, 202.
11. *Ibid.,* CIII, 427; CVI, 583.
12. *Ibid.,* XCII, 28.
13. *United States Statutes at Large,* XXXIV, pt. i, 596.
14. *Laws of Ohio,* XCVIII, 315.

In 1867 the duty of keeping a permanent record of birth and deaths was given to the probate judge, a duty which in 1908 was delegated to the state bureau of vital statistics; these records are in Lake County probate court only from 1867 to 1908, therefore.[15]

An important addition to the jurisdiction of the probate court was made by an emergency act of the assembly in April 1941.[16] The court was enabled to, after a hearing on the merits of the application, to correct existing birth records and to established birth dates formally where no public record exists, but where proof brought before the court is regarded as sufficient. This action was taken in response to the need for authentic documents to support claims to American births for employment, social security and military service.

The judge of probate court is elected for a term of four years. Qualifications for the office were raised in 1931 with an amendment to the probate code restricting eligibility to a practicing attorney, or to a person who "shall have previously served as probate judge immediately prior to his election."[17]

In Lake County, the probate judge receives a salary of $3525 annually, and his staff of one deputy and six clerks received an aggregate salary of $8122.[18] Of the business transacted in the court in 1940 shows 110 wills probated, 500 estates administered, 39 guardians appointed, 7 adoptions, 476 marriage licenses issued, 53 estates released from administration, 21 wills deposit for safekeeping, 5 certificates issued to doctors and 5 to trained nurses, 4 ministers licenses to perform marriage ceremonies, and 6 dance hall licenses issued.[19] During 1940 the court committed 34 metal cases to various institutions in the state, and sent 1 epileptic to Gallipolis, Ohio.[20] For accommodation of its unfortunates, Lake County depends almost wholly upon the state institution in Cleveland, Lima, and Gallipolis.

For diversity and magnitude of business only the auditor's office exceeds the probate court in Lake County. Its records are correspondently numerous and diverse, filing 496 volumes and 833 file boxes.

---

15. *Ibid.,* LXIV, 63-64; XCIX, 296-307; G.C. sec, 10501-15. *See also* entry 197.
16. Ohio general assembly, House Bill 101.
17. *Laws of Ohio,* CXIV, 320; CXVI, 481.
18. Commissioners' Journal AA (1938-1939), 245.
19. Annual Report to Secretary of State, 1940.
20. Annual Report to Secretary of State, 1940.

Calendars and Dockets

160. COURT CALENDAR
1884—. 15 volumes. (1-15).
Record of cases to appear before probate court, showing date of hearing, names of litigants, courts memorandum of disposition of case, also volume and page numbers of Probate Court Journal, entry 169. Arranged chronologically by dates of hearings. No index. Handwritten on printed forms. Average 300 pages. 14 x 10 x 1.5. 11 volumes, 1884-1929, attic; 4 volumes, 1930—, Probate court office.

161. CIVIL DOCKET
1840—. 6 volumes. (A, 1-5).
Docket of proceedings in civil and lunacy cases before common pleas court 1840-1851, and before probate court 1852—, showing case number, title of case, dates of entries, proceedings, volume number or letter and page number of Probate Court Journal, entry 169, and Fee Book, entry 207. Also serves as indexed to Civil Papers, entry 173, by showing case number and file box number. Arranged numerically by case numbers and chronologically thereunder by dates of entries. Index alphabetically by titles of cases. Handwritten on printed forms. Average 500 pages. 18 x 13 x 3. Probate court vault.

162. CRIMINAL DOCKET
1852-1931. 4 volumes. (A-D). Discontinued; jurisdiction transferred to court of common pleas in 1931.
Docket of proceedings in criminal matters before probate court, showing case number, title of action, dates of entries, volume letter or number and page number of Criminal Journal, entry 170, Criminal Record, entry 175, fee Book, entry 207. Also serves as an index to Criminal Papers, entry 174, by showing case number. Arranged numerically by case numbers and chronologically thereunder by dates of entries. Index alphabetically by names of defendants. Handwritten on printed forms. Average 500 pages. 18 x 13 x 3. Probate court vault.

163. PROBATE DOCKET
1840-1891. 8 volumes. (1-8).
Docket of estate matters, showing case number, name of administrator or executor, name of decedent, volume letter or number and page number of Probate Court Journal, entry 169, Probate Court Final Record, entry 176, Fee Book, entry 207,

and a memorandum of proceedings with date of hearing. Arranged numerically by case numbers. Indexed alphabetically by names of decedents. Handwritten on printed forms. Average 250 pages. 14 x 9 x 1.5. Probate court office.

164. ADMINISTRATION DOCKET
1840—. 18 volumes. (A, B, 1-16).
Docket of administration of estates, showing case number, name of decedent, name of administrator or executor, volume letter or number and page number of Probate Court Journal, entry 169, Probate Court Final Record, entry 176, Fee Book, entry 207, and a memorandum of proceedings with date of hearing. Arranged numerically by case numbers. Indexed alphabetically by names of decedents; also separate index, entry 165. Handwritten on printed forms. Average 500 pages. 18.5 x 13.5 x 3. Probate court office.

165. GENERAL INDEX, ADMINISTRATION DOCKET
1840— 2 volumes. (1, 2).
Index to Administration Docket, entry 164, Estate Papers, entry 188, showing date, case number, name of the decedent, names of administrator or executor, volume letter or number and page number of docket, and file box number of case papers. Arranged alphabetically under tabs by names of decedents. Typed. Average 250 pages. 17 x 12 x 2. Probate court office.

166. GUARDIANS' DOCKET
1840—. 6 volumes. (A, 1-5).
Docket of proceedings and guardianship matters, showing case number, name, age, and residence of ward, names of parents, dates of entries, trustees' bonds, court orders, and volume letter or number, and page number of Probate Court Journal, entry 169, and Fee Book, entry 207. Arranged numerically by case numbers and chronologically thereunder by dates of entries. Indexed alphabetically by names of words; also separate index, entry 167. Handwritten on printed forms. Average 500 pages. 18.5 x 13.5 x 3. Probate court office.

167. GENERAL INDEX CARD, GUARDIANS' DOCKET
1840—. 1 volume.
Index to Guardians' Docket, entry 166, and Guardians' [Papers], entry 189, showing date of instrument or entry, case number, names of ward and guardian, volume letter or number and page number of docket, and file box number of case papers.

Arranged alphabetically by names of wards. Typed. 600 pages. 18.5 x 13.5 x 3. Probate court office.

168. EXECUTION DOCKET
1853-1892. 1 volume. Discontinued.

Record of execution proceedings in civil and criminal cases before probate court, showing date of hearing, case number, title of case, volume and page numbers of Probate Court Journal, entry 169, Probate Court Record, entry 176; includes pleas, sentences, and sheriff's cost bills. Arranged chronologically by dates of hearings. Indexed alphabetically by titles of cases. Handwritten on printed forms. 600 pages. 18 x 12 x 3. Probate court vault.

Court Proceedings

169. PROBATE COURT JOURNAL
1852—. 63 volumes. (A-Z, 27-63).

Record of proceedings in civil cases before probate court, showing title of case, kind of action, date of hearing, names of plaintiffs and defendants or principles; court orders in civil cases, adoption, inheritance tax, and lunacy hearings; reports of county visitors, 1913—, of auditor on unknown depositors, 1888—. Also contains Adoption Records, 1852—, and Lunacy Record, 1852-1904. Arranged chronologically by dates of hearings. Indexed alphabetically by titles of cases or names of principles. 1852-1906, handwritten; 1907—, typed. Average 600 pages. 16.5 x 11 x 3. 45 volumes, 1852-1927, attic; 18 volumes, 1928—, Probate court vault.

170. CRIMINAL JOURNAL
1852-1931. 5 volumes. (A-E). Discontinued; jurisdiction transferred to court of common pleas in 1931.

Record of journal entries and proceedings in criminal matters before probate court, showing date of hearing, title of case, name of defendant, and journal entry. Arranged chronologically by dates of hearings. Indexed alphabetically by names of defendants. Handwritten on printed forms. Average 500 pages. 18 x 13 x 3. Probate court office.

171. COURT JURY BOOK
1854-1891. 1 volume. Discontinued.

Record of probate jurors, showing term of court, title of case, names of jurors, mileage, days and attendance, and amount of fees. Arranged chronologically by court terms. No index. Handwritten on printed forms. 200 pages. 13.5 x 9 x 1.5. Attic.

172. WITNESS RECORD
1853—. 4 volumes. (1-4).

Record of witnesses subpoenaed in court cases, showing term of court, title of case, kind of action, date of hearing, name of witness, mileage, days of attendance, amount of fee, date certificate given, and signature of witness for certificate. Arranged chronologically by dates of hearings. Indexed alphabetically by titles of cases. Handwritten on printed forms. Average 250 pages. 16 x 11.5 x 2. 1 volume, 1853-1899, attic; 3 volumes, 1900—, Probate court vault.

173. CIVIL PAPERS
1853—. 68 file boxes. (1-68).

Original papers filed in civil cases, showing case number, names of plaintiff and defendant, orders of the court, charge, and final disposition of case; includes motions to set aside sales, arbitration causes, and contested election. All papers of each case are filed together in a jacket, showing file box number, case number, and volume and page numbers of Civil Docket, entry 161. Arranged numerically by case numbers. For index, see entry 161. Handwritten and typed on printed forms. 10 x 4.5 x 13.5. Probate court vault.

174. CRIMINAL PAPERS
1853-1931. 4 file boxes. (1-4). Discontinued.

Original papers issued in criminal cases filed in probate court, including summonses, warrants to arrest, affidavits of information, transcripts from magistrates' court, subpoenas and all other *writs*, defendants' pleas, execution for cost, certificates of sentences to penal institutions, and itemized cost bills; all documents show court term, name of defendant, offense charged, date issued, case number, and date filed. All papers of each case are filed together in a jacket, showing file box number, case number, and volume letter and page number of Criminal Docket, actually 162. Typed on printed forms. 14 x 20 x 22. Probate court vault.

175. CRIMINAL RECORD
1852-1931. 7 volumes. (A-D, 5-7). Discontinued; criminal jurisdiction transferred to court of common pleas in 1931.

Record of proceedings in criminal matters before probate court, showing title of case, date of hearing, name of defendant, court orders, sentence, volume letter and page number of Criminal Journal, entry 170, affidavit of arresting officer, information of prosecuting attorney, warrants, sheriff's returns, and sheriff's cost bill. Arranged chronologically by dates of hearings. Indexed alphabetically by names of defendants. 1852-1915, handwritten on printed forms; 1916-1931, typed on printed forms. Average 500 pages. 18 x 13 x 3. Probate court vault.

176. PROBATE COURT FINAL RECORD
1853—. 34 volumes. (A-P, 17-34).

Final record of civil matters before probate court, showing title of case, case number, kind of action, date of hearing, plea application, list of exhibits, notice of claim, court findings, final orders, and settlements; also includes record of change of names. Arranged chronologically by dates of hearings. Indexed alphabetically by titles of cases, or names of principals. 1853-1912, handwritten on printed forms; 1913—, typed on printed forms. Average 500 pages. 16.25 x 11.5 x 3. Probate court vault.

Wills

177. WILL RECORD
1853—. 38 volumes. (A-P, 17-38).

Copies of wills offered for probate, showing name of testator, application to admit to probate, date of hearing, petition, proceedings, testimony of witness to will, text of will, and signature of decedent. Arranged chronologically by dates of hearings. Indexed alphabetically by names of testators. 1853-1912, handwritten; 1913—, typed. Average 500 pages. 16.25 x 12 x 2.5. Probate court vault.

178. INDEX TO RECEIPT FOR WILLS DEPOSITED
1880—. 1 volume.

Record of wills deposited by living with probate court, showing date deposited, name and address of testator, date taken out, signature of person receiving will, and date returned for probate Arranged alphabetically by names of testators. No index. Handwritten on printed forms. 100 pages. 14 x 9 x 1. Probate court vault.

179. [WILLS]

1840—. In Estate Papers, entry 188.

Original wills which have been probated, showing date of will, text of will, signatures of witnesses and testators, date probated, file box number, and case number.

Estates and Guardianships

Appointments, Bonds, and Letters

180. EXECUTORS' ADMINISTRATORS' APPLICATIONS, BONDS AND LETTERS

1852—. 34 volumes. (1-17, 1-17). Some volumes subtitled. With Will Annexed.

Record of executors' and administrators' applications for appointment, executors' and administrators' bonds, and letters testamentary and letters of administration. Applications show date of application, title of case, volume and page numbers of Administration Docket, entry 164, names of heirs, degree of kinship of heirs. and amount of assets; bonds show name of executor or administrator, amount and condition of bond, signatures of sureties, and date of approval of bond; letters testamentary and letters of administration show name of decedent, name of executor or administrator, duties, and date appointed by court. Arranged chronologically by dates of applications. Indexed alphabetically by names of decedents. 1852-1912, handwritten on printed forms; 1913—, typed on printed forms. Average 500 pages. 18.5 x 12.5 x 3. Probate court vault.

181. EXECUTORS' APPLICATION, BOND AND LETTERS

1940—. 16 volumes. (1-15).

Record of executors' applications for appointment and letters testamentary, showing date of application, name of testator, name of executor, and copy of letter of authority; bonds show date, amount of bond, and names of sureties. Arranged chronologically by dates of applications. Indexed alphabetically by names of executors. Handwritten on printed forms. Average 500 pages. 18 x 14 x 3. Probate court office.

183. GUARDIANS' APPLICATION, BOND AND LETTERS
1852—. 8 volumes. (A-E, 6-8).

Record of proceedings and appointment of guardians for minors, imbeciles, idiots, and other incompetents, including copies of applications for appointment, showing date of application, title of case, name and address of applicant, relationship to minor or ward, name, age, and address of ward, and amount of estate of ward; guardians' bonds, showing names of guardian and ward, names the sureties, amount and condition of bond, and date; letters of guardianship, showing name of appointee, name of ward, and date of application. Arranged chronologically by dates of applications. Indexed alphabetically by names of wards. 1852-1912, handwritten on printed forms; 1913—, typed on printed forms. Average 500 pages. 18.5 x 12.5 x 3. Probate court vault.

183. NOTICE RECORD
1873—. 11 volumes. (1-11).

Record of publication of notices of appointment of executor or administrator by probate court, showing title of estate, date of filing appointment, names of appointees and statement of duties, and notarized oath of publisher of notice. Arranged chronologically by dates of filing of appointments. Indexed alphabetically by names of appointees. Handwritten on printed forms. Average 300 pages. 16 x 12 x 2.5. 9 volumes, 1873-1929. 2 volumes, 1930—, Probate court vault.

Inventory, Sale Bills, and Claims

184. INVENTORY AND APPRAISEMENT RECORD
1886—. 37 volumes. (1-28, 33-41). 10 volumes subtitled With Widows; 7 volumes, Without Widows; 1 volume, With Spouse, 2 volumes, Without Spouse. Title varies; Record of Inventory and Sale Bill, 1886-1909, 13 volumes; Record of Sale Bill and Inventory, 1920-1936, 1 volume.

Record of appraisement and inventory in estate settlement matters, showing name of estate, title of case, and date of hearing; also letters testamentary and of administration, orders to appraise, notices of appraisement, oaths of appraisers, schedules of assets and liabilities with recapitulation, and orders of the court. Arranged chronologically by dates of hearings. Index alphabetically by names of estates. Handwritten and typed on printed forms. Average 500 pages. 18 x 13 x 3. 31 volumes, 1886-1927, attic; 6 volumes, 1928—, Probate court vault.

185. SCHEDULE OF CLAIMS, DEBTS AND LIABILITIES
1932—. 5 volumes. (1-5).
Schedule of claims, debts, and liabilities filed in estate matters in probate court, showing name of decedent, volume and page numbers of Administration Docket, entry 164, names and addresses of creditors, nature of claim, amount of claims and interest, amount allowed, date of allowance or rejection, rate of interest allowed, date of maturity, and date submitted. Arranged chronologically by dates submitted. Indexed alphabetically by names of decedents. Handwritten on printed forms. Average 550 pages. 13.5 x 10.5 x 3. Probate court vault.

Accounts and Settlements

186. EXECUTORS', ADMINISTRATORS', AND GUARDIANS' ACCOUNT RECORD
1852—. 43 volumes. (A-Z, 27-43).
Record of proceedings in estate settlements (final and partial) in probate court, showing title of case, date of hearing, itemized account rendered court, cost bills, and orders of court. Arranged chronologically by dates of hearings. Indexed alphabetically by names of decedents or wards. 1852-1912, handwritten; 1913—, typed. Average 600 pages. 16 x 12.5 x 3. 29 volumes, 1852-1920, attic; 14 volumes, 1921—, Probate court's volt.

187. REAL ESTATE RECORD
1842—. 34 volumes. (1-34).
Record of land ordered sold by probate court, showing name of decedent or ward, date of each proceeding, description of property, and name of purchaser of land. Arranged chronologically by dates of proceedings. Indexed alphabetically by names of decedents or wards. 1842-1912, handwritten on printed forms; 1913—, typed on printed forms. Average 600 pages. 16.5 x 12 x 3. Probate court office.

Case Papers

188. ESTATE PAPERS
1840—. 600 file boxes. (1-600).
Original papers filed in proceedings of estate administration cases, including applications for appointment as administrator or executor, notices of appointment, bonds filed, letters of administration or testamentary, inventories and sale bill,

accounts filed, final settlements, and cost bills. All show date, name of decedent, name of administrator or executor, case number, and file box number. All papers of each case are filed together in a jacket, showing final box number and case number. Also contains [Wills], entry 179. Arranged numerically by case numbers. For index, see entry 165. Handwritten and typed on printed forms. 10 x 4.5 x 13.5. Probate court vault.

189. GUARDIANS' [Papers]
1853—. 140 file boxes. (1-140).
Original papers issued in guardianships, consisting of applications for appointment as guardian, notices of appointment, bonds filed, letters of guardianship, inventories and appraisements, accounts, and cost bills. All show date, name of ward, name of guardian, case number, and file box number. Arranged numerically by case numbers. For index, see entry 167. Handwritten and typed on printed forms. 10 x 4.5 x 13.5. Probate court vault.

Inheritance Taxes

190. INHERITANCE TAX RECORD
1919—. 18 volumes. (1-18).
Record of procedure followed in securing itemized statement of assets and liabilities filed for determination of inheritance taxes, showing name of decedent, date of hearing, net value of estate, personal property, and real estate, itemized statement of debts, names of heirs, age, and relationship to decedent, claims for exemption from inheritance tax, and volume and page numbers of Probate Court Journal, entry 169. Arranged chronologically by dates of hearings. Indexed alphabetically by names of decedents. Typed on printed forms. Average 500 pages. 18.5 x 12.5 x 3. Probate court vault.

Dependents

191. LUNACY RECORD
1902-1932. 4 volumes. (1-4). 1852— also in Probate Court Journal, entry 169.
Record of proceedings in lunacy matters in probate court, showing title of case, name of defendant, date of hearing, affidavit of lunacy, and names and kinship of nearest relative; includes order for and warrants to arrest, sheriff's returns and fee

bills, orders after hearing, medical certificates, subpoenas for witnesses, returns of service, applications for admission to state hospital, and warrants to convey and returns thereon. Arranged chronologically by dates of hearings. Indexed alphabetically by names of defendants. 1904-1912, handwritten on printed forms; 1913-1932, typed on printed forms. Average 500 pages. 18.5 x 13 x 3. Probate court office.

192. RECORD OF WARDS – CHILD WELFARE BOARD
1922-1936. 1 volume.

List of minor wards of county, showing case number, name of ward, names of parents, name of foster home, and dates of admission and departure. Arranged numerically by case numbers. Indexed alphabetically by names of wards. Handwritten on printed forms. 200 pages. 16 x 12 x 2. Probate court vault.

193. RECORD OF WARDS, CHILD WELFARE BOARD
1922—. 1 volume.

Record of all epileptic, imbecile, idiotic, incompetent, dependent, or orphaned minor wards of the probate court, showing date of entry, name and address of ward, date of birth, sex, color, race, education of ward, date became ward of court, for what reason, and date and reason of final discharge. Arranged chronologically by dates of entries. Index alphabetically by names of wards. Handwritten. 200 pages. 16.25 x 12 x 2. Probate court office.

194. ADOPTION RECORD
1928—. 1 volume. (1).

Record of papers filed in adoption proceedings, showing title of case, name of petitioner, and date of hearings; includes court orders, petitions, answers and consents, reports of next friend, histories of petitioners, findings of court, and approvals. Arranged chronologically by dates of hearings. Indexed alphabetically by names of petitioners. Typed. 500 pages. 18 x 13 x 2.5. Probate court vault.

Naturalization

195. NATURALIZATION RECORD
1860-1906. 6 volumes. (1-6).
Record of naturalization of aliens, including copies of declarations of intention, showing date of issue, name of alien, nativity, and names of witnesses to residence in the United States; copies of affidavits and oath of allegiance to the United States, showing date of issue of final papers. Arranged chronologically by dates of issue of final papers. Indexed alphabetically by names of applicants. Average 400 pages. 18 x 12.5 x 3. Probate court vault.

For similar naturalization records, 1907—, see entries 138, 139.

196. NATURALIZATION DOCKET
1860-1869, 1903-1906. 3 file boxes. Title varies; Naturalization Record, 1860-1869, 1 file box.
Original declarations of intention of aliens to become naturalized citizens of the United States, showing date, name of alien, case number, nativity, date of entry into the United States, and date of filing. Also contains [Birth and Death Reports], 1868-1869, entry 198. Arranged numerically by case numbers. No index. Handwritten on printed forms. 10 x 4.5 x 13.5. Probate court vault.

Vital Statistics

Births and Deaths

197. RECORD OF BIRTHS AND DEATHS
1867-1908. 2 volumes. (1, 2).
Records of births, showing date recorded, name, sex, date, place of birth, and color of child, names of residence of parents, and name of township. Record of deaths, shows date recorded, name of decedent, last address, sex, color, occupation, place of birth and death, and cause of death. Births arranged by township and chronologically thereunder by date of birth; deaths, arranged chronologically by dates of death. Births indexed alphabetically by names of infants; deaths, indexed alphabetically by names of decedents. Handwritten on printed forms. Average 300 pages. 18 x 13 x 3. Probate court vault.

For subsequent records, see entries 381, 382.

198. [BIRTH AND DEATH REPORTS]

1868-1869. 2 bundles in 1 file box, Naturalization Docket, entry 196. Discontinued.

Original weekly statistical reports from township sextons to the probate court, showing date of report, number of births in past week, number of boys and girls, number of deaths in past week, number of communicable and contagious disease cases being cared for in past week, number of deaths due to accidents, name of township, and signature of sexton making report. Arranged alphabetically by names of townships and chronologically thereunder by dates of reports. No index. Handwritten on printed forms. 11 x 3 x 3. Probate court vault.

Marriages

199. MARRIAGE LICENSES AND RECORDS

1840—. 19 volumes. (A-K, 12-19). Title varies; Licenses, 1840-1867, 2 volumes.

Record of applications and licenses to marry issued by probate court and certificates of marriages performed, showing name of applicants, date of application, date of issue of license and certificate, and name of officiating minister or other official. Arranged chronologically by dates of applications. Indexed alphabetically by names of male applicants; also separate index, entry 200. Handwritten on printed forms. Average 500 pages. 16 x 12 x 3. Probate court office.

200. GENERAL INDEX TO MARRIAGES

1840—. 2 volumes. (1, 2).

Index to Marriage Licenses and Records, entry 199 and Marriage Certificates, Consents and Refusals, entry 201, showing names of groom and bride, date of application, date and number of certificate, volume letter or number and page number of record, and file box number of marriage papers. Arranged alphabetically by names of grooms and brides. Handwritten on printed forms. Average 500 pages. 18 x 13 x 3. Probate court office.

201. MARRIAGE CERTIFICATES, CONSENTS AND REFUSALS

1925—. 5 file boxes. (1-5).

Original papers pertaining to marriages, including applications for marriage licenses, showing name of applicants, dates of application and issuance of license, certificate number, and name of officiating minister or justice of peace; parents' consent to marriage of minors, showing names of parents and minor, name of other party to contract, and date of filing; certificate of performance of marriage, showing certificate number, date of marriage, names of contracting parties, signature of officiating minister or magistrate and volume and page numbers of Marriage License and Records, entry 199. Arranged chronologically by dates filed. For index, see entry 200. 10 x 4.5 x 13.5. Probate court vault.

Licenses

202. MINISTER'S LICENSE
1846—. 4 VOLUMES. (1-4).

Records of licenses to ministers to perform marriages in Lake County, showing date of issue, name of minister, and church affiliation. Arranged chronologically by dates of issue. No index. 1846-1875, handwritten; 1876—, handwritten on printed forms. Average 200 pages. 10 x 7.5 x 1.5. 2 volumes, 1846-1874, attic; 2 volumes, 1875—, Probate court vault.

203. RECORD OF MEDICAL CERTIFICATES
1896—. 1 volume.

Copies of certificates to practice medicine and surgery in the state issued by State Medical Board, showing certificate number, name of applicant, college degree and name of college, date of graduation, date of certificate, and date recorded. Arranged chronologically by dates of recording. Indexed alphabetically by names of licensees. Handwritten on printed forms. Average 400 pages. 16.25 x 11 x 2.5. Probate court vault.

204. NURSES' REGISTER
1916—. 1 volume.

Copies of certificates issued by State Medical Board to graduate nurses on passing examinations, showing certificate number, name of nurse, date of graduation, name of college or training school, and date recorded; includes limited practitioners' licenses, showing license number, name of licensee, residence, branch authorized to practice, date issued by board, signatures of officials, and date and place of recording. Arranged chronologically by dates of recordings. Indexed alphabetically by names of nurses or practitioners. Handwritten on printed forms. 325 pages. 16.25 x 12 x 2. Probate court vault.

Fiscal Accounts

205. CASH BOOK

1879—. 16 volumes. (2 unnumbered, 1-14).
Record of money received and disbursed by probate court, showing date of entry, by whom paid, to whom due, total amount, distribution to accounts, name of each account, date of disbursement, to whom paid, and signature of payee; also includes cash record of juvenile court, 1937—. Arranged chronologically by dates of entries. Indexed alphabetically by names of payers. Handwritten on printed forms. Average 500 pages. 18.5 x 12.5 x 3. 11 volumes, 1879-1928, attic; 5 volumes, 1929—, Probate court vault.

206. COST BILLS, ESTATES, MISCELLANEOUS

1907-1909. 2 volumes. (1, 1). Discontinued.
Record of cost bills for administering estates and miscellaneous matters in probate court, showing title of case, name of estate, itemized account of charges for services rendered, and date recorded. Arranged under tabs of types of actions and chronologically thereunder by dates of recordings. Indexed alphabetically by names of cases. Handwritten on printed forms. 500 pages. 18 x 13 x 3. Attic.

207. FEE BOOK

1873—. 14 volumes. (1-4, 1-10). Title varies slightly.
Record of fees received by probate court, showing name of payer, title of case, name of principal, type of action, date of entry, and total receipts. Arranged chronologically by dates of entries. Indexed alphabetically by titles of cases or names of principles. Handwritten. Average 500 pages. 14.5 x 10 x 3. 10 volumes, 1873-1907, attic; 4 volumes, 1908—, Probate court office.

Miscellaneous

208. ANNUAL REPORT OF COUNTY VISITORS

1913—. 1 file box. (Civil I, 162A-171A).
Copies of annual reports of board of county visitors to probate court, showing date of report, detailed conditions of county institutions visited, activities within the institution, recommendations, discrepancies found, moral and physical aspects, and signatures of county visitors. Arranged chronologically by dates or reports. No index. Typed. 10.5 x 4.75 x 13.5. Probate court vault.

209. REPORTS [Miscellaneous]

1928—. 4 file boxes.

Miscellaneous reports, including auditor's report to probate judge on crippled children enumerated in the county school districts, showing name, sex and age of youth, name and address of parent or guardian, date of last school attendance, date report filed, and date sent to health commissioners; inheritance tax reports to auditor from probate judge, giving name of court, name of judge, inclusive dates of reports, case number, value of estate, tax assessment, tax collected, no tax found, amount of fee, probate judge's certificate and receipt for funds received from county treasurer; reports from Cleveland and Athens state hospitals to probate judge, showing number of patients enrolled, number of males and females, and date of report; duplicate copies of the reports filed by Haskins and Sells to the Andrews school for Girls and annual reports to the school's finances to the probate judge, showing date of report, amount of receipts and expenditures, and amount of money on hand at end of the year; also includes applications for clerk hire from probate court to county commissioners, showing date of applications, number requested, and classification; and statement for newspapers to the probate judge of the amounts received for the publication of legal notices, giving dates of publication, volume and page numbers of cash Book, entry 205, title of case, and amount received. Arranged by subjects and chronologically thereunder by dates of reports or papers. No index. 10 x 4.5 x 13.5. Probate court vault.

210. CORONER'S REPORT

1908-1911. 1 file jacket. Discontinued.

Coroner's reports to probate court of inventory of effects found on body of deceased, showing name of deceased, date of inquest, list of articles found on body, record of money found on body, next friend's receipt for same, and date of filing. Arranged chronologically by dates of filing. No index. Handwritten on printed forms. 11 x 4 x 2. Probate court vault.

211. PATENT REGISTER

1868-1869. 1 volume. Discontinued.

Record of affidavits in patent right matters in probate court, showing number of patent, type and name of patent, name, age, residents, and occupation of affiant, name of employer, date of affidavit, date of letters for patent, to whom issued, and date of filing. Arranged chronologically by dates of filing. Indexed alphabetically by names of affiants. Handwritten on printed forms. 300 pages. 14 x 9 x 2. Attic.

212. CORRESPONDENCE

1922—. 6 file boxes. (1-6).

Copies of all correspondence pertinent to business of probate court, showing dates, names of correspondence, and subject matter. Arranged alphabetically by names of correspondences and subjects. No index. 11.5 x 16.5 x 24. Probate court office.

213. ATLAS OF LAKE COUNTY, OHIO

1895. 1 volume.

Political maps of county, showing townships, corporations, roads, streets, alleys, railroads, streams, section and range lines, and numbers, and boundary lines of land tracts with area and names of owners; corporations or hamlets, showing boundary lines of corporation or hamlet, lot lines with lot numbers, streets names, and location of public buildings; also county directory, giving brief summary of industrial pursuits of each township and town with short biography of prominent citizens. Published by H.B. Stranahan. Arranged alphabetically by names of townships and towns. No index. Printed. 114 pages. 17.25 x 15.25 x .65. Attic.

The juvenile court, which originated in Chicago in 1899, was signally successful and was widely copied. In Ohio it was established in 1902 by an act of the assembly for Cuyahoga County,[1] and in 1904 was extended to the whole state.[2] In larger counties domestic relations and juvenile cases have been assigned to one or more of the common pleas judges, but in the less populous counties, where there is no court or domestic relations, juvenile cases are brought before the probate judge, as being concerned with the legal affairs of minors.

Whether juvenile court is lodged with the court of domestic relations or with the probate court, the purposes and procedures are the same. Hearings are informal, the court acting as friendly advisor rather than judicial referee; and a probation officer whose chief concerned is a constructive program for the delinquent is provided to the court. The court assumes jurisdiction over offenders under 18 years, and may continue supervision until they come of age.[3] Charges vary from mere pranks to very serious offenses, and the disposition of the offenders accordingly ranges from a simple warning to the parents, to placing the child in a reformatory.[4] Cases warranting serious consideration are carefully studied and handled, with the happy result that many first offenses are also last offenses.

In recent years aid to dependent children has been a great help to juvenile court, since poverty is for obvious reasons the most important contributing factor in juvenile crime. With the establishment of aid to dependent children, also, came a formal definition by the legislature of the terms dependent child and delinquent child,[5] which has been extremely useful and dealing with juvenile delinquency.

Juvenile court is held in Lake County by the probate judge. In the last five years cases coming before the juvenile court judge have averaged 114 per year.[6] Many of these cases are put on probation in their own homes, some are turned over to the Child Welfare Board, and a few are sent to the Bureau of Juvenile Research in Columbus.[7] The county maintains no detention home, but the private dwelling of the juvenile probation officer is used as one for children whose final disposition has not been decided.

---

1. *Laws of Ohio,* XCV, 785.
2. *Laws of Ohio,* XCVII, 561.
3. *Ibid.,* XCII, 561; XCIX, 192; CIII, 859; G.C. sec. 1643.
4. G.C. secs. 1652, 1653.
5. *Laws of Ohio,* XCIV, 192; G.C. secs. 1644, 1645.
6. Juvenile Appearance Docket, 1936-1940, entry 214.
7. Juvenile Journal, 1936-1940, entry 215.

214. JUVENILE APPEARANCE DOCKET
1908—. 5 volumes. (1-5).

Record of all papers filed, orders, and proceedings in juvenile matters, showing case number, title of case, kind of action, name, age, and residence of minor, names of parents, guardians, or custodians, date of filing, volume and page numbers of Juvenile Journal, entry 215. Also contains Juvenile Court Record, 1908-1916, and 1920—, entry 216. Arranged numerically by case number. Indexed alphabetically by names of minors. Handwritten on printed forms. Average 400 pages. 18.5 x 13 x 3. Probate court vault.

215. JUVENILE JOURNAL
1906—. 5 volumes. (1-5).

Records of journal entries and proceedings in juvenile matters, showing title of case, kind of action, name of minor, date of hearing, proceedings, and orders of court. Also includes information on wards of the Child Welfare Board, 1924-1926, found in Journal, 1924—, entry 408. Arranged chronologically by dates of hearings or meetings. Indexed alphabetically by names of minors or other principles. Average 400 pages. 18.5 x 13 x 3. Office juvenile officer.

216. JUVENILE COURT RECORD
1917-1919. 1 volume. 1908-1916 and 1920—, in Juvenile Appearance Docket, entry 214.

Complete record of juvenile matters, showing name of minor, title of case, and date of hearings; includes complaints, orders of court, petitions, summonses, warrants, sheriff's returns and fee bills, and findings of court. Arranged chronologically by dates of hearings. Indexed alphabetically by names of minors. Handwritten on printed forms. 300 pages. 16 x 11 x 2. Probate court vault.

217. JUVENILE [Cases–Original Papers]
1923—. 25 file boxes. (1-25).

Original papers filed in juvenile court cases, including complaints, warrants to arrest, cost bills, citations, subpoenas, medical and health records, journal entries, and all other papers pertinent to case. All papers of each case are filed together in a jacket, showing file box and case numbers, title of case, and dates of filing. Arranged numerically by case numbers. No index. Handwritten on printed forms. 10 x 4.5 x 13.5. Office juvenile officer.

218. [RECORD OF DELINQUENTS AND DEPENDENTS
1938——. 2 file boxes. (labeled by contained letters of alphabet).
Card record of delinquent, dependent, and crippled children, showing case number,
method of disposition, identifying date of child, case history of child and parents,
and other pertinent information. Arranged alphabetically by names of children. No
index. Handwritten on printed forms. 6.25 x 9.25 x 14. Office juvenile officer.

219. MOTHERS' PENSION RECORD
1919-1936. 3 volumes. (1; 2 unnumbered). Discontinued; superseded by aid
to dependent children.
Record of papers filed and mothers' pension matters, showing date of filing, name
of applicant, findings and orders of court, applications for partial support, name of
children, ages, and schooling, investigator's reports, and amount of award.
Arranged chronologically by dates of filing. Indexed alphabetically by names of
applicants. Typed. Average 300 pages. 16.5 x 11.5 x 2.5. 1 volume, 1919-1933,
probate court's vault; 2 volumes, 1934-1936, aid to dependent children office.
For subsequent records, see entry 220.

Aid to dependent children (superceding the mothers' pension law of 1914 to 1936) was set up for Ohio in April 1936, by an act of the state legislature accepting the provisions of the social security act by which the United States government offered to assist properly administered state aid to dependent children.[1]

Lake County complied with the requirements of the act as early as July 1936, when the agency was organized by judge Elton H. Behm of the probate court, under state and federal regulations. The staff consists of the county investigator and an assistant, who receive an aggregate annual compensation of $2268.[2] They are appointed by the juvenile court judge, who is the local administrator of aid to dependent children.[3]

Children are eligible if under 16 years of age, and if they are deprived for various stipulated reasons of parental or other support; however, a child over 16 and under 18 may still receive aid at the discretion of the county administrator.[4] Persons receiving aid for dependent children must be in need of this assistance; must be morally, mentally, and physically able to care for a child or children; and must have adequate home facilities for so doing.[5] To comply with this act the county is required to provide 15/100 of a mill of the tax duplicate in order to participate; the state makes an annual appropriation on a population basis and the federal government contributes one dollar for every two dollars provided by the state and county.[6] To states with approved plans, the federal government makes grants for aid to dependent children under 16 years of age equal to one-third of the total expenditures of the state, both for assistance and administration, estimating its maximum monthly payment at $18 for the first child and $12 for each additional child.[7] These figures simply place an upper limit on the amounts taken as a basis for computing federal grants. The state is entirely free to set its own rate of individual payments, depending upon the needs of the family.[8] In Lake County the average payment for each child for one month was $10.34 during 1940.[9]

---

1. G.C. secs. 1683-2--1683-10; 1359-31–1359-45.
2. Payroll, 1940, entry 283.
3. G.C. sec. 1358-31.
4. G.C. sec. 1359-32.
5. G.C. sec. 1359-34.
6. G.C. secs. 1359-36, 1359-37.
7. G.C. sec. 1359-38.
8. G.C. sec. 1359-33.
9. Aid to Dependent Children Payroll (not inventoried, a current record not kept permanently).

The law sets no limit on the amount of aid to be given; it specifically requires the aid to be given on the basis of individual need.[10]

The average number of children aided through 1940 was 267.[11] Because to the county or the entire year was $13,235, and the same amount in 1941, the remainder of the total cost being supplied according to plan in unequal amounts by the state and federal governments.[12]

The law requires a case worker to visit each child four times each year, but problem cases requiring closer supervision are visited more frequently, as the case demands.

---

10. G.C. sec. 1359-33.
11. Aid to Dependent Children Payroll, see footnote 9.
12. Budget Summary, 1940-1941 (not inventoried, a current record not kept permanently).

220. AID TO DEPENDENT CHILDREN
1936—. 2 file boxes. (1, 2).
Original applications and case papers of needy children, showing case number, date, and the name and address of applicants; includes personal, family, and statistical information; reports of investigators; reports to county commissioners; and correspondence. Arranged alphabetically by names of applicants. No index. Handwritten on printed forms. 11.5 x 16 x 24. Aid to dependent children's office.

221. [INDEX TO CHILDREN AND BLIND FILES]
1936—. 2 file boxes. (labeled by contained letters of alphabet).
Card record, showing case number, type of case, date of application, name of applicant, address, and amount of grant. Also contains [Card Index, Aid to the Blind], entry 31. Arranged alphabetically by names of applicants. Typed on printed forms. 4 x 5 x 7. Aid to dependent children's office.

A jury commission for selection of jury list has functioned in Lake County since authorization of such an agency in 1894.[1] The commission, consisting originally of four, but now of two members, is appointed by the court of common pleas and serves during its pleasure.[2] Members of the commission must be electors of the county and under 70 years of age. The salary paid varies with the population of the counties, but under the jury code of 1931,[3] may not exceed $2200 a year. In Lake County commissioners are paid $5 for each day served.[4]

At the beginning of each year the commissioners are required to prepare from a list of voters provided by the board of elections a new and complete jury list, known as the annual jury list, and an index to this list. It must be arranged alphabetically by precincts, districts, and townships, and record the name, occupation, business address, and residence of each prospective juror. A duplicate list is certified by the commissioners and filed with the clerk of court of common pleas.[5]

The commission is further required to prepare a slip or card for each name on the annual jury list, and to place these cards in a jury wheel, which is, as its name signifies, a sort of hollow wheel so design as to mix the slips or cards when revolved. The wheel is kept carefully locked when not in use. The name slips are thoroughly mixed and the names are withdrawn in the presence of a judge of the court of common pleas, the clerk of courts, and the sheriff.[6]

Usually 110 jurors are called for each term of court in Lake County, but only 60 of these are selected.[7] The first 15 names drawn comprise the grand jury, and the remainder of the list supplies if necessary names for whatever petit juries may be required. The list is held in the custody of the journal clerk, and the prospective jurors are then summoned to appear before the commissioners to be examined as to their mental and physical ability to serve on a jury.[8]

---

1. *Laws of Ohio,* XCI, 176; [Common Pleas] 0 (1894), 240, entry 131.
2. *Laws of Ohio,* LXXXVIII, 200; CIII, 513; CXI, 106.
3. *Ibid.,* CXIV, 193-213.
4. Appropriation Ledger 1940, entry 269.
5. *Laws of Ohio,* CXIV, 205; G.C. sec. 11419-41.
6. G.C. secs. 11419-22; 11419-24.
7. Jury Book, 1940, entry 91.
8. Information obtained from clerk of court.

222. JURY REPORTS
1927—. 2 file drawers.

Miscellaneous files regarding jury commission including; clerk's term reports to jury commission, showing date of report, term of court, list the jurors called, names and addresses of jurors chosen, number of days and dates served, amount of fee, names of jurors excused or discharged, names and addresses of those who did not serve, names of persons fined in cases, signatures of jury commissioners, judge, and clerk; letters from judge to jury commission, showing date, setting a time to draw jurors, manner or method of drawing, and code reference for authority to do so; journal entries of impaneling grand jury, showing term of court, names of jurors chosen, names of those excused, name of jury foreman, and date filed; venires to sheriff for petit jurors, showing names and addresses of jurors drawn. Arranged chronologically by court terms. No index. Handwritten and typed on printed forms. 9.5 x 9 x 11. Clerk of court's office.

At each session of the court of common pleas, usually four each year, the jury commissioner is requested to select 15 electors to serve as a grand jury.[1] Usually the first 15 persons drawn from the jury wheel are selected for this duty. In Lake County, the grand jury can usually conclude its work in two or three days, but may be required to serve longer. Each juror receives three dollars for each day served.[2] When the grand jury has reviewed all cases presented by the prosecuting attorney, it recesses, but maybe recalled at any time during the session of court. The function of the grand jury is to make a preliminary examination of all persons bound over, either with bail or without, who are charged with capital or infamous crimes.[3]

The prosecuting attorney presents the charges in secret session,[4] which is generally dominated by him, since the defendant may not be represented by council, nor is he permitted to call witnesses. Twelve of the 15 grand jurors mut concur in finding an indictment.[5]

The governor or general assembly may order a new grand jury to conduct any investigation, and, upon written request of the attorney-general, the common pleas court, or any judge thereof they order a special grand jury which is completely independent of the regular one but proceeds in exactly the same way.[6]

In 1939, in Lake County, there were 35 true bills returned by the grand jury and in 1940 there were 23, covering almost the entire range of offenses against person and property.[7]

Since 1869 it has also been the duty of the grand jury to visit the county jail once at each term of court at which they may be in attendance, examine its state and condition and inquire into the discipline and treatment of prisoners, and return a written report to the court.[8]

The grand jury keeps no separate records; for Jury Book, 1842-1856, 1864—, see entry 91. For *praecipes* and subpoenas for grand jury witness, entries 93 and 94; for reports of grand jury, 1932—, entry 104; for jury commission record, 1927—, entry 222.

---

1. G.C. sec. 13436-2.
2. Jury Book, 1940, entry 91.
3. G.C. sec. 13436-5.
4. G.C. sec. 13436-7.
5. G.C. sec. 13436-17.
6. G.C. sec. 13436-14.
7. Criminal Appearance and Execution Docket, VII, *passim.*
8. G.C. sec. 13436-20.

At each session of the court of common pleas the jury commissioners select that number of persons eligible for jury duty which in their judgment will serve the requirements of the current term of courts. A venire is issued to the sheriff to cause these persons to appear on the day fixed for trial.[1] From the persons so summoned a jury of twelve is impaneled. The prosecuting attorney and council for the defense may challenge peremptorily six persons each in capital cases, and four in other cases. Challenges may also be made for causes prescribed by law, such as having an interest in the case, former conviction of crime, and relationship or affinity to one of the parties in the case.[2] The jury may reach a verdict either in the courtroom or in secret session in the custody of a court officer. If the jurors disagree as to testimony, or desire to be further instructed in the law, they may return to the court for additional information.[3] In criminal cases the verdict must be unanimous, in civil cases it may be nine to three.[4]

Trial by jury may be dispensed with when waived by the defendant and criminal cases, or by agreement of both parties in civil cases. Juries are waived in 80 percent of the criminal trials and in 10 percent of the civil cases in Lake County.[5] There is a definite trend toward submission of issues to a decision by the court rather than by a jury. In Lake County only three venires were called in 1940.[6] The cost of trial by jury is one factor involved; the other is a growing preference for judicial rather than jury decisions. For the years 1936 through 1940, the records show an average of 19 jury trials for criminal offenses each year and eight jury trials of civil cases.[7]

Jurors serve throughout the term of court for which they are called, and additional venires may be requested by the court. Attempts to avoid jury duty in Lake County are few, and usually for the reason that the prospective juror cannot well be spared from his work.[8]

The petit jury keeps no separate records; for Jury Book, 1842-1856, 1864—, see entry 91; Jury List, 1879-1903, 1932—, see entry 92; Jury Commission Record, 1927—, see entry 222.

---

1. G.C. sec. 13443-1.
2. G.C. secs. 13443-4; 13443-6; 13443-8.
3. G.C. secs. 11420-3, 11420-6.
4. G.C. sec. 11420-9; *Laws of Ohio,* CXIII, 195.
5. Information attained from county prosecuting attorney; *see* Common Pleas Court Journal, entry 131.
6. Common Pleas Court Journal, L, 558; LI, 238; LII (n. p.), January 27, 1941.
7. Common Pleas Court Journal, XLIV-LI, (1936-1940), *passim.*
8. Information obtained from county prosecuting attorney.

Since 1936 the office of county prosecuting attorney has been elective for a four-year term.[1] He is removable for cause by the court of common pleas, which, in the event of the office falling vacant, appoints a successor pending the next election.[2] He is required to furnished bond of not less than $1000.[3] He may appoint his own assistants, clerks, and stenographers, and fix their salaries, subject to the approval of the county commissioners,[4] and since 1911 he has had authority to appoint county detectives to aid in the investigation of criminal matters.[5]

The prosecuting attorney is required to report annually to the county commissioners the number of prosecutions completed in criminal court, the amounts collected in fines and cost, and the amounts forfeited.[6] He may be required to report annually also to the attorney general as to all prosecutions in his county.[7]

The most important duty of the prosecuting attorney is to inquire into and to prosecute crimes and misdemeanors. In cases of felony, he must obtain an indictment from the grand jury; if successful, he attempts to win a conviction in trial before the court of common pleas.[9] In cases of misdemeanors he may initiate prosecution in the court of common pleas by information alone.[10] At any time, even after a case has started, he may, with the consent of the court, enter a *nolle prosequi;* the matter of pressing a case to a conclusion is thus within the discretion of the prosecuting attorney.[11]

In civil matters the prosecuting attorney acts for both state and county. He may bring suit in the name of the state when he considers public moneys have been in any way mishandled; and for the county against persons violating contracts to which the county is a party, or using county property illegally.[12] Another of his civil duties is conducting foreclosure proceedings against delinquent taxpayers.[13]

---

1. G.C. sec. 2909.
2. G.C. secs. 2911, 2912.
3. G.C. sec. 2911.
4. G.C. sec. 2914.
5. G.C. sec. 2915-1.
6. *Laws of Ohio,* LXXVIII, 120; G.C. sec. 2926.
7. *Laws of Ohio,* XC, 225; G.C. sec. 2925.
8. G.C. sec. 2916.
9. G.C. sec. 2916.
10. G.C. sec. 13437-34.
11. G.C. sec. 13437-32.
12. G.C. sec. 2921.
13. G.C. sec. 5624-15.

The prosecuting attorney has served since 1906 in an advisory capacity to all county boards and officials and to township officers who may require his opinion in writing on matters connected with the official duties.[14] He prepares official bonds for all county officers.[15] It is an advisory capacity, also, that he serves on the budget commission and the board of trustees of the sinking fund.[16]

The prosecuting attorney of Lake County receives a salary of $2210 annually and his bond is fixed at $3000. He has one assistant prosecutor and two stenographers on his staff, who received an aggregate annual compensation of $4660.[17]

He disposed of approximately 250 civil cases, in which Lake County was a party, in 1940.[18] Proceedings for foreclosure and delinquent taxpayers, totaled 175.[19] In his capacity as legal advisor to county officials he delivers an average of one written and three verbal opinions daily.[20]

---

14. *Laws of Ohio,* XCVIII, 160-161; G.C. sec. 2917.
15. G.C. sec. 2920.
16. G.C. secs. 5624-15, 2976-18.
17. Payroll, 1940, entry 283.
18. Report of Judicial Statistics to Secretary of State, 1940, entry 12.
19. *Ibid.*
20. Information obtained from office of prosecuting attorney.

223. PROSECUTING ATTORNEY'S FILE
1929—. 12 bundles. Subtitles; 2, Active County; 2, Active Road; 2, Closed Sewer; 2, Closed Road; and 4, Closed County.

Documents and correspondence pertaining to business of prosecuting attorney: two file boxes contain originals and copies of papers issued by common pleas court in active county cases, such as court declarations are particulars, *writs* issued, court orders and decrees, journal entries, sheriff's returns on *writs*, and itemized cost bills; six file boxes contain originals and copies of papers issued by common pleas court in active and closed road and sewer litigations, such as property damage, right-of-way violations, violations of contracts and agreements, request for removal by landowners, signatures on petitions for road work, *writs*, subpoenas, and itemized cost bills; four file boxes contain original and copies of all papers issued in closed criminal cases by county courts, such as warrants to arrest, summons, affidavits of information, transcripts for magistrates' court, subpoenas and other *writs*, defendants' pleas, executions for cost, certificates of sentence to penal institution, and itemized cost bills; also resolutions passed by county commissioners pertaining to contested matters, showing date of meeting, members present, copy of resolution, result of vote taken; original and copies of papers issued by common pleas court in test cases concerning bond issues for building of Lake County Memorial Hospital, such as court declarations of particulars, *writs* issued, court orders and decrees, journal entries, and itemized cost bills. All papers show date of issue, names of litigants, case number, kind of action, and date filed. Arranged by subjects and numerically thereunder by case numbers. For index, see entry 224. 12 x 16.5 x 24. Prosecuting attorney's file room.

224. COUNTY FILE
1929—. 1 file box.

Card index to Prosecuting Attorney's File, entry 223, showing title of case, title or subject, case number, and name of principal or writer. Arranged alphabetically by titles of cases, names of writers, or subjects. Handwritten and typed on printed forms. 4 x 5 x 14. Prosecuting attorney's file room.

It is the duty of the coroner to hold preliminary investigations over the bodies of all persons found within the county who appear to have died by violence or casualty. Like the sheriff, he is a county officer who derives directly from a predecessor in the government of the Northwest Territory. When appointment of a coroner was first authorized[1] the office shared jurisdiction with the sheriff, as the coroner of the territorial government had done, in addition to being required to perform the particular duties of his own office. He was elected for a two-year term.[2] In 1805 a statute was passed which defined the duties of the coroner, and separated his office from that of the sheriff, unless the office of sheriff shall fall vacant, when he was required to execute temporarily the duties of the sheriff.[3] The latter provision, those seldom invoked, remained law until 1887.[4] Very few changes have been made in the coroner's duties since that time. In 1921 he was made official custodian of the morgue, in such counties as maintain a morgue;[5] in 1936 the term of office was extended to four years;[6] and in 1937 a law was enacted requiring the coroner to be a licensed physician.[7] On authorization of the prosecuting attorney he may perform autopsies.

The coroner is required to report his findings, with the testimony of witnesses, to the clerk of courts.[8] These reports constitute the only permanent records of the coroner, all others being current material which he keeps in his home or office.

---

1. *Ohio Const., 1802,* Art. VI, sec. 1.
2. *Ibid.*
3. *Laws of Ohio,* III, 156-161.
4. *Ibid.,* LXXXIV, 208-210.
5. *Ibid.,* CIX, 543.
6. G.C. sec. 2823.
7. *Laws of Ohio,* CXVII, 43.
8. G.C. secs. 2856, 2857.

The corner of Lake County receives a compensation from the county on the basis of services performed, but which fees are paid.[9] In Lake County the average amount paid annually to the coroner during the period from 1936 to 1940, inclusive, was $375.[10] Bond is fixed at $5000. In 1940 Lake County's coroner investigated 55 deaths, one of which was homicide, and 17 suicides; five were due to traffic accidents, and 32 were due to other accidental causes. Three autopsies were performed during the year.[11]

The coroner keeps no separate records; for records of inquest, see entries 123, 124, 210.

---

9. Commissioners' Journal, AA (1938-1939), 245, entry 1.
10. Figures supplied by coroner from personal records.
11. Coroner's Inquest, 1940, entry 124.

The office of sheriff is one of the oldest in county government, appearing as it does in the Northwest Territory governmental organization in 1792 with almost exactly the same functions as today.[1] The sheriff, at that time appointed by the governor, attended upon the court, executed *writs*, warrants, and the like; and policed and arrested criminals. In 1803 the constitution provided for the continuance of the office, which made it elective for a term of two years.[2] The constitution of 1851 did not alter the term but stipulated that the sheriff might serve no more than four out of any period of six years.[3] In 1936 the term became four years,[4] which it has remained. The salary is fixed by the county commissioners within the maximum of $6000, according to the population of the county.[5] The Lake County sheriff receives $2295 annually, and the commissioners have fixed his bond at $15,000.[6]

The powers and duties of the sheriff today are substantially the same as established by the constitution of 1802. The sheriff is required to attend the court of common pleas, appellate court, and probate court if required by the probate judge.[7] He may adjourn the court of common pleas from day to day upon the failure of the judge to appear at regularly scheduled sessions.[8] He executes services orders, warrants, *writs*, and subpoenas from the above named courts as well as from the governor and other state officers and boards.[9] Fees received for this and other services set by law are placed in the county treasury.[10] The sheriff also assists the jury commissioners.[11] He must seek to suppress affrays, riots, unlawful assemblies, and apprehend and jail all felons and traitors.[12] His police powers are coextensive with the county.[13]

---

1. Pease, *op. cit.,* 8.
2. *Ohio Const., 1802,* Art. VI, sec. 1.
3. *Ohio Const., 1851,* Art. X, sec. 3.
4. *Laws of Ohio,* CXVI, pt. ii, 184.
5. G.C. sec. 2994, 2996, 2997.
6. Commissioners' Journal, AA (1938-1939), 245.
7. G.C. secs. 1530, 2833, 10501-26.
8. G.C. sec. 2855.
9. G.C. secs. 2834, 118, 285, 346, 2709, *et al.*
10. G.C. secs. 61, 1275-1, 1307-1, -1530, 1661, 2527-5, 2838, 2845, 2852, 3171, 5348-10, 5544-13, 8323-3, 8572-112, 11374, 11692, 11787, 12189, 1344-12, 3045.
11. G.C. secs. 11419-23, 11419-24.
12. G.C. secs. 2833, 12811, 13432-1.
13. For the most important police powers, see G.C. secs. 2833, 3345, 4112, 12811.

He and the mayor stand on equality as enforces of state laws and municipalities.[14]

The sheriff may appoint and fix the salary of one or more deputies who are directly responsible to him and are bonded to him.[15] In Lake County there are seven deputies on the sheriff's staff, all approved by the county commissioners, and one clerk.[16] The sheriff, on emergency, may call to his aid such persons as he needs (*posse comitatus*), for the apprehension of criminals, and the suppression of riots.[17] Vacancies occur upon failure to give proper bond, nonacceptance, or death, and are filled by the county commissioners pending the next election.[18] The sheriff is removable by the common pleas court after a hearing on the ground of financial defalcation, willful refusal or neglect of duty in criminal cases, or by the governor after a hearing for permitting lynching.[19]

The sheriff is in charge of the courthouse and is official custodian of the county jail.[20] The present jail of Lake County was completed in 1908, and contains 19 cells with room for two prisoners in each.[21] The jail population was 882 in 1940, which is slightly less than the average during the last five years.[22]

Unless otherwise specified all records are located in the sheriff's office, county jail, 74 East Erie Street, Painesville, Ohio.

---

14. Estrich, *op cit.,* XXXVI, 645.
15. G.C. secs. 2830, 2831, 2981.
16. Information obtained from sheriff's office.
17. G.C. secs. 2833, 12811.
18. G.C. secs. 2827, 2828, 12196.
19. G.C. secs. 3036, 3049, 12850, 12851, 2855-1, 2855-2.
20. G.C. secs. 2833; 3157-3176, *passim.*
21. Commissioners' Record G (1906-1913), 7.
22. Jail Register, VI, ((1936-1940), *passim,* entry 228.

Dockets

225. FOREIGN EXECUTION DOCKET

1840—. 8 volumes. (A-C; 1-5).

Records of executions issued by courts other than Lake County courts on property located in Lake County to satisfy judgments rendered, showing title of case, date recorded, from what court, volume and page numbers of docket of court of record, case number, names of plaintiff, defendant, and attorneys, and amount of judgment; also returns and sheriff's bill and fees. Arranged chronologically by dates of recording. Indexed alphabetically by names of plaintiffs and defendants. 1840-1913, handwritten on printed forms; 1914—, typed. Average 500 pages. 18 x 12 x 3. 7 volumes, 1840-1924, attic; 1 volume, 1925—, County jail, sheriff's office.

226. FOREIGN SUMMONS DOCKET
1877—. 12 volumes. (1-12).
Sheriff's record of summonses issued by courts other than Lake County on residents of Lake County, showing date recorded, what county, what court, name of person summoned, case number, date *writ* was received, and date served; also returns and sheriff's cost and fee bill. Arranged chronologically by dates of recording. No index. Handwritten on printed forms. Average 300 pages. 16.5 x 11.5 x 2. 2 volumes, 1877-1917, attic; 10 volumes, 1918—, County jail, sheriff's office.

227. APPEARANCE DOCKET
1885-1908. 5 volumes. (1-5). Discontinued.
Record of service of *writs*, showing title of case, volume and page numbers of docket of court of record, names of litigants, date received, kind of *writ* or *writs*, date served, date returned, mileage, and service fee. Arranged chronologically by dates received. Indexed alphabetically by titles of cases. Average 100 pages. 16 x 11 x 1. Attic.

228. JAIL REGISTER
1868—. 6 volumes. (1-6).
Register of persons committed to county jail, showing name of prisoner, date committed, period confined, by what authority held in jail, date of discharge, by what authority discharged, offense charged, whether first offense (yes or no), offenses (classified), sentence of court, acquittal or release, age, sex, color, social condition, education, date and place of nativity, height, weight, complexion, scars or marks of identification, number of meals served each prisoner for period of incarceration, total number of meals served by month, and year, and sheriff's fees; includes, 1913—, arrest of parole violators. Arranged chronologically by dates of commitments. No index. Handwritten on printed forms. Average 300 pages. 18 x 15 x 1.5. 1 volume, 1868-1908, attic; 5 volumes, 1900—, County jail, sheriff's office.

229. RECORD OF ARREST
1925-1928. 1 volume.

Record of arrest, showing date of arrest, name, occupation, sex, color, and age of prisoner, name of arresting officer, offense, case number, date of trial, plea, disposition, judgment, sentence, fine, and cost. Arranged alphabetically by names of prisoners and chronologically thereunder by dates of arrests. No index. Handwritten on printed forms. 300 pages. 18 x 13 x 2.

230. [BERTILLON RECORDS]
1931—. 1 file box.

Bertillon system of recording information about convicted criminals, showing photograph of convicted prisoner, prison number, prisoner's name, alias, address, age, height, weight, sex, color, and any particular recognizable features for identification, date convicted, for what cause, decision of court, term served, date released, and imprints of fingers. Arranged alphabetically by names of prisoners. No index. Handwritten and typed on printed forms. 11 x 16 x 24.

Fiscal Accounts

231. CASH BOOK
1873—. 7 volumes. (1-7).

Sheriff's record of cash: receipts show date received, case number, title of case, names of litigants, nature of suit, judgments, sheriff's fees due, court costs, and manner of payment; disbursements show to whom paid, date paid out, and amount. Arranged chronologically by dates of entries. Indexed alphabetically by titles of cases. Handwritten on printed forms. Average 500 pages. 17.5 x 12 x 2. 1 volume, 1873-1912, attic; 6 volumes, 1913—, County jail, sheriff's office.

232. RECORD OF ACCRUED FEES
1904—. 3 volumes. (1-3).

Sheriff's record of fees accrued, showing date accrued, case number, in what matter, to whom charged, total fee in civil and criminal cases, from foreign *writs*, from probate and juvenile cases, and from sundries; also shows date of payment. Arranged chronologically by dates of accrual. Indexed alphabetically by titles of cases. Handwritten on printed forms. Average 250 pages. 18 x 13 x 1.5.

Miscellaneous

233. [REPORT OF MEALS]
1936—. 1 file drawer.
Copies of weekly reports made to commissioners of meals served prisoners, showing date of report, name of prisoner, number of prisoner, number of meals served, cost per meal, time prisoner served, date discharged, and amount of cost and fees; monthly reports of meals served, showing total number of meals served during month, cost per meal, total costs, and number of prisoners confined during month. Arranged chronologically by dates of reports. No index. Handwritten on printed forms. 11.5 x 16.5 x 23.5.

234. [DAILY REPORTS–SHERIFF'S DEPARTMENT]
1936—. 1 file drawer.
Daily reports of deputies of traffic accidents or offenses investigated, showing date, location, time, weather conditions, road conditions, type of accident or offense, names of persons involved, license numbers of vehicles involved, direction of travel of each party, detailed account of accident or offense, names of witnesses, and signature of deputy. Arranged chronologically in jackets by month and chronologically thereunder by days of the month. No index. Handwritten on printed forms. 11.5 x 16.5 x 23.5.

235. AUTO LICENSE RECORD
1936—. 1 volume.
Record of all automobile and truck licenses issued in county, showing license number, name, and post office address of licensee, make of automobile or truck, year, and serial and motor numbers. Arranged numerically by license numbers. No index. Handwritten on printed forms. 325 pages. 13 x 9 x 5.25.

The office of dog warden was established in Lake County in 1927.[1] Prior to that date the duties were performed by the sheriff.[2] The warden is under civil service, and is appointed by the commissioners to serve at their discretion. His salary has been set at $1824.[3] He is assisted by one deputy and an assistant.[4]

It is the duty of the dog warden to enforce the licensing of all dogs in the county; to impound and dispose of all unlicensed dogs; to investigate claims for damage to livestock; and to enforce the orders of health authorities for rabies quarantine.[5] Owners may redeem dogs imprisoned by the warden or his deputy by paying costs assessed and providing a registration tag.[6]

In the year 1940, 2000 dogs were seized. Three of these were redeemed, two sold,[7] and the rest were disposed of as provided by law, after being held for the period of three days required.[8]

The total appropriation for the office in 1940 was $3947.05.[9]

The dog warden keeps no separate records; for report to commissioners on dogs impounded and animal claims investigated, see entry 8.

---

1. G.C. sec. 5652-8; Commissioners' Journal, T (1926-1927), 248E, entry 1.
2. *Laws of Ohio,* CVII, 535.
3. Payroll, 1940, entry 283.
4. Commissioners' Journal AA (1938-1939), 293, entry 1.
5. G.C. secs. 5657-7, 5652-9, 5652-16.
6. G.C. sec. 5652-11.
7. General [Weekly Report of County Dog Warden], 1940, *passim,* entry 8.
8. G.C. sec. 5652-7.
9. Commissioners' Journal AA (1938-1939), 293, entry 1.

The office of auditor was established in Ohio in 1820, when the general assembly, by joint resolution, appointed an auditor for each county, to serve one year.[1] The following year the office became elective, for the same term.[2] It has remained elective, though the term has changed several times and is now four years, as set by law in 1919.[3] Vacancies are filled by vote of the county commissioners until the next succeeding election.[4] The auditor is required to furnish bond, and is responsible for the deputies whom he is permitted to appoint, as well as for himself. In Lake County the commissioners have fixed his bond at $5000, and his salary at $3080.[5] There is a full-time staff of eight deputies, two clerks, and one stenographer, who receive an aggregate annual compensation of $14,623.41.[6] In addition to discharging the duties of his office, the auditor is required to serve on the budget commission, the board of trustees of the sinking fund, and on the board of revision. He is secretary of the first two and is required to keep a full record of their proceedings.[7]

The auditor keeps a close check on all phases of county finance. First among his duties in this respect is the assessing of taxes. Since the adoption of the centralizing tax act of 1915, when he was made the chief assessing officer of the county, it has been his duty to appraise all the real and tangible personal property of the county[8] except public utilities which are assessed by the State Tax Commission.[9] The auditor is also required to compute inheritance taxes on order from the probate court[10] and to determine special assessments or road and ditch improvements.[11] All transfers of real property must be cleared through the auditor's office before the deeds may be recorded.[12]

---

1. *Laws of Ohio,* XVIII, 71.
2. *Ibid.,* XIX, 116.
3. *Ibid.,* CVIII, pt. ii, 1294.
4. G.C. sec. 2562.
5. G.C. sec. 2559; Record of Official bonds, entry 306; Payroll, 1940, *passim,* entry 283.
6. Payroll, 1940, *passim,* entry 283.
7. G.C. secs. 5625-19, 2976-19–2976-27, 5580.
8. G.C. secs. 5548, 5548-1; *Laws of Ohio,* CVI, 246.
9. G.C. sec. 5425.
10. G.C. sec. 5341.
11. G.C. secs. 3298-15b, 6484, 6923.
12. G.C. sec. 2573.

He receives and examines periodic settlements from the treasurer, showing the amounts of taxes collected and uncollected.[13] As a member of the budget commission, he has a part also in determining the correctness and permissibility by law of the apportioning of tax money to the various taxing districts, including the state, county, city, townships, or other units;[14] as a member of the board of revision, he is concerned with adjustment and alteration of assessments.[15]

All bills and other claims against the county must have the approval of the auditor, who issues warrants on the county treasurer for moneys payable from the treasury.[16] County money due to the state is similarly handled. Bills or vouchers for payment from funds controlled by commissioners or the board of county infirmary directors must be deposited with the auditor five days before they are approved by the boards.[17] The auditor keeps a running account with the treasurer, receiving from him a daily statement which records all payments into the treasury, listing the dates, by whom paid, and to which fund. These items are all entered in the auditor's account as charges to the treasurer.[18] He is himself responsible to the commissioners and must report to them monthly on the state of county finances.[19]

The auditor holds county borrowing to a sound basis and keeps the commissioners informed of details and totals of bond issued.[20] He signs bonds, keeps a complete bond register, and delivers bonds, when due, to the treasurer for redemption.[21] He has many other minor duties, among them the familiar one of issuing vendors' licenses, dog licenses, cigarette licenses, and cosmetic licenses.[22]

---

13. G.C. secs. 2596, 2643.
14. G.C. sec. 5348-11.
15. Board of Revision, entries 352-255 .
16. G.C. sec. 2570; *Laws of Ohio,* LXVII, 103.
17. *Laws of Ohio,* XCVII, 25.
18. G.C. secs. 2568, 2569.
19. G.C. sec. 2569.
20. G.C. secs. 2293-2, 2293-9, 2293-10.
21. G.C. sec. 2441.
22. G.C. secs. 13166, 13167; 5652-8; 5894-5, 5543-1.

Property Transfers

236. TRANSFER RECORDS
1840—. 65 volumes. (1-65).

Auditor's record of real estate transfers, showing names of grantor and grantee, range, township, section, lot numbers, acreage, description of tract, tax valuation, date of transfer; 1933—, also shows card number of Special Assessment Cards, 1933—, entry 253, and consideration; includes 1915—, record of auditor's deeds, showing appraised value for sale of property for delinquent taxes, name of owner, exact location and description of property, tax valuation, amount of delinquent taxes and penalties due, date sold, name of purchaser, and amount of sale. Arranged alphabetically by names of townships and alphabetically thereunder by names of grantors or for delinquent tax sales by names of purchasers. No index. Handwritten on printed forms. Average 500 pages. 24 x 14.5 x 3. 26 volumes, 1840-1916, attic; 39 volumes, 1916—, Auditor's transfer room.

237. [DAILY TRANSFER RECORD SHEET]
1928—. 3 volumes. Initiated 1928.

Daily record of real estate transfers from which transfer record is posted, showing date of transfer, special assessment card number, names of grantor and grantee, range, township, section and lot numbers, acreage, description of tract, tax valuation, date of transfer, and consideration. Arranged chronologically by dates of transfers. No index. Handwritten on printed forms. Average 320 pages. 17 x 11 x 3. Auditor's transfer room.

238. CERTIFICATE OF TRANSFER OF OWNERSHIP OF DOGS
1928-1930. 1 volume.

Copies of certificates of transfer of ownership of dogs, showing date of certificate, names of vendor and vendee, license number, age, sex, color, and breed of dog. Arranged chronologically by dates of certificates. Indexed alphabetically by names of vendees. Handwritten on printed forms. 100 pages. 11.5 x 9 x 1.5. Attic.

Maps

239. TAX MAPS

1910—. 17 volumes. Subtitled by names of subdivisions.

Plat maps taxing districts and subdivision of Lake County, showing township by sections with boundary lines of sections and townships and boundary lines of land tracts with name of present owner of each tract, acreage, roads, railroads, and streams; also villages, towns, and city wards, showing streets, alleys, streams, railroads, lot lines, and lot dimensions. Prepared by county engineer's office. Arranged alphabetically by names of subdivisions. No index. Blueprint. Scale varies, 1 inch equals 50 feet to 1 inch equals 500 feet. Average 150 pages. 30.5 x 18.5 x 1.5. Auditor's transfer room.

Tax Records

Tax Appraisement and Tax Rates

240. FIELD SHEETS [Reappraisement of Lands in Lake County]

1925—. 79 volumes. Initiated 1925.

Tax enumerator's field reports, showing date, page number of Tax Maps, entry 239, name of taxing district, name and address of owner, range, township, section and lots numbers, acreage, land value, building value, total value, and value as revised by the board of revision. Arranged alphabetically by names of taxing districts. No index. Handwritten on printed forms. Average 800 pages. 17 x 11 x 5. Auditor's transfer room.

241. APPRAISERS' FIELD SHEETS

1925—. 1 bundle.

Original appraisers' field sheets used in reappraisement of lands and buildings of Cleveland, Painesville, and Ashtabula railroad property in Lake County, showing track mileage, valuation of land and buildings, and names of taxing districts. Arranged alphabetically by names of taxing districts. No index. Handwritten. 11 x 8 x 4. Attic.

242. TAX RATES
1906-1934. 2 file boxes. Discontinued.
Record of rates of taxation, showing date of entry, name of taxing district, name of owner, range, township, section and lot numbers, acreage, description of tract, land and building value, and total value for taxation. Arranged alphabetically by names of taxing districts and chronologically thereunder by dates of entries. No index. Typed on printed forms. 10 x 4.5 x 13.5. 1 file box, 1906-1923, attic; 1 file box, 1924-1934, Auditor's main office.

Tax Returns

243. ASSESSOR'S RETURN OF TAXABLE PROPERTY
1840-1862. 14 volumes. (Dated).
Assessor's returns of taxable real property, showing name of taxing district, name of property owner, range, township, section and lot numbers, acreage, description of tract, land, and building value, and total value for taxation. Arranged by names of taxing districts and alphabetically thereunder by names of property owners. No index. Handwritten on printed forms. Average 150 pages. 13 x 9 x 1.5. Attic.

244. ASSESSOR'S RETURN OF TAXABLE PERSONAL PROPERTY
1849-1861. 3 volumes.
Assessor's returns of taxable personal property, showing name of taxing district, name of property owner, description of property, value, and total value for taxation. Arranged alphabetically by names of taxing districts and alphabetically thereunder by names of property owners. No index. Handwritten on printed forms. Average 300 pages. 14 x 10 x 2.5. Attic.

245. INDIVIDUAL RETURN OF TAXABLE PROPERTY
1927—. 130 volumes, 16 file boxes (Dated).Volumes subtitled by names of taxing districts.
Individuals' returns of taxable personal property, showing date, name of taxing district, name and address of property owner, items of taxable property, total listed value, tax rate, amount of tax, and taxpayers oath. Arranged alphabetically by names of taxing districts and alphabetically thereunder by names that taxpayers. No index. Handwritten on printed forms. Volumes average 300 pages. 14 x 9 x 4; file box, 11 x 16 x 24. 130 volumes, 1927-1931, attic; 16 file boxes, 1931—, Auditor's work room.

Tax Lists and Duplicates

246. AUDITORS TAX LIST
1840—. 308 volumes. (labeled by years and by consecutive numbers under each year). Subtitled by names of taxing districts.

Record of tax assessments on real property, showing name of taxing district, name of property owner, year, description of property, acreage, lot number, value, value as equalized by board of revision and tax commission, amount assessed, special assessments, delinquent taxes, penalties, and total due; also includes personal property assessments, 1840-1931, showing name of property owner, list of taxable chattels, and value. Also contains delinquencies, 1840-1883, entry 258. Arranged by names of taxing districts and alphabetically thereunder by names of property owners. No index. 1840-1898, handwritten; 1899-1913, handwritten on printed forms; 1914—, typed on printed forms. Average 400 pages. 17.25 x 4.5 x 3. 167 volumes, 1840-1906; 1933—, Auditor's main office; 141 volumes, 1907-1932, attic.

247. AUDITOR'S GENERAL PERSONAL TAX DUPLICATE
1932—. 1 volume.

General tax list, showing year, name of taxing district, tax rate, assessment certificate number, number of taxing districts shown on assessment certificate, on class list, grain list, name of taxpayer, address, assessed value (dollars only), total tax for year, amount, advanced payment, amount, tax due, amount, when paid, unpaid tax for year, remarks, and line number. Arranged by names of taxing districts and alphabetically thereunder by names of taxpayers. Handwritten on printed forms. 250 pages. 19 x 16.5 x 3. Auditor's work room.

248. AUDITOR'S CLASSIFIED PERSONAL TAX DUPLICATE
1932—. 1 volume.

Classified tax list, showing year, name of taxing district, assessment certificate number on general list, grain list, name and address of taxpayer, tax rate, income yield, amount of tax, assessed value (dollars only) classified under productive investments, unproductive investments, deposits, credits, money and other taxable and intangibles, amount of total tax for year, amount of advanced payment, next lower amount of tax due, date paid, amount of unpaid taxes for year, and remarks. Arranged by names of taxing districts and alphabetically thereunder by names of taxpayers. No index. Handwritten on printed forms. 50 pages. 16.5 x 19 x 3. Auditor's work room.

249. DUPLICATE OF TAXES ON DOGS
1878-1880. 1 volume. Discontinued.

Duplicates of taxes levied on dogs, showing year, name of taxing district, name of owner, number and value of dogs, amount of tax, and date paid. Arranged alphabetically by names of taxing districts and alphabetically thereunder by names of owners. No index. Handwritten on printed forms. 100 pages. 18 x 12 x 1. Attic.

For dog and kennel register, see entry 300.

250. AUDITOR'S CIGARETTE DUPLICATE
1920—. 2 volumes.

Auditor's cigarette tax assessment duplicate, showing name of licensee, business address, name of owner of real estate, description of real estate, date license issued, amount of tax, date paid, and receipt number. Arranged numerically by receipt numbers. No index. Handwritten on printed forms. Average 50 pages. 18 x 12.5 x 1. 1 volume, 1920-1928, attic; 1 volume, 1929—, Auditor's main office.

251. SPECIAL ASSESSMENT RECORD
1912—. 10 volumes.

Record of special assessments levied on real estate for public improvements, as highways, streets, and sewers, showing name of improvement, name of taxing district, name of property owner, description of property, number of acres or foot frontage, value, amount of assessment, amount of each annual installment, years delinquent, amount delinquent, and penalty. Arranged alphabetically by names of taxing districts and alphabetically thereunder by names of property owners. No index. Handwritten on printed forms. Average 800 pages. 22.5 x 14.5 x 5. 4 volumes, 1912-1918, attic; 6 volumes, 1919—, Auditor's transfer room.

252. SPECIAL ASSESSMENTS
1914—. 15 file boxes.

Original records of special assessments levied on real estate for public improvements as highways, streets, and sewers, showing name of improvement, name of taxing district, name of property owner, description of property, number of acres or foot frontage, value, amount of assessment, amount of each annual installment, years delinquent, amount delinquent, penalty, and date filed. Arranged alphabetically by names of taxing districts and chronologically thereunder by dates of filing. Handwritten and typed on printed forms. No index. 10 x 4.5 x 13.5. Auditor's main office.

253. SPECIAL ASSESSMENT CARDS

1933—. 20 file boxes. Subtitled by names of taxing districts. Prior records
destroyed.

Card record of special assessments levied on real property for public improvements
as highways, streets, or sewers, showing name of improvement, name of taxing
district, card number, name of property owner, description of property, number of
acres or foot frontage, value, amount of assessment, amount of each annual
installment, years delinquent, amount delinquent, and penalties. Arranged
alphabetically by names of taxing districts and numerically thereunder by card
numbers. No index. Handwritten and typed on printed forms. 10.5 x 17 x 28.
Auditor's transfer room.

Exemptions, Additions, Deductions

254. APPLICATION FOR EXEMPTED PROPERTY

1922—. 1 file box.

Applications for the exemption of property from taxation as schools, churches,
cemeteries, armories, and public buildings, showing name of taxing district,
subdivision or addition, description, location, total value of land and buildings, and
date filed. Arranged chronologically by dates of filing. No index. Handwritten and
typed on printed forms. 10 x 4.5 x 13.5. Auditor's main office.

255. AUDITOR'S LIST OF EXEMPTED PROPERTY

1924—. 1 volume.

List of tax exempt properties including churches, schools, county and municipal
lands and buildings, charitable institutions, and libraries, showing name of taxing
district, what buildings and lands, description of tract or lot, name of property
owner, and land and building value. Arranged alphabetically by names of taxing
districts. No index. Typed on printed forms. 100 pages. 17.5 x 14.5 x 2. Auditor's
main office.

256. ADDITIONS AND DEDUCTIONS

1881—. 5 volumes.

Record of additions and deductions in assessment of property by reason of new
buildings or improvements, or by destruction of building by fire or storm, or
revision by board of equalization, showing name of taxing district, date, name of
property owner, range township, section, lot numbers, reason for revision or

additional assessment, acreage, value and amount of addition or deduction. Arranged alphabetically by names of taxing districts. No index. Handwritten. 300 pages. 16 x 12 x 1. 3 volumes, 1881-1924' attic; 2 volumes, 1925——, Auditor's main office.

257. ADDITIONS AND REMITTERS
1881——. 4 bundles, 9 file boxes.
Original and duplicate copies of orders for additions or remitters, showing name of taxing district, name of taxpayer, location and description of property, amount of tax, interest rate, for what period, amount to be added or remitted, date of order, notation of error, and miscellaneous correspondence pertaining to the case. Arranged chronologically by dates of instruments. No index. Handwritten or printed forms. Bundles, 7 x 11 x 13; file box, 10 x 4.5 x 13.5. 4 bundles, 1881-1923, attic; 9 bundles, 1924——, Auditor's main office.

Delinquent Taxes

258. DELINQUENCIES
1883——. 29 volumes. (1-29). 1840-1883 in Auditor's Tax List, entry 246. Auditor's record of unpaid taxes, showing name of taxing district, name of property owner, range, township, section and lots numbers, acreage, description of tract, property value, amount of taxes and penalty due, treasure's reason for not collecting, and penalty; also contains Tax List-Delinquent Personal, 1920——, entry 259. Arranged alphabetically by names of taxing districts and alphabetical thereunder by names of property owners. No index. Handwritten on printed forms. Average 600 pages. 17.5 x 14.5 x 4. Auditor's main office.

259. TAX LIST–DELINQUENT PERSONAL
1900-1919. 5 volumes. 1920——, in Delinquencies, entry 258.
Record of unpaid personal taxes, showing name of taxing district, name and address of owner, description of properties, value, amount of tax and penalty due, treasurer's reason for not collecting, and penalty. Arranged alphabetically by names of taxing districts and alphabetical thereunder by names the taxpayers. No index. Handwritten on printed forms. Average 450 pages. 17.5 x 14 x 4. Attic.

260. DELINQUENT SPECIALS
1927—. 6 volumes. (15-30).

Duplicate of delinquent special taxes levied on real estate for public improvements as highways, streets, and sewers, showing name of taxing district, name of property owner, name of improvement, range, township, section and lot numbers, acreage, description of tract, acreage taxed, value, years delinquent, total tax, and penalty due. Arranged alphabetically by the names of improvements and alphabetically thereunder by names of property owners. No index. Handwritten on printed forms. Average 500 pages. 16.5 x 12 x 4. Auditor's main office.

261. AUDITOR'S DUPLICATE OF MISCELLANEOUS COLLECTIONS UPON REAL PROPERTY
1906—. 91 volumes. (labeled by volume numbers under each taxing district). Subtitled by names of taxing districts.

Auditor's record of payment of delinquent taxes on real property, showing name of taxing district, name of property owner, range, township, section and lot numbers, acreage, description of tract, acreage taxed, tax value, years delinquent, total tax due, penalties due, and date and amount paid. Arranged alphabetically by names of taxing districts and alphabetically thereunder by names of property owners. No index. 1906-1913, handwritten on printed forms; 1914—, typed on printed forms. Average 400 pages. 17.5 x 14.5 x 3. 58 volumes, 1906-1910, 1930-1933, attic; 33 volumes, 1911-1929, 1934—, Auditor's main office.

262. TRIENNIAL TAX CERTIFICATES
1932—. 8000 sheets in piles. Initiated 1932.

Copies of triennial land tax certificates of delinquent taxes to prosecuting attorney, showing name of property owner, description of property, itemized account of delinquencies, item, general taxes, special assessments, penalties,8% interest on general taxes, special assessments, only to date of August settlements, total fee for making lists, grand total, and name of township. Arranged in piles by townships and alphabetically thereunder by names of property owners. No index. Handwritten on printed forms. Sheets 14 x 17. Prosecuting attorney's stenographers room.

263. FORFEITED LANDS [Redeemed]
1910-1924. 1 file box.

Certificates of redeemed forfeited lands, showing date of certificate, name of owner, number and description of lot, location of lot, value, amount of delinquent taxes, penalties, total amount paid, date of transfer by auditor, and notice of redemption to auditor of state. Arranged chronologically by dates of transfers. No index. Handwritten and typed on printed forms. 10 x 4.5 x 13.5. Auditor's main office.

264. RECORD OF TAX SALES–DELINQUENT LAND SALE
1839-1914. 5 volumes.

Record of lands on which taxes are delinquent, showing name of owner, acreage, range, township, section and lot numbers, acreage taxed, value, description of tract, amount of tax due, penalty, interest, and total due; also copies of advertisements offering lands for sale for taxes; delinquent land sales, showing name of owner, acreage, range, township, section and lot numbers, acreage taxed, value, description, amount due, quantity sold, amount sold for, and name of purchaser; also date redeemed, by whom redeemed, or date of issue of auditor's deed, and signature of auditor. Arranged alphabetically by names of taxing districts. No index. 1839-1897, handwritten; 1897-1914, handwritten on printed forms. Average 350 pages. 16 x 12 x 2.5. Auditor's main office.

265. AUDITOR'S INHERITANCE TAX CHARGES
1908—. 4 volumes.

Copies of auditor's certificates of inheritance tax charges to treasurer as certified by the probate court, showing date and number of certificate, case number, title of case, name of decedent, amount of tax assessed, name of person to whom tax charged, amount charged, and date paid. 1908-1919, arranged numerically by certificate numbers; 1920—, arranged alphabetically by titles of cases. No index. Typed on printed forms. Average 100 pages. 11.5 x 11.5 x 2.5. 1 volume, 1908-1919, attic; 3 volumes, 1920—, Auditor's main office.

266. SAFE DEPOSIT BOX INVENTORY AND TAX COMMISSIONERS RELEASE OF PROPERTY
1934—. 4 file boxes.

Original inventories of safe deposit boxes of estates and release of property from lock boxes as authorized by tax commissioner, showing date of inventory and release, safety deposit box number, names of depositories and renters, title of case, and description of property removed. Arranged chronologically by dates of documents. No index. Handwritten on printed forms. 5.5 x 14 x 17.5. Auditor's work room.

Settlements

267. SCHOOL SETTLEMENT RECORD
1881—. 3 volumes.
Record of annual and semiannual settlements of school funds, showing name of township or special school district; also auditor's statement of distribution of February settlement on annual settlement (August 31), showing balance on hand at beginning of year, amount of February settlement, amount of August settlement, amount from all sources, expenditures of each fund, balance of each fund, and total balance or deficit. Arranged alphabetically by names of taxing districts and chronologically thereunder by dates of entries. No index. 1881-1903, handwritten; 1904—, handwritten on printed forms. Average 600 pages. 18 x 11.5 x 2.5. 2 volumes, 1881-1929, attic; 1 volume, 1930—, Auditor's main office.

268. [SEMIANNUAL SETTLEMENTS]
1930—. 1 file box. Prior records destroyed.
Original statements of auditor's semiannual settlements with the county treasurer, showing date, total amount of state tax, county tax in mills, township and school tax, city or village tax, undivided classified fund, undivided general fund, total, auditor's fee, net amount of undivided classified taxes collected, recapitulated distribution, general statement of treasurer's accounts, total net collection reported, recapitulation of treasurer's account, and copy of abstract of settlement sent to state auditor; includes statements of semiannual apportionments of municipal, school, and township taxes, showing date, source of receipts, bond settlements, special assessments, total distribution, and amount distributed. Arranged chronologically by dates of settlements. No index. Handwritten on printed forms. 11.5 x 16 x 28. Auditor's main office.

Business Administration of Office

Appropriations and Certificates of Funds

269. APPROPRIATION LEDGER
1919—. 5 volumes.

Record of appropriations to each fund or department by county commissioners and expenditures from each fund, showing name of fund or department, amount credited to each, amount debited to each, date of entries, name of payee, goods or services supplied, warrant number, amount of warrant, appropriation or authorization, debit, credit, and unencumbered balance. Arranged alphabetically by names of funds and chronologically thereunder by dates of entries. No index. Handwritten on printed forms. Average 250 pages. 14.5 x 12 x 2. 2 volumes, 1919-1935, attic; 3 volumes, 1936—, Auditor's main office.

270. TRANSFERS [Of Funds]
1930—. 1 file box.

Copies of auditor's authorization to the treasurer to make transfers from one fund account to another, showing names of funds from which and to which to make transfer, amount to be transferred, and reason for transfer; includes copies of minutes of meetings of county commissioners, showing date of meeting, members present, copy of resolution authorizing transfers or appropriation of funds, and record of vote taken on resolution; also includes auditor's authorization for purchase orders, showing date of order, order number, to whom issued, goods or services ordered, auditor's certificate of appropriation and name of department. Arranged chronologically by dates of authorization. No index. Typed, some on printed forms. 10 x 4.5 x 13.5. Auditor's main office.

271. RECORD OF AUDITOR'S CERTIFICATE OF UNAPPROPRIATED FUNDS
1913-1925. 2 volumes. (1, 2). Discontinued.

Copies of auditor's certificate to county commissioners of amounts and various construction funds, showing date of certificate, number of certificate, name of fund, names of contractors, dates of contracts, volume and page numbers of Commissioners' Record, entry 1, amounts certified, and purpose of fund. Arranged numerically by certificate numbers. Indexed alphabetically by names of contractors. Handwritten on printed forms. Average 250 pages. 18 x 11.5 x 2. Attic.

Purchase Orders, Bills, Claims

272. AUDITOR'S RECORD OF ORDERS
1881-1903. 3 volumes. (E-G).

Auditor's record of purchase orders issued by the county commissioners, showing date of order, consecutive number, item, from whom purchased, for what, amount of bill, date approved, date paid, and debit to each fund. Arranged chronologically by dates of orders and also numerically by consecutive numbers. No index. Handwritten on printed forms. Average 300 pages. 18 x 14 x 2. Attic.

273. GENERAL [Purchase Orders]
1925—. 14 file boxes.

Auditor's copies of purchase orders issued by county commissioners to be checked against invoices before payment is made, showing date of order, number of order, name of creditor, goods or service supplied, amount of bill, date of approval, and date and amount paid. Arranged numerically by order numbers. No index. Handwritten and typed on printed forms. 11 x 16 x 24. 12 file boxes, 1925-1934, attic; 2 file boxes, 1935—, Auditor's main office.

274. AUDITOR'S DOCKING OF BILLS FILED–COMMISSIONERS
1904—. 6 volumes.

Auditor's record of bills filed with commissioners by creditors for payment from county funds, showing date of bill, consecutive number, name of creditor, goods or services supplied, amount of bill, date filed, date approved, amount approved, date paid, and warrant number; also contains; Auditor's Docket of Bills Filed–Sewer, Water, 1904-1922, 1933—, entry 277; Register of Sheep Claims, 1924—, entry 278. Arranged chronologically by dates of filing and also numerically by consecutive numbers. No index. Handwritten on printed forms. Average 480 pages. 18 x 13 x 2. 4 volumes, 1940-1930, attic; 2 volumes, 1931—, Auditor's main office.

275. AUDITOR'S DOCKET OF BILLS FILED–INFIRMARY
1904—. 3 volumes.

Auditor's record of bills filed with county commissioners against infirmary account, showing date of bill, consecutive number, name of creditor, goods or services supplied, amount of bill, date filed, date approved, amount approved, date paid, and warrant number. Arranged chronologically by dates of bills and also numerically by consecutive numbers. No index. Handwritten on printed forms. Average 350 pages. 18 x 12.5 x 2. 2 volumes, 1904-1933, attic; 1 volume, 1934—, Auditor's main office.

276. DOCKET, BILLS FILED – CHILD WELFARE
1924—. 2 volumes. (1, 2).

Record of bills filed with county commissioners for board, supplies, clothing for children, and board in private homes, showing date and number of bill, name of creditor, for what, amount of bill, date filed, date approved, amount approved, dates paid, and warrant number. Arranged numerically by consecutive build numbers. Indexed alphabetically by names of children. Handwritten on printed forms. Average 320 pages. 18.25 x 13 x 2. 1 volume, 1924-1935, attic; 1 volume, 1936—, Auditor's main office.

277. AUDITOR'S DOCKET OF BILLS FILED–SEWER, WATER
1923-1932. 1 volume. 1904-1922, 1933– in Auditor's Docket of Bills Filed– Commissioners, entry 274.

Auditor's record of bills filed with county commissioners against sewer and water account, showing date of bill, consecutive number, name of creditor, goods or services supplied, amount of bill, date filed, date approved, amount approved, date paid, and warrant number. Arranged chronologically by dates of bills and also numerically by consecutive numbers. No index. Handwritten on printed forms. 350 pages. 18 x 12.5 x 2. Attic.

278. REGISTER OF SHEEP CLAIMS
1899-1923. 1 volume. 1924– in Auditor's Docket of Bills Filed – Commissioners, entry 274.

Auditor's copies of claims filed for compensation for sheep killed or injured by dogs, showing date claim filed, name of claimant, number of sheep killed, number of sheep injured, value, testimony of witnesses, amount allowed, and warrant number. Arranged chronologically by dates of filing. No index. Handwritten on printed forms. 320 pages. 16 x 11.5 x 2. Attic.

General Accounts

279. RECEIPTS JOURNAL
1937—. 2 volumes.

Daily record of money received by auditor, showing name of fund, name and number of account, date of entry, name of payer, number of receipts, and number of bill. Arranged by names of funds and chronologically thereunder by dates of entries. No index. Handwritten on printed forms. Average 175 pages. 14.5 x 12 x 2. Auditor's main office.

280. AUDITOR'S LEDGER
1844-1888, 1904—. 10 volumes. (B; 1-9).

Auditor's fund account ledger; fund credits, showing date credited, source, pay-in order number, and amount; fund debits, showing date debited, goods or services supplied, order number, and amount. Arranged alphabetically under tabs by names of funds and chronologically thereunder by dates of entries. No index. 1844-1888, handwritten; 1904—, handwritten on printed forms. Average 400 pages. 18 x 12 x 3. 8 volumes 1844-1888, 1904-1931, attic; 2 volumes, 1932—, Auditor's main office.

281. AUDITOR'S JOURNAL OF WARRANTS INTO TREASURY
1907—. 20 volumes. (2-9, 1-12).

Auditor's daily record of payments into county treasury, showing date of entry, name of fund, by whom paid, for what, pay-in-order number, amount debited to treasurer, and amount credited to each fund. Arranged chronologically by dates of entries also numerically by-pay-in order numbers. No index. Handwritten and typed on printed forms. Average 200 pages. 18 x 12.5 x 1.5. 8 volumes, 1907-1931, attic; 12 volumes, 1932—, Auditor's main office.

282. RECORD OF FEES
1907-1931. 2 volumes. (1,2).

Auditor's daily record of fees collected, showing date of entry, by whom paid, for what service, and amount; includes fees for transfers, deeds, licenses, certificates, and sundries. Arranged chronologically by dates of entries. No index. Handwritten on printed forms. Average 160 pages. 18 x 11.5 x 1.5. Attic.

283. PAYROLL
1924——. 8 file boxes.

Original monthly departmental reports of payrolls to county auditor, showing date
of report, name of department, names and occupations of employees, and amounts
due each. Arranged chronologically by dates of reports. No index. Typed on printed
forms. 10 x 4.5 x 13.5. Auditor's main office.

Special Accounts

284. RECORD OF INDIGENT SOLDIERS, SAILORS, MARINES,
WIVES
1901——. 3 volumes. (1-3).

Record of grants made by county commissioners to indigent service men and their
widows or wives, showing date, name of service man, name of recipient,
relationship, amount allowed by county commissioners, and record of monthly
payments. Arranged alphabetically by names of townships and alphabetically
thereunder by names of recipients. No index. Handwritten on printed forms.
Average 240 pages. 16 x 11.5 x 2. 2 volumes, 1901-1934, attic; 1 volume, 1935——,
Auditor's main office.

285. INDIGENT MOTHERS OF SMALL CHILDREN
1914——. 3 volumes.

Auditor's record of payments to indigent mothers of young children, showing date
of entry, case number, probate court orders, number of warrant, name and address
of payee, number of children, amount of grant, monthly benefits, and period of
grant. Arranged chronologically by dates of entries. Indexed alphabetically by
names of mothers. Handwritten on printed forms. Average 50 pages. 16 x 12 x 1.
1 volume, 1914-1932, attic; 2 volumes, 1924——, Auditor's main office.

286. MOTHERS' PENSION
1929——. 1 file box.

Original orders to auditor from probate judge authorizing payment to indigent
mothers of dependent children, showing date of order, case number, name of payee,
number of children, monthly benefit, record of payments, and date filed; includes
1936——, auditor's copies of monthly report of payment for dependent children,
showing date of report, case number, name of payee, amount, and warrant number;

1936— carbons of notices of modification and terminations of grants issued by the Bureau of Aid to Dependent Children, showing reason for and nature of modification. Arranged chronologically by dates of instruments. No index. Handwritten and typed on printed forms. 10 x 4.5 x 13.5. Auditor's main office.

287. LEDGER – INDIGENT BLIND
1906-1936. 1 volume.

Auditor's record of amounts paid to indigent blind persons, showing name and address of recipient, amount paid, dates paid, and warrant number of each payment. Arranged chronologically by dates of payments. Indexed alphabetically by names of recipients. Handwritten. 315 pages. 15.5 x 11 x 2. Auditor's main office.

Warrants and Vouchers

288. AUDITOR'S JOURNAL OF WARRANTS ISSUED
1904—. 21 volumes. (1-21).

Auditor's daily record of warrants issued on county treasurer for payment from county funds, showing date of entry, name of fund, name of payee, goods or services supplied, warrant number, amount credited treasurer, and amount debited each county funds; also includes record of orders of state treasurer for distribution of motor vehicle license fees, 1925-1932. Arranged chronologically by dates of entries and numerically by warrant numbers. No index. Handwritten on printed forms. Average 200 pages. 18.5 x 12.5 x 1.5. 17 volumes, 1904-1935, attic; 4 volumes, Auditor's main office.

289. AUDITOR'S COURT WARRANTS
1904—. 3 volumes. (1-3).

Record of court warrants issued for jury and witness fees for common pleas court, petit jury and grand jury, grand jury witnesses, and witnesses in criminal cases; for probate court jury, criminal witnesses, and witnesses in lunacy and epilepsy cases; witnesses in minor courts and coroner's witnesses and jurors, all showing name of court, date, number of warrant, name of witness or juror, date of appearance, nature of case, and amount of fee paid. Arranged chronologically by dates of warrants and numerically by warrant numbers. No index. Handwritten on printed forms. Average 250 pages. 18 x 13 x 1.5. 2 volumes, 1904-1931, attic; 1 volume, 1932—, Auditor's main office.

290. WARRANTS
1927—. 1080 bundles, 54 file boxes. (labeled by contained warrant numbers).

Auditor's warrant on county treasurer for payment of bills and claims authorized by county commissioners, showing warrant number, date, name of payee, amount, purpose, and name of fund; also includes commissioners' purchase orders with payees' bill attached, showing date, name of payee, amount of order, and goods or services supplied. Arranged numerically by warrant numbers. No index. Handwritten and typed on printed forms. File boxes, 10 x 4.5 x 13.5; bundles, 10 x 5 x 4. 1080 bundles, 1927-1934, attic; 54 file boxes, 1935—, Auditor's main office.

291. COURT WARRANTS [Redeemed]
1936—. 1 file box.

Cancelled warrants issued for payment of witness and juror fees, mileage fees, showing date of payment, warrant number, name of court, name of witness or juror, date of appearance, nature of case, amount of fee paid, and date redeemed. Arranged chronologically by dates of payments and numerically by warrant numbers. No index. Handwritten on printed forms. 10 x 4.5 x 13.5. Auditor's main office.

292. REDEEMED WARRANTS
1916—. 41 file boxes. (labeled by contained warrant numbers).

Redeemed warrants on county treasurer for payment of bills and claims authorized by county commissioners or other county executives by voucher, showing warrant number, date of warrant, name of payee, amount, goods or services supplied, fund debited, and date cancelled. Arranged numerically by warrant numbers. No index. Handwritten on printed forms. 3 file boxes, 22 x 18 x 24; 38 file boxes, 10 x 4.5 x 13.5. 3 file boxes, 1916-1930, attic; 38 file boxes, 1931—, Auditor's main office.

293. HOUSING RELIEF
1933—. 2 file boxes.

Vouchers issued by county commissioners authorizing payment and tax allowance for direct housing relief, showing number and date of instrument, name of indigent tenant, name of property owner, description and location of property, name of taxing district, volume, page and line number of Auditors Tax List, entry 246, value, amount of tax, amount of warrant, and effective period. Arranged chronologically by dates of instruments and numerically by voucher numbers. No index. Handwritten on printed forms. 10 x 4.5 x 13.5. Auditor's main office.

Licenses

294. PEDDLERS' LICENSES
1863-1865, 1881, 1882, 1884-1916, 1918, 1920-1923, 1925—. 2 file boxes. Original applications for licenses to sell goods as traveling merchants, showing date of application, name and address of applicant, if ex-soldier, company, regiment or vessel, description of merchandise, value, mode of travel, term of license, amount of fee, and date of filing. Arranged by dates of applications. No index. Handwritten on printed forms. 10 x 4.5 x 13.5. 1 file box, 1863-1865, 1881, 1882, 1884-1916, 1918, 1920-1923, 1925-1927, attic; 1 file box, 1928—, Auditor's main office.

295. APPLICATION, CIGARETTE, WORT, MALT, COSMETIC
1931—. 1 bundle, 1 file box.
Original applications to auditor for license to deal in cigarettes, brewers' wort, malt liquors, and cosmetics, showing date of application, name and address of applicant, whether wholesale or retail, business address, term of license, fee, and date of filing. No index. Handwritten on printed forms. Bundle, 9 x 12 x 5; file box, 10 x 4.5 x 13.5. 1 bundle, 1931-1936, attic; 1 file box, 1937—, Auditor's main office.

296. CIGARETTE LICENSES
1906—. 2 volumes, 4 bundles.
Copies of retail cigarette licenses, showing date issued, license number, name and address of licensee, name and place of business, and term of license. Arranged chronologically by dates of issue and numerically by license number. No index. Handwritten on printed forms. Average 100 pages. 18 x 11.5 x 1. 1 volume, 1906-1919, attic; 1 volume, 4 bundles, 1920—, Auditor's main office.

297. BREWERS' WORT OR MALT LICENSE
1934—. 1 volume.
Copies of retail licenses to deal in malt liquors, showing date issued, license number, name and address of licensee, name and place of business, term of license, and fee. Arranged chronologically by dates of issue and numerically by license number. No index. Handwritten on printed forms. 50 pages. 15 x 9 x 1. Auditor's main office.

298. BEVERAGE DEALERS' LICENSE
1934-1935. 1 volume. Discontinued; law repealed.
Copies of beverage dealers' licenses, showing the date issued, license number, name and address of licensee, name and place of business, term of license, and fee. Arranged chronologically by dates of issue and numerically by license number. No index. Handwritten on printed forms. 185 pages. 15 x 9 x 2. Auditor's main office.

299. COSMETIC DEALERS' LICENSE
1933-1934. 1 volume. Discontinued; law repealed.
Copies of cosmetic licenses, showing date issued, license number, name and address of licensee, name and place of business, term of license, and fee. Arranged chronologically by dates of issue and numerically by license number. No index. Handwritten on printed forms. 50 pages. 15 x 9 x 1. Auditor's main office.

300. DOG AND KENNEL REGISTER
1917—. 1 bundle, 10 volumes.
Register of dog tag applications, showing application number, date of application, name and address of applicant, number and sex of dogs kept, address where dogs kept, registration fee, penalty (if any), tag numbers, date of registration, and date and number of duplicate tags issued. Arranged chronologically by dates of applications. Indexed alphabetically by names of dog owners. Handwritten on printed forms. Average 200 pages. 14.5 x 11.5 x 1.5. 6 volumes, 1 bundle, 1917-1935, attic; 4 volumes, 1936—, Auditor's main office.
For dogs tax duplicate, 1878-1880, see entry 249.

301. [Application For] DOG LICENSE
1930—. 13 file boxes.
Original applications to auditor for the registration of dogs, showing application number, date, name and address of owner, age, sex, color and breed of dog (if known), amount of fee paid, penalty (if any), number of tag, date of registration, date duplicate tag issued, and date of transfer of ownership. 1930-1936, arranged numerically by application numbers; 1937—, arranged alphabetically by names of owners. No index. Handwritten on printed forms. 10 x 4.5 x 13.5. Auditor's main office.

302. AUDITOR'S INDEX TO MOTOR VEHICLE LICENSES
1932-1933. 2 volumes. Discontinued.
Auditor's record of motor vehicle licenses issued in Lake County, showing name and address of owner, license number, make of car, serial number, motor number, fee, and date license issued. Arranged alphabetically by names of licensees. No index. Handwritten on printed forms. Average 200 pages. 16 x 12 x 2. Attic.

303. [Vendor's] LICENSES
1934—. 1 file box.
Carbon copies of vendors' licenses issued by the county auditor, showing date issued, license number, name of licensee, street address, kind of business, code number, and auditor's and deputy auditor's signatures. Arranged chronologically by dates issued and numerically by license numbers. No index. Handwritten on printed forms. 11.5 x 16 x 28. Auditor's work room.

Reports

304. AUDITOR'S AND TREASURER'S FINANCIAL REPORTS
1931—. 9 file boxes.
Financial reports, including: copies of weekly reports of the auditor and treasurer to the county commissioners, showing date filed, title of report, outstanding warrant account, warrant number, distribution by funds with heading for each fund, total amount of court warrants and general warrants outstanding, warrant number last issued, and warrant number last redeemed; monthly financial statements of the auditor and treasurer to the county commissioners, showing date filed, title of report, names of funds, balances, overdrafts, receipts and disbursements during month, outstanding warrant account, and treasurer's and auditor's certificate of accuracy; bank statements of account, showing name of bank, name of account, date filed, dates of checks, amounts of checks, to whom paid, number of checks, deposits credited to accounts, balance forwarded, date, and balance in each account; cancelled checks 1933—, returned by the bank to auditor, showing date, check number, name of payee, amount, and signature of treasurer. Arranged chronologically by dates of filing. No index. Typed on printed forms. 10 x 4.5 x 13.5. Auditor's main office.

305. TREASURER'S DAILY REPORT
1931—. 9 file boxes.

Daily statements of treasurer to auditor, showing date of report, balance at close of previous day, source of receipts, and disbursements from each fund. Arranged chronologically by dates of statements. No index. Handwritten on printed forms. 10 x 4.5 x 13.5. Auditor's main office.

Bonds

306. RECORD OF OFFICIAL BONDS
1840-1904, 1926—. 2 volumes. (3; 1 unlabeled).

Copies of surety bonds filed with the county auditor by the county treasurer, sheriff, coroner, prosecuting attorney, clerk of courts, and probate judge, showing date of bond, names of principal and sureties, what office, amount of bond, and conditions and term of the bond. Arranged chronologically by dates of bonds. Indexed alphabetically by names of officials. 1840-1904, handwritten; 1926—, typed. Average 400 pages. 14.25 x 9.5 x 2. 1 volume, 1840-1904, attic; 1 volume, 1926—, Auditor's main office.

307. TOTAL BONDS ISSUED
1899—. 1 volume.

Record of total number of bonds issued, showing amount, purpose, date issued, interest, and total issued. Arranged chronologically by dates of issue. No index. Handwritten on printed forms. 12 pages. 16 x 14 x .5. Auditor's main office.

308. RECORD OF COURTHOUSE AND JAIL BONDS
1907-1934. 1 volume.

Record of bonds issued by county commissioners in connection with building of courthouse and jail, showing date of bond, bond number, amount, date due, interest rate, when redeemed, number of coupons, amount, and to whom sold. Arranged numerically by bond numbers. No index. Handwritten on printed forms. 450 pages. 14.5 x 10 x 2. Auditor's main office.

309. RECORD OF BONDS ISSUED

1909—. 15 volumes. (3-17).

Auditor's record of bonds issued by county for various improvements, showing name of bonds, purpose of issue, amount of issue, date of issue, date of sale, buyer, numbers of bonds, denominations, rate of interest, maturity dates, record of redemption, and interest payments. Arranged chronologically by dates of issue. No index. Handwritten on printed forms. Average 425 pages. 16 x 14 x 2.25. Auditor's main office.

310. TRANSCRIPTS OF BONDS ISSUED

1905-1919. 1 file box.

Transcripts of minutes and proceedings of the board of county commissioners in matters pertaining to issuing bonds for improvements and buildings, showing date of meeting, members present, resolutions passed declaring improvements necessary, resolutions passed for vote on improvements, result of vote taken, and approval of the minutes; also includes copies of notices to electors, showing date of publication, details of proposed tax levy with purpose of levy, amount of levy, date of election, and publisher's oath of publication; sheriff's returns on posting of notices of election with copies of form of ballot; copies of minutes of meetings of county commissioners to canvas vote on proposal, showing date of meetings, members present, and approval of the minutes; clerks of courts certificates of appointment of building commission by common pleas court, showing date and names of appointees; copies of minutes of meetings of county commissioners, showing date of meeting, members present with copy of resolution for issuing bonds, showing number of bonds, amount of each bond, and consecutive numbers, date due, rate of interest, notice of date and place of sale of bonds, and publisher's oath of publication of notice; auditor's certificate of sale, showing date, name of purchaser, number of bonds purchased, consecutive numbers, denominations, rate of interest, and date due; copies of auditor's certificate to the commissioners of amount to be added to the tax duplicate and total levy for the county; copies of the bonds from the auditor to the county commissioners with purpose, rate of interest, date due and amount; county commissioners' authorizations to the auditor to have bonds lithographed; auditor's certificates to the commissioners of no threatened or pending litigation. No obvious arrangement. Typed, some on printed forms. 10 x 4.5 x 13.5. Auditor's main office.

311. COUPONS

1929—. 24 file boxes.

Cancelled coupons from bonds issued by Lake County for roads, jail building, fairgrounds, and sewer and water bonds, showing date due, amount of coupon, bond and coupon numbers, depositor's and depositories' names and addresses, for what purpose issued, where payable, and auditor's warrant number. No index. Handwritten on printed forms. 10 x 4.5 x 13.5. Auditor's main office.

312. HOSPITAL RECORD

1922-1923. 1 volume. Discontinued.

Auditor's record of minutes of Lake County Hospital Association, showing date of meetings, and business transacted; also includes record of appointment of building commission, showing names and addresses of appointees, date appointed, and length of term; record of petitions to county commissioners and to the governor of the state for building Lake County Memorial Hospital, showing names and addresses of petitioners; special election proceedings, showing copy of petition as submitted to the electors of Lake County for approval or rejection, and total vote for and against; bonds of trustees, showing date and term of appointment, amount of bond, and names the sureties; proceedings in the sale of bonds, showing date sold, amount sold, to whom sold, denominations of bonds, number of bonds, rate of interest, and date due; certification of the auditor to the treasurer of the amount needed for the construction of Lake County Memorial Hospital. Arranged chronologically by dates of meetings. No index. Typed. 520 pages. 17 x 12 x 3.5. Attic.

Weights and Measures

313. RECORD OF SEALER OF WEIGHTS AND MEASURES
1912-1928. 1 volume.

Copies of reports of deputy sealer of weights and measures to auditor, showing date of inspection, name of firm, individual, or corporation, address, kind of business, types of weighing and measuring devices tested, kind of commodities reweighed or measured, number found correct, number found incorrect, and whether under or over. Arranged chronologically by dates of reports. No index. Handwritten on printed forms. 132 pages. 32 x 18 x 1.5. Attic.

Miscellaneous

314. RECORD OF SCHOOL ENUMERATORS
1852-1920. 3 volumes. (1-3).

Enumeration list of school age unmarried youths between 6 and 21 years of age, showing number of youths, ages, number of males, number of females, and the same information for each township and taxing district in Lake County. Arranged alphabetically by names of taxing districts and chronologically thereunder by dates of enumerations. No index. 1852-1906, handwritten; 1907-1920 Handwritten on printed forms. Average 250 pages. 16 x 10 x 2. Attic.

For other enumeration reports, 1842-1872, see entry 377.

The office of treasurer was created by legislative act in 1803.[1] The holder of the office was appointed for one year by the associate judges in 1803 and by the county commissioners in 1804, and was removable by the appointing power.[2] The office became elective in 1827 for a term of two years.[3] In accordance with the constitution of 1851, the legislature, in 1859, fixed the term at two years,[4] which it remained until 1936, when the term of all county officials was changed to four years.[5] The salary is determined by law according to the population of the county.[6] The Lake County treasurer's salary in 1941 was $2080, and his bond was set at $50,000.[7]

The duties of the treasurer today remain very much the same as when the office was created in 1803. He must give public notice of the tax duplicates. On receiving from the auditor a duplicate of the taxes assessed on the property of the county, he prepares and post notices in the townships and inserts the notice for six weeks in the newspaper of the largest circulation in the county.[8] He receives the money and payment of these taxes and issues receipts.[9] Since 1858 the treasurer has been authorized to demand semiannual payment of taxes, and the commissioners to extend the time for paying taxes for not more than 30 days after the time fixed by law.[10]

After each semiannual collection of taxes the treasurer reports to the auditor the amount of taxes received in each taxing district since the last collection, listed according to source of tax i. e., liquor, cigarette, property, etc. Immediately after settlement with the auditor, and upon proper warrant from the auditor, the treasurer pays to the various boards and subdivisions of the county, and to the state, the amounts due to them.[11]

---

1. *Laws of Ohio,* I, 97.
2. *Ibid.,* II, 154.
3. *Ibid.,* XXV, 25-32.
4. *Ibid.,* LVI, 105.
5. *Ibid.,* CXVI, pt. ii, 184.
6. *Ibid.,* XCVIII, 89.
7. Payroll, 1941, entry 283; Record of Official Bonds, 1941, entry 306.
8. *Laws of Ohio,* I, 98; XXIX, 291; LII, 124.
9. G.C. sec. 2650; *Laws of Ohio,* XXIX, 292; LXXVI, 70.
10. *Laws of Ohio,* LV, 62; LVI, 101.
11. G.C. sec. 2689; *Laws of Ohio,* LVI, 101, CXIV, 732.

It is the treasurer's duty also to collect delinquent taxes. He may assess a penalty for nonpayment, to be paid to the treasurer's fund. If the treasurer cannot collect the delinquent taxes, he turns the account over to the clerk of courts, who proceeds according to law.[12] The Wittemore Act. However, passed as a depression emergency measure in 1933, provided for the payment of delinquent real estate taxes in installments, without interest or penalty. This was later extended to include delinquent personal and classified taxes.[13]

The treasurer has charge of all funds belonging to the county as well as those collected by taxation. Since 1894 the commissioners have been authorized to deposit county moneys with local banks and trust companies for safe keeping under stipulated conditions.[14] Lake County maintains active accounts under this ruling

The treasurer makes a daily accounting to the auditor of all moneys received and disbursed, from whatever source and for whatever purpose,[15] and of the balance remaining in the treasury. Once a year, he reports to the county commissioners.[16] Still further checks are made on the treasurer. Every six months the auditor and county commissioners are required to make a thorough examination of the books of the treasurer,[17] and every year, the board of inspection in the office of the state auditor conducts an examination of the finances of the treasury, as well as of all other county offices.[18]

The treasurer, like the auditor, serves on the budget commission, the county board of revision, and on the board of trustees of the sinking fund,[19] and he is the official custodian of the bonds furnished to the state by the various county officials.

In Lake County the treasurer has a staff of eight assistants, three of whom are deputy treasures, and five clerks. Their aggregate annual compensation is $10,484.07.[20]

---

12. G.C. sec. 2660; *Laws of Ohio,* LVI, 175; XCIX, 435.
13. *Laws of Ohio,* CXV, 161-164; CXVI, pt. ii, 230, 332.
14. *Laws of Ohio,* XCI, 403; CII, 59; CXV, pt. ii, 14-21.
15. G.C. sec. 2642; *Laws of Ohio,* XCVII, 457.
16. G.C. sec. 2684.
17. G.C. sec. 2699, R.S. sec. 1129; *Laws of Ohio,* LXXI, 137.
18. G.C. sec. 284.
19. G.C. secs. 5625-19; 5580; 2976-18.
20. Payroll, 1940, *passim,* entry 283.

Tax Records

Tax Duplicates and Lists

315. TREASURER'S TAX LIST
1840—. 308 volumes. (1-308).
Treasurer's duplicate of tax bills for assessment on real estate, showing name of
taxing district, line number, name of property owner, tract, lot, block, description
of property, footage, acreage, value assessed, amount of state, county, and general
taxes, delinquency, penalty, and total tax. Arranged alphabetically by names of
taxing districts and alphabetical thereunder by names of property owners. No index.
1840-1898, handwritten; 1899-1913, handwritten on printed forms; 1914—, typed
on printed forms. Average 400 pages. 17.5 x 14.5 x 3. 292 volumes, 1840-1935,
auditor's main office; 16 volumes, 1936—, Treasurer's main office.

316. DUPLICATE OF SPECIAL TAXES
1906-1910. 1 volume. Discontinued.
Record of taxes assessed on real property for improvement, showing line number,
name of property owner, range, tract, survey, lot number, description of property,
total tax, date and amount due, and date paid. Arranged alphabetically by names of
taxing districts and alphabetically thereunder by names of property owners. No
index. Handwritten on printed forms. 400 pages. 16 x 12 x 2. Attic.

317.   TREASURER'S   ASSESSMENT   DUPLICATE   [Traffic   in
      Intoxicating Liquors]
1884-1919. 7 volumes. (1-7). Discontinued.
Treasurer's record of applications for licenses to deal in intoxicating liquors by
retail, showing name of applicant, location of business, name of taxing district,
receipt number, date of commencing business, amount of tax, penalty, and date of
payment of tax. Arranged alphabetically by names of taxing districts and
alphabetical thereunder by names of applicants. No index. Handwritten on printed
forms. Average 40 pages. 18 x 11.5 x .5. Attic.

318. TREASURER'S CIGARETTE TRAFFIC TAX DUPLICATE
1920-1934. 3 volumes. Discontinued.
Treasurer's record of applications for licenses to deal in cigarettes by retail,
showing receipt number, name of applicant, location of business, name of property

owner, description of property, date of assessment, amount, and date of payment of tax. Arranged numerically by receipt numbers. No index. Handwritten on printed forms. Average 50 pages. 18.5 x 11.5 x .5. Attic.

319. CARD MAILING LIST
1928—. 35 file boxes. (labeled by contained letters of the alphabet). Subtitled by names of taxing districts.

Treasurer's mailing list of taxpayers, showing name and address of taxpayer, amount of tax due each half, and description of property. Arranged alphabetically by names of taxing districts and alphabetical thereunder by names of taxpayers. No index. Handwritten on printed forms. 4.5 x 5.5 x 23. Treasurer's main office.

Auditions and Remitters

320. ADDITIONS
1928—. 29 bundles.

Auditor's notice to treasurer of additions to be collected on real estate, personal property, and special assessments, showing date, order number, name of owner, name of taxing district, type of tax, value, amount of addition, and reason for addition. Arranged numerically by consecutive order numbers. No index. Typed on printed forms. 11 x 7 x 3. 27 bundles, 1928-1939, attic; 2 bundles, 1940—, Treasurer's main office.

321. REMITTERS
1925—. 14 bundles.

Original remitters submitted to treasurer by auditor for money to be remitted to taxpayers due to overcharge or because buildings were destroyed since last assessment, showing date, number of remitter, amount to be remitted, and reason for remittance. Arranged numerically by consecutive remittance numbers. No index. Typed on printed forms. 11 x 7 x 4. 12 bundles, 1925-1939, attic; 2 bundles, 1940—, Treasurer's main office.

Delinquent Taxes

322. UNDERTAKINGS TO PAY TAXES
1933—. 10 volumes.
Record of undertakings to pay full principal amount of delinquent real property tax and assessments, less penalties, interest, and other charges in annual installments, showing note signed by taxpayer, date of signature, name of property owner, name of township, and description of property. Arranged alphabetically by names of taxing districts, alphabetically thereunder by names of property owners, and chronologically thereunder by dates of agreements. No index. Handwritten on printed forms. Average 400 pages. 18.5 16.5 x 3. Treasurer's main office.

323. DUPLICATE OF TAXES DELINQUENT ON PERSONAL PROPERTY
1904—. 6 volumes. (1-6).
Record of delinquent taxes on personal property, showing names of taxpayer, years delinquent, valuation and description of property, total tax, penalty, total amount due, and amount and date collected. Arranged alphabetically by names of taxing districts, and alphabetically thereunder by names of taxpayers. No index. 1904-1913, handwritten on printed forms; 1914—, typed on printed forms. Average 500 pages. 16.5 x 11.5 x 3. 5 volumes, 1904-1922, attic; 1 volume, 1923—, Treasurer's main office.

324. DELINQUENT LAND TAX CERTIFICATES
1918—. 14 volumes.
Copies of auditor's certificate of delinquent land tax, showing name of taxing district, name of property owner, description of property, location, valuation, and amount of tax. Arranged alphabetically by taxing districts and alphabetically thereunder by names of owners. No index. Typed on printed forms. Average 300 pages. 18.5 x 12.5 x 2. Treasurer's vault.

Inheritance Tax

325. INHERITANCE TAX CHARGE
1926—. 2 volumes.
Copies of certificates of inheritance tax as certified by auditor and submitted to treasurer, showing number of certificate, name of estate or decedent, amount of tax,

and to whom charged; also a list of payers, showing date of accrual of tax, amount fixed by court, discount or interest, total amount, and date paid. Arranged alphabetically by names of estates or decedents, and numerically thereunder by certificate numbers. No index. Typed on printed forms. Average 250 pages. 12 x 11 x 3. Treasurer's main office.

326. INHERITANCE TAX CHARGE
1929—. 1 bundle, 1 file box.

Original statements of inheritance tax charges submitted by auditor to treasurer in reference to taxes fixed upon estates by probate court, showing description of estate and amount of tax, name of decedent, date of accrual of taxes, amount fixed by court, discount or interest, total amount and date paid, and name of taxing district. Arranged alphabetically by names of decedents. No index. Handwritten on printed forms. Bundle, 11 x 10.5 x 1.5; file box, 11 x 16 x 24. 1 bundle, 1929-1933, attic; 1 file box, 1934—, Treasurer's main office.

Sales Tax

327. VENDOR'S PURCHASE ORDERS OF SALES TAX
1935. 2 file boxes.

Triplicate copies of vendor's purchase orders of sales tax stamps, showing name of vendor, license number, date of order, quantity, amount of value, denominations, total gross, amount less discount, date, and total net due. Arranged chronologically by dates of orders. No index. Handwritten on printed forms. 19.5 x 17.5 x 16.5. Attic.

328. DAILY AND WEEKLY SALES RECORD INVENTORY
1935—. 2 volumes.

Inventory record of sales tax stamps, showing date of record, amount received, amount sold, and amount on hand of each denomination each day of week, with total value sold, and total value on hand. Arranged chronologically by dates of inventories. No index. Handwritten on printed forms. Average 52 pages. 17.5 x 14.5 x .75. Treasurer's main office.

329. DAILY RECORD OF SALES TAX RECEIPTS
1835—. 2 volumes. (1, 3).

Itemized, detailed record of sales tax receipts, showing vendor's license number, amount of each denomination of stamps purchased, total value, vendor's discount, and amount collected; total of each denomination sold, total discount, and total amount or value collected. Arranged chronologically by dates of purchases. No index. Handwritten on printed forms. Average 365 pages. 17.5 x 14.5 x 2.5. 1 volume, 1935, attic; 1 volume, 1936—, Treasurer's vault.

330. ADVICE TO STATE TREASURER ON SALES TAX REMITTANCE
1935. 1 file box.
Treasurer's copies of weekly reports of sales tax stamps to state treasurer, showing total gross amount of sales for week, total vendor's discounts and total net amount of sales for the week. Arranged chronologically by dates of reports. No index. Handwritten. 11 x 16 x 24. Attic.

Tax Collections

331. RECORD OF TAXES COLLECTED [Form 7]
1904—. 9 volumes. (1-9).
Record of road, inheritance, delinquent personal, special, and all other taxes except cigarette and liquor tax, showing name of taxing district, date, amount, kind of tax, and total of each kind of tax paid and received from all county taxing districts, name of taxpayer, and receipt number. Arranged alphabetically by names of taxing districts and chronologically thereunder by names of tax collections. No index. Average 340 pages. 15 x 14.5 x 2.5. 8 volumes, 1904-1934, attic; 1 volume, 1935—, Treasurer's main office.

332. RECORD OF TAXES COLLECTED [Forms 8 and 9]
1904-1910. 1 volume.
Record of taxes collected on liquor and cigarettes, showing name of taxing district, name of payer, date paid, amount of tax, and business address. Arranged alphabetically by names of taxing districts. No index. Handwritten on printed forms. 100 pages. 18 x 12 x 1.5. Attic.

333. TAX BILLS
1929—. 22 file boxes. Subtitled by names of taxing districts.
Receipts of tax bills paid by taxpayers of county, showing line number, tract, lot, acreage, frontage, delinquent half-tax and whole tax, name of taxpayer, name of

taxing district, volume and page numbers of Treasurer's Tax List, entry 315; date of payment is stamped on some and on others it is perforated. Arranged alphabetically by names of taxing districts and alphabetically thereunder by names of taxpayers. No index. Handwritten. 11 x 16 x 24. 13 file boxes, 1929-1936, treasurer's vault; 9 file boxes, 1937—, Treasurer's main office.

334. UNDERTAKINGS [County Treasurer]
1934—. 3 volumes. (1-3).
Record of treasurer's undertakings to collect delinquent taxes under the Wittemore Act, showing description of real property, general tax, county assessments, and total principal and penalty; under the heading "principal and penalty," shows name of property owner, amount of principal, date paid, and penalties to be remitted; also shows name of property owner, date of payment of first installment, balance due, and subsequently the same for balance of year, showing dates, month, and year of each payment. Arranged alphabetically by taxing districts and chronologically thereunder by dates of payments. No index. Handwritten on printed forms. Average 400 pages. 17.5 x 16 x 2. Treasurer's main office.

335. EXCISE TAXES COLLECTED
1876-1880. 1 volume.
Record of excise taxes collected on liquor, wine, and malt beverages, showing date, name of payee, location of business, rate of tax, and total amount paid. Arranged alphabetically by names of taxpayers. No index. Handwritten. 200 pages. 15 x 11 x 1. Attic.

Fiscal Accounts

336. JOURNAL OF WARRANTS REDEEMED
1904—. 27 volumes. (1-27).
Record of warrants redeemed, showing line number, date of warrant, name of payee, purpose of warrant, warrant number, amount, distribution to various funds, and date redeemed. Arranged chronologically by dates of warrants and numerically thereunder by warrant numbers. No index. 1840-1904, handwritten; 1904—, handwritten on printed forms. Average 300 pages. 20 x 15 x 2. 21 volumes, 1904-1936, attic; 6 volumes, 1937—, Treasurer's main office.

337. JOURNAL OF COURT WARRANTS REDEEMED
1904—. 3 volumes. (1-3).

Record of court warrants redeemed, showing date of warrant, name of payee, warrant number, amount, of what court, for what purpose, such as paying of witnesses, petit and grand jurors, lunacy, minor, and coroner's court. Arranged chronologically by dates of warrants and numerically thereunder by warrant numbers. No index. Handwritten on printed forms. Average 350 pages. 18 x 12 x 1.5. 1 volume, 1904-1924, attic; 2 volumes, 1925—, Treasurer's main office.

338. JOURNAL OF RECEIPTS
1904—. 14 volumes. (1-12, 16, 20).

Daily record of receipts into treasury, showing dates, line number, name of payer, purpose, pay-in order number, debits and credits to various funds, and daily balance. Arranged chronologically by dates of entries and also numerically by pay-in order numbers. No index. Handwritten on printed forms. Average 200 pages. 20.5 x 16 x 1.5. 12 volumes, 1904-1936, attic; 2 volumes, 1937—, Treasurer's main office.

339. DAILY CASH BALANCE
1840—. 24 volumes. (1840-1904, 7 volumes dated; 1904—, 1-17). Title varies; Treasurer's Account, 1840-1904, 7 volumes.

Daily record of receipts, disbursements, and cash balance, showing date of entry, amounts received and disbursed, and cash on hand. Arranged chronologically by dates of entries. No index. Handwritten on printed forms. Average 325 pages. 16.5 x 12 x 2. 19 volumes, 1840-1930, attic; 5 volumes, 1931—, Treasurer's main office.

340. TREASURER'S ORDERS
1840-1904. 6 volumes. (A-F). Discontinued.

Itemized record of orders drawn on treasurer, showing to whom paid, amount, for what purpose, date, and order number. Arranged chronologically by dates of orders. No index. Handwritten on printed forms. Average 300 pages. 14 x 11 x 1.5. Attic.

341. CASH BOOK
1840—. 20 volumes. (A-G, 1-13).

Record of money received and disbursed, showing the various types or sources of receipts, total disbursements, balance of various accounts, and date. Arranged chronologically by dates of entries. No index. 1840-1888, handwritten; 1889—, handwritten on printed forms. Average 250 pages. 18 x 12 x 1.5. 9 volumes, 1840-

1904, attic; 11 volumes, 1905—, Treasurer's vault.

342. TREASURER'S LEDGER
1840-1869, 1904-1914, 1929—. 14 volumes. (A, 1, 2, 4-14). Title varies: Ledger, 1840-1869, 1 volume.

Record of treasurer's accounts with various funds, showing dates of entries, names of funds, amount of credit or debit to each fund, and balance or overdraft in each fund. Arranged by names of funds and chronologically thereunder by dates of entries. No index. 1840-1869, handwritten; 1904-1914, 1929—, handwritten on printed forms. Average 500 pages. 18 x 12.5 x 3. 7 volumes, 1840-1869, 1904-1914, 1929-1931, attic; 7 volumes, 1932—, Treasurer's main office.

343. RECEIPTS
1925—. 3 file boxes.

Receipts for money expended by treasurer each month for soldiers' relief fund, showing date, amount, and signature of recipient. Arranged alphabetically by names of recipients and chronologically thereunder by dates of receipts. No index. Handwritten on printed forms. 7 x 13 x 17. 1 file box, 1925-1933, attic; 2 file boxes, 1934—, Treasurer's main office.

344. PAY-INS
1930—. 7 bundles.

Pay-in orders from auditor for money to be paid to treasurer, showing name of payer, number of order, amount to be paid, and fund to be credited with payment. Arranged numerically by consecutive order numbers. No index. Handwritten on printed forms. 11 x 8 x 3. 3 bundles, 1930-1932, attic; 4 bundles, 1933—, Treasurer's main office.

Reports

345. DAILY STATEMENT
1927—. 3 bundles, 2 file boxes.

Copies of daily statements of treasurer to auditor at close of each day's business, showing receipts, sources, disbursements, list of active and inactive deposits, and total. Arranged chronologically by daily entries. No index. Handwritten on printed forms. Bundles, 11 x 8.5 x 5; file boxes, 14 x 9 x 20. 1 bundle, 1927-1931, attic; 2 bundles, 2 file boxes, 1932—, Treasurer's main office.

346. FINANCIAL REPORT, AUDITOR'S AND TREASURER'S
1926—. 3 file boxes, 1 bundle.

Treasurer's copies of monthly financial reports to auditor, showing date of report, active and inactive bank accounts, outstanding warrants, warrant number, amount, and fund charged; also statement of daily transactions with balance of county funds, deposits, withdrawals; also list of cancelled checks for month. Arranged chronologically by dates of reports. No index. Handwritten. Bundle, 18 x 14 x 12.5, file boxes, 11 x 16 x 24. 3 file boxes, 1926-1936, attic; 1 bundle, 1937—, Treasurer's vault.

Bonds

347. TOWNSHIP CLERK'S BONDS
1923—. 1 volume.

Record of bonds township clerks, showing name of clerk, amount of bond, name of bonding company or sureties, and oath of clerk. Arranged chronologically by dates of bonds. Indexed alphabetically by names of clerks. Handwritten on printed forms. 70 pages. 14 x 8.5 x .5. Treasurer's main office.

348. RECORD OF OFFICIAL BONDS
1840—. 7 volumes.

Copies of fidelity bonds of county officials, showing name of officer, office held, names of sureties, amount, condition, date of bond, oath, and signature of notary public. Arranged chronologically by dates of bonds. Indexed alphabetically by names of officers bonded. 1840-1906, handwritten; 1906—, typed. Average 300 pages. 16 x 11 x 2. 3 volumes, 1840-1925, attic; 4 volumes, 1926—, Treasurer's main office.

349. RECORD OF OFFICIAL BONDS
1840—. 5 bundles, 1 file box.

Original fidelity bonds of county officers, showing name of officer, names of sureties, certificate of approval of prosecuting attorney, oath of official, date, and amount of bond. Arranged chronologically by dates of bonds. No index. Handwritten on printed forms. Bundles 8.5 x 5 x 4; file box, 10 x 4.5 x 13.5. 5 bundles, 1840-1912, attic; 1 file box, 1913—, Treasurer's vault.

In 1911 a law was passed by the state legislature authorizing the establishment in each county of a budget commission to be composed of the county auditor, the mayor of the largest municipality of the county, and the county prosecuting attorney.[1] In 1915 the treasurer replaced the mayor on the commission.[2] The county auditor as secretary is required to keep a full and accurate record of the proceedings.[3] Under the present law, passed in 1927, the commission receives and examines the annual budget of the county, municipal, township, and school authorities, together with an estimate of the amount to be raised for state purposes in each subdivision.[4] If the total exceeds the sum authorized to be raised, the commission adjusts the amount, and may revise the estimates. The commission may reduce all items in the budget but it is prohibited from increasing the total of the budget or of any item in it.

The adjusted budget is certified to the taxing authority in each subdivision. If the budget is satisfactory, each taxing authority authorizes by ordinance or resolution the necessary tax levies. However, the taxing authorities may appeal from the decision of the budget commission to the State Tax Commission.[5]

They total budget approved by the county budget commission of Lake County for 1941 was $294,749.10.[6] This does not include villages and townships which have their own budgets set up by their own trustees.

---

1. *Laws of Ohio,* CII, 271.
2. *Ibid.,* CVI, 180.
3. G.C. sec. 5649-3b.
4. *Laws of Ohio,* CXII, 399.
5. G.C. secs. 5625-25, 5625-28.
6. Auditor's Tax List, 1941, entry 246.

350. RECORD OF PROCEEDINGS

1911-1932, 1927—. 2 volumes. (1, 2). 1 file box.
Minutes of regular and special meetings of the budget commission showing date of meeting, proceedings, actions and resolutions taken, reports made, and disposal of budgets for various taxing districts. Arranged chronologically by dates of meetings. No index. Handwritten on printed forms. Average 400 pages. 16.56 x 11.5 x 1. 2 volumes, 1911-1923, attic; 1 file box, 1927—, Auditor's private office.

351. BUDGET ESTIMATES
1923—. 13 bundles.
Estimates of budgets of various taxing districts, including school boards, as submitted for approval for budget commission, showing real and personal property valuation for each taxing district, operating expenses of each, and tax rates for each. Arranged alphabetically by names of taxing districts. No index. Handwritten and typed. 7 x 4.5 x 2.5. Auditor's main office.

BOARD OF REVISION

An agency for the appeal of taxpayers from defects and inequities in tax assessments was first authorized by law in Ohio in 1825,[1] and was originally known as a board of equalization. Under the present system, authorized by law in 1917, the agency, now known as a board of revision, is composed of the county treasurer, the county auditor, and the president of the county commissioners.[2] It is the duty of the board to hear all complaints relating to assessments or valuations of both real and personal property as they appear upon the tax duplicates of the current year. The board is authorized to investigate all complaints and may increase or decrease any valuation or correct any assessment complaint of, or may order a reassessment by the original assessing official.[3] No valuation is increased without giving personal notice to the owner of the property affected by the increase in assessment.[4] Should a complaining taxpayer wish to take issue with a decision of the board of revision, he must appeal to the Tax Commission of Ohio within 30 days of the time the board renders its decision.[5]

The board of revision must review the returns of assessments of both personal and real property for the current year as submitted by the auditor, who is not permitted to make up his tax list and duplicate until the board has completed its work and submitted to him all returns laid before it with revisions.[6]

---

1. *Laws of Ohio,* XXIII, 64.
2. G.C. sec. 5580.
3. G.C. sec. 5597.
4. G.C. sec. 5599.
5. G.C. sec. 5610.
6. G.C. sec. 5605.

In its investigations the board has authority to examine witnesses under oath, regarding their own or others' real property.[7] The decisions of the board are subject to appeal to the State Tax Commission.[8] The auditor as secretary of the board is required to keep an accurate record of proceedings, and is required to keep in his office separate records of all minutes and evidence offered in each complaint,[9] which are open to inspection by the public.[10]

---

7. G.C. sec. 5695.
8. G.C. sec. 5610.
9. G.C. secs. 5880, 5603.
10. G.C. sec. 5591.

352. BOARD OF EQUALIZATION RECORD
1846—. 3 volumes.

Minutes of county board of equalization, 1846-1913, board of revision, 1914—, with record of revision of real and personal property valuations for taxation, showing date of meeting, name of property owner, name of taxing district, description of property, amount added to or deducted from original valuation, and reason for revision. Arranged chronologically by dates of meetings. No index. 1846-1900, handwritten; 1901—, typed. 1 volume, 250 pages. 16.25 x 12 x 1.5; 2 volumes, average 250 pages, 12.25 x 8 x 1. 1 volume, 1846-1913, attic; 2 volumes, 1914—, Auditor's main office.

353. RECORD – BOARD OF REVISION [City of Painesville], 1904—. 2 volumes. (1, 2).

Minutes of board of review of the city of Painesville, showing date of meeting, order of business, adjustments made on taxation values of real and personal properties, name of property owner, and amount of addition or deduction. Arranged chronologically by dates of meetings. No index. Typed. Average 400 pages. 17 x 11.5 x 2. 1 volume, 1904-1812, attic; 1 volume, 1913—, Auditor's main office.

354. COMPLAINTS – APPRAISALS
1914—. 3 file boxes.

Originals and copies of complaints to the board of revision of assessments on real property, showing date of filing, name of taxing district, name and address of property owner, description, location, assessed value of property, amount of deduction asked, assessor's report, and miscellaneous correspondence pertaining to the case. Arranged chronologically by dates of filing. No index. Handwritten and typed on printed forms. 10 x 4.5 x 13.5. Auditor's main office.

355. BOARD OF REVIEW NOTICE OF HEARING
1904-1912. 4 volumes.

Record of notices from board of review sent to property owners for hearings on tax additions or deductions, showing name of taxing district, name and address of property owner, amount of addition or deduction, and the time and place of hearing. Arranged alphabetically by names of taxing districts and alphabetically thereunder by names of property owners. No index. Handwritten on printed forms. Average 250 pages. 18 x 8 x 1. Attic.

Members of the county board of elections serve as deputies of the secretary of state, who is the chief election official of the state,[1] and are appointed by him biennially for a term of four years. The board consists of four qualified voters, two from each of the two major parties. They are removable by the secretary of state for cause. Compensation is appropriated by the county commissioners and is based on population, which, in Lake County, with 73 precincts, and 30,872 registered voters, entitles them to receive $600 annually.[2]

The board is authorized to establish election precincts, fix places of registration, and provide for the purchase, preservation, and maintenance of voting booths, ballot boxes, books, maps, flags, and other equipment.[3] On or before September 1 of each election year, the members of the board appoint precinct election officials for one-year terms, four to be judges, and two to be clerks. Two judges and one clerk must be appointed from each major party.[4] The board receives and checks on the sufficiency of nominating petitions; receives and canvasses returns; abstracts returns; certifies the winner; and reports to the secretary the official returns.[5] It may also investigate irregularities and violations of election laws.[6]

In the event of a close vote, the board can be required, at the request of a candidate, to make a recount of the votes for the office in question. The cost of the recount is from $5 to $10 per precinct, as determined by the board. If an error of more than 2 percent is found, no charge is made to the candidate requesting the recount, and the losing candidate may at any time request a cessation of the count.[7]

All records are located in the board of election office, unless otherwise specified.

---

1. *Laws of Ohio,* LXXXVIII, 449; G.C. sec. 4785-8.
2. G.C. sec. 4785-18.
3. G.C. sec. 4785-13.
4. G.C. sec. 4785-25.
5. G.C. sec. 4785-13.
6. G.C. sec. 4785-13.
7. G.C. secs. 4785-162, 4785-164.

Minutes

356. MINUTES OF BOARD OF ELECTIONS
1896—. 4 volumes.

Minutes of board of elections, showing date of meeting, business transactions, financial reports, appointments of officers to board of elections, resolutions and actions taken thereon, appointments of committees, and bills passed for payment. Arranged chronologically by dates of meetings. No index. Handwritten and typed. Average 300 pages. 15 x 9.5 x 1.5.

Electors' Records

357. POLL BOOKS AND TALLY SHEETS
1936—. 122 volumes. Subtitled by voting districts.

Lists of registered voters, showing name and address of voter, voting districts, name of political party, and signature of voter. Tally sheets show total votes received by each candidate and issue in each voting district, also signatures of clerks and judges of elections. Poll books arranged alphabetically by names of electors; tally sheets, arranged by offices and issues. No index. Handwritten on printed forms. Average 12 pages. 17.5 x 10.5 x .25.

For clerk of courts' official copy, 1930—, see entry 115.

358. REGISTERED ELECTORS, MENTOR-ON-LAKE
1936—. 1 volume.

Complete list of registered voters in election district, Mentor-On-Lake, showing name and address of voter, and political party affiliation. Arranged alphabetically by names of registrants. No index. Typed on printed forms. 50 pages. 14 x 13 x ?.

359. REGISTER OF ABSENT AND DISABLED VOTERS
1936—. 1 volume.

Register of applications to vote absentee ballots by absent and disabled voters, showing name of applicant, date of application, application number, present temporary address, home address and voting district, and reason for absence. Arranged numerically by application numbers and also chronologically by dates of applications. No index. Handwritten on printed forms. 50 pages. 13.5 z 8.5 z .5.

360. ABSTRACT OF VOTES
1936—. 1 bundle.

Certified abstracts of total votes cast for candidates and issues, showing list of offices, lists of votes by precincts, date of elections, and type of election, whether primary, special, or regular, and total votes cast for each candidate and issue. No obvious arrangement. No index. Handwritten and typed on printed forms. 17 x 22 x 3. Secretary's office, 177 Main Street, Painesville, Ohio.

Miscellaneous

361. RECORD OF APPOINTMENTS AND PAYROLL
1930—. 2 volumes.

Record of appointments of judges and clerks of elections, showing voting district, name and address of appointee, political party affiliation, date qualified, type of service, rate of pay, total amount due, and date of order on treasurer. Arranged by voting districts and alphabetically thereunder by names of appointees. No index. Handwritten on printed forms. Average 250 pages. 16.5 x 11.5 x 1.5.

The Lake County board of education was established under the provisions of an act of the legislature passed in 1914, providing for the creation of county school districts. This act provided that the county school district should embrace all of the territory of the county not included in any cities or village having a population of 3000 or more, and desiring exemption. The board consisted originally of five members, elected for five-year terms by the presidents of all the school boards of the county.[1] In 1921 the law was amended to provide for election of members of the board by popular vote.[2]

The powers of the board include appointment of a county superintendent of schools for a term of three years; creation and modifications of school districts, subject to the wishes of the voters of the district; annual certification to the auditor of the number of superintendents and teachers employed, and their salaries; and the amount apportioned to each school district for the payment of the salaries of the county and district superintendents. The board also may publish, with the advice and consent of the county superintendent, a minimum course of study to serve as a guide to local board members. Each member of the county board of education receives, as compensation for his services, three dollars for each day in session, and a traveling allowance for 10 cents a mile.[3]

Lake County schools have improved from year to year in personnel, attendance, and school facilities. Records for 1940 show a staff of 246 teachers and superintendents; 21 centralized elementary school buildings and 6 high schools; and a total attendance of 6,270 pupils. The year's payroll was $341,007.[4]

All records are located and the board of education office unless otherwise specified.

---

1. *Laws of Ohio,* CIV, 133.
2. *Ibid.,* CIX, 242.
3. G.C. secs. 4744, 4735, 4735,-1, 4736, 4744-2, 4737, 4734.
4. [Financial Reports], 1940, entry 365.

362. RECORD OF PROCEEDINGS

1914—. 2 volumes.

Minutes of county board of education, showing date of meeting, members present, resolutions presented and action taken, bills passed for payment, and other pertinent matters. Arranged chronologically by dates of meetings. No index. Typed. 11.5 x 9.5 x 1.5.

363. ANNUAL STATISTICAL REPORT OF PUBLIC SCHOOLS

1912—. 1 file drawer.

Copies of county superintendent's annual reports to state department of education on school statistics, showing date of report, number of schools in county, number of schoolrooms, number of consolidated schools, number of high schools, number of teachers, number of principals, number of pupils in county, number of weeks in school, and date report filed. Arranged chronologically by dates of filing. No index. Handwritten. 11 x 16 x 24.

364. ANNUAL REPORT OF COUNTY SUPERINTENDENT OF SCHOOLS

1912—. 1 file box.

Copies of county superintendents annual report to state department of education, showing date of report, total enrollment, name of teachers, salaries, total cost for teachers, transportation, and janitor service; tax receipts (general fund), estimated income from public school fund, general notes, and date report filed; also 1931-1935, shows cost per pupil. Arranged chronologically by dates of filing. No index. Handwritten. 11 x 16 x 24.

365. [FINANCIAL REPORTS]

1912—. 1 file drawer.

Copies of county superintendents annual financial report to state department of education, showing date filed, each balance on hand as of June 30th previous year, itemized receipts and itemized expenditures certified by county superintendent. Arranged chronologically by dates of filing. No index. Handwritten on printed forms. 11 x 16 x 24.

366. ANNUAL REPORT, TEACHERS
1934—. Estimated 488 reports in 1 file box.

Teachers annual reports to county superintendent, of attendance, promotion, and home record of pupils in township and village schools, showing name of school, school district, name of teacher, name of pupil, grade, age, and number of days attending school each month; record of examinations, showing grade received in each study, and record of promotion; also home record, showing name of pupil, date of birth, date entered school, name of parent or guardian, and residence. Arranged alphabetically by names of school districts and alphabetically thereunder by names of schools and teachers. No index. Handwritten on printed forms. 11 x 16 x 24.

367. CERTIFIED STATISTICAL REPORT FOR DISTRIBUTION OF THE STATE PUBLIC FUNDS TO COUNTY SCHOOL DISTRICTS
1934—. 1 file drawer.

Copies of annual statistical reports from county superintendent to state department of education, showing name of school, number of teachers, actual aggregate days of attendance, actual average daily attendance, number of days in session in school year, total tax duplicate of district, total tax levy in mills for current school operations, all purposes, and total expenditures for transportation of pupils during school year, date of report, and county superintendent's oath. Arranged chronologically by dates of reports. No index. Handwritten on printed forms. 11 x 16 x 24.

Teachers' records

368. CERTIFICATES, TEACHERS'
1897—. 1 file box.

Teaching certificates issued by county board and state board of examiners, showing name of teacher, number and kind of certificate, signatures of board of examiners and director of education, and seal. Arranged alphabetically by names of teachers. No index. Handwritten and typed on printed forms. 11 x 16 x 24.

369. LAKE COUNTY CERTIFICATES
1897-1934. 1 file box. Discontinued; law repealed.
Record of examination by county board of examiners, showing date of examinations, names of teachers, and grades made in examinations for teaching certificates; also certificates issued by Lake County board of examiners, showing date, name of teacher, term of certificate, and type. Arranged chronologically by dates of examinations. No index. Typed on printed forms. 11 x 16 x 24.

370. OLD TEACHERS' REPORTS AND CERTIFICATES
1853-1864. 2 envelopes.
Copies of teachers' certificates and contracts to teach in common schools, showing date, name of teacher, and kind of certificate or contract; also includes pupils' attendance records as reported by teachers. Arranged chronologically by school years. No index. Handwritten, some on printed forms. 9 x 4 x 1. Attic.

Pupils' Records

371. PERMANENT RECORD OF PUPILS
1923—. 2 bundles, 4 file boxes. Initiated 1923.
Active and inactive individual advancement cards of students in school together with record of their grades, showing date, school district, and name of pupils. Arranged by school districts and alphabetically thereunder by names of pupils. No index. Handwritten on printed forms. 2 drawers contain active records, 2 drawers and 2 bundles inactive records. Bundles, 11 x 10 x 8.5; file drawer, 11 x 16 x 24. 1923-1928, 2 bundles, attic; 1929—, 4 file boxes, Board of education office.

372. CO-OPERATIVE HIGH SCHOOL REGISTER
1908-1923. 18 volumes. Prior and subsequent records kept at each high school.
Individual advancement cards of students for some of the schools in different school districts of Lake County with record of their grades, showing name of pupil, address, grade, and remarks. These records are made in duplicate and are very incomplete. No obvious arrangement. No index. Handwritten on printed forms. Average 50 pages. 14.5 x 11 x .25. Attic.

373. REPORT Of PUPILS TUITION
1934—. 2 file drawers.

Record of pupils attending high or grade schools out of their legal district, and paying contracted tuition for the privilege, showing semester attendance, date, name of school, grade, and date of report. Arranged chronologically by dates of reports. No index. Handwritten and typed on printed forms. 11 x 16 x 24.

Fiscal Accounts

374. SCHOOL FUND ACCOUNT
1921-1925. 4 volumes. Discontinued.

Record of appropriations to county board of education and of operating expenses of the board, showing date of entry, total receipts from all sources and total expenditures itemized by funds. Arranged chronologically by dates of entries. No index. Handwritten on printed forms. Average 98 pages. 14 x 16 x .5. Attic.

375. SCHOOL LEDGER
1931—. 1 volume.

Record of amounts apportioned by the board of education for various purposes, showing date of entry, name of vendor or payee, purpose, date of purchase, purchase order, warrant number, amount of warrant, and appropriation or authorization. Arranged chronologically by dates of entries. No index. Handwritten on printed forms. 250 pages. 11.5 x 14.5 x 2.

376. LAKE COUNTY SCHOOLS [Contracts for transportation of Pupils]
1936—. 1 file box.

Contracts made by Lake County school board with owners and operators of vehicles for transportation of pupils to and from school, showing date, name of school, school district, name of bus operator, and contract amount to be paid monthly; specifications giving route number and names and direction on each road or street traveled on each route. Arranged alphabetically by names of school districts and chronologically thereunder by dates of contracts. No index. Handwritten on printed forms. 11 x 16 x 24.

Miscellaneous

377. ENUMERATION REPORTS

1842-1972. 2 bundles. Discontinued.

Enumeration records of the youths of Lake County between the age of five and 18 years, showing date of report, name, address, age, sex, name of parent or guardian, and school attending. Arranged chronologically by dates of reports. No index. Handwritten on printed forms. 8 x 4 x 2. Attic.

For auditor's enumeration list, 1852-1920, see entry 314.

378. RURAL SCHOOL DISTRICT BOARD OF EDUCATION POLL BOOK AND TALLY SHEET

1925-1929. 192 volumes. (Dated). Discontinued. Subtitled by name of school districts.

Poll books and tally sheets of school board elections in rural school districts; poll books show names of electors casting ballots in each election; and tally sheets show number of votes received by each candidate for school board position; also school district and date of election. These records are not complete. Arranged alphabetically by names of school districts and chronologically thereunder by dates of entries. No index. Handwritten on printed forms. Average 12 pages. 17 x 10.5 x .25. Attic.

The county board of health in Ohio, as organized today, go back to the act passed by the legislature in 1919, and amended later in the same year, which provided that all villages and townships combine to form a general health district.[1]

A district advisory council consisting of the mayors of the villages, and the chairman of the board of trustees of the townships, appoints a district board of health composed of five members, one of whom must be a physician, and all of whom serve without compensation.[2] This board appoints a district health commissioner, a licensed physician who serves as secretary to the board; he is designated deputy state registrar of vital statistics and must report monthly to the state registrar of vital statistics.[3]

On his recommendation, public health nurses are employed, the prevalence of communicable diseases is studied, provisions are made for the treatment of venereal diseases, and regulations are drawn up for the prevention and suppression of nuisances. The board also inspects public charitable, benevolent, penal, and correctional institutions, and may also institute inspection of dairies, stores, restaurants, hotels, and any other places where food is manufactured, handled, or sold. It is authorized to carry on necessary laboratory test, either by establishing a laboratory, or by contracting with existing laboratories, publicly or privately maintained.[4]

The health department is maintained by public taxation. Each year the board submits an itemized estimate of its needs for the coming year to the budget commission, which fixes the amount it will receive. This sum is collected from the townships and villages in the district on the basis of their respective real estate valuations.[5]

In 1941 the total appropriation for Lake County health department amounted to $9774.32, $1000 of which is paid by the state.[6] The commissioner is appointed for one year at an annual salary of $2750. His staff includes two public health nurses who receive an aggregate annual salary of $2700, one sanitary officer, one milk inspector, and one clerk.[7]

---

1. *Laws of Ohio,* CVIII, pt. I, 238.
2. *Ibid.,* CVIII, pt. ii, 1085.
3. G.C. sec. 1261-32; *Laws of Ohio,* CVIII, pt. I, 238-242.
4. *Laws of Ohio,* CVIII, pt. ii, 1088, 1089.
5. *Ibid.,* CVIII, pt. ii, 1091.
6. Appropriation Ledger, 1941, entry 269.
7. Payroll, 1941, entry 283.

The department conducts preschool and medical clinics. Rabies serum is furnished by the county commissioners and is kept in the board of health office.[8]

There is no tuberculosis sanatorium in Lake County. Since 1929 one public health nurse assisted by a stenographer, has worked in this field, under the direction of the health commissioner but not responsible to him.[9] The work is organized under the Ohio Public Tuberculosis and Health Association. Both are paid out of a fund appropriated by the county commissioners and entirely independent of the board of health. They draw an annual aggregate salary of $2810[10] from the county. All other expenses of care and treatment of tuberculosis cases are paid from the funds of the Association, which are derived from the sale of Christmas seals and private contributions. A clinic is held monthly by a visiting Cleveland specialist to whom the nurses bring their cases. Patients requiring hospital care are sent to Lake County Memorial Hospital.[11]

All records are located and board of health office.

---

8. Information secured from the health commissioner's office.
9. Commissioners' Record V (1928-1930). 291. Entry 1.
10. Payroll, 1941, entry 283.
11. Information secured from health commissioner's office.

Minutes

379. MINUTES OF LAKE COUNTY BOARD OF HEALTH
1920—. 3 volumes.

Minutes of board of health, showing date of meeting, names of members present, resolutions passed, bills passed for payment, and proceedings in such matters as come before the board for consideration. Arranged chronologically by dates of meetings. No index. Handwritten and typed. Average 200 pages. 12 x 9 x 1.

Vital Statistics

380. [INDEX TO VITAL STATISTICS]
1920—.1 volume.

Index to Birth Records, entry 381, and Death Records, entry 382, showing date of birth or death, name of child or decedent place of birth or death, registration number of birth, and volume and page numbers of record. Arranged alphabetically by names of children or decedents. Handwritten on printed forms. 200 pages. 17 x 13 x 1.5.

381. BIRTH RECORDS
1920—. 68 volumes. (1-68).

Record of birth in county health district, showing name of child, sex, date of birth, registration number, name, address, race, age, birthplace and occupation of parents, and certificate of attending physician. Arranged numerically by registration numbers. For index, see entry 380. Typed on printed forms. Average 100 pages. 8.5 x 7 x .5.

For record of births, 1867-1908, see entry 197.

382. DEATH RECORDS
1920—. 47 volumes. (1-47).

Record of deaths in county health district, showing name and last address of decedent, place of death, date of death, cause the death, manner and date of burial, and full personal and statistical particulars. Arranged chronologically by dates of death. For index, see entry 380. Typed on printed forms. Average 100 pages. 8.5 x 7 x .5.

For record of deaths, 1867-1908, see entry 197.

383. REGISTER OF CASES OF INFECTIOUS AND CONTAGIOUS DISEASES
1920—. 2 volumes.

Record of reported communicable diseases, showing name of disease, name, address, age, sex, and race of patient, district number, name of attending physician, name of township, and date reported. Arranged alphabetically by the names of townships and chronologically thereunder by dates of reports. Indexed alphabetically by names of patients. Handwritten on printed forms. Average 150 pages. 19.5 x 12.5 x 1.5.

384. CARD RECORD TOXIN AND ANTI-TOXINS
1924-1926. 4 file boxes. Discontinued.

Card record of toxins given in cases of contagious diseases affecting school children, showing name of child, date, consent of parent or guardian, kind of disease, and name of school. Arranged alphabetically by names of schools and alphabetically thereunder by pupils. No index. Handwritten and typed on printed forms. 4.5 x 5.5 x 11.5.

385. SCHOOL HEALTH RECORD
1930-1936. 2 packing boxes, 16 file boxes.
Record of health of pupils in schools in Lake County (excluding Fairport, Painesville, Willoughby, and Wickliffe), showing name and address of pupil, name of school and grade, complete personal history, date of report, and doctor's and nurse's notes; includes diphtheria records, 1933-1936. Arranged alphabetically by schools and numerically thereunder by grades and alphabetically thereunder by names of pupils. No index. Handwritten on printed forms. Packing boxes, 12 x 17 x 28; file boxes, 2 x 18 x 24.

Permits

386. PERMITS, SEPTIC TANKS
1928—. 1 volume.
Record of all septic tank permits issued, showing permit number, name and address of applicant, device, date issued, fee, and dates paid. Arranged numerically by permit numbers. Indexed alphabetically by names of applicants. Handwritten on printed forms. 100 pages. 11.5 x 9.25 x .5.

387. PERMITS, RESTAURANTS
1930—. 1 volume.
Copies of permits issued to restaurants, showing permit number, fee, name of owner, location of restaurant, date of permit, and date paid. Arranged numerically by permit numbers. Indexed alphabetically by names of applicants. Handwritten on printed forms. 100 pages. 11.5 x 9.25 x .5.

Fiscal Accounts

388. CASH BOOK
1934—. 1 volume. Prior records missing.
Record of receipts from all sources and expenditures of this office, showing date and nature of receipt or disbursement, and debit and credit and balance. Arranged chronologically by dates of entries. No index. Handwritten on printed forms. 100 pages. 14.5 x 11.5 x 1.

Tuberculosis Division

389. [REGISTER]
1930—. 1 volume. Initiated 1930.
Register of tuberculosis cases reported to the county board of health and county tuberculosis association, showing date and by whom reported, case number, name and address of patient, occupation, number exposed, source of infection, age, sex, color, home and social conditions, name of physician, type of case, laboratory report, x-ray results, treatment, and final disposition. Arranged numerically by case numbers. Indexed alphabetically by names of patients. Handwritten on printed forms. 100 pages. 18 x 11 x 1.25.

390. HEALTH RECORD, LAKE COUNTY TUBERCULOSIS
1931—. 1 volume.
Record of clinic attendance, showing date of entry, location of clinic, number of male and female adults and children attending, new, return, and total patients; positive contact, advanced, incipient, and arrested cases, physician's name, clinical records, and final disposition. Arranged chronologically by dates of entries. Indexed alphabetically by names of patients. Handwritten. 152 pages. 14.25 x 11 x .5.

391. LAKE COUNTY TUBERCULOSIS AND HEALTH ASSOCIATION RECORD
1929—. 4 file boxes. (labeled by contained letters of alphabet).
Complete case papers of all tuberculosis patients, showing date of entered, name and address of patient, date and place of birth, color, sex, names and addresses of parents, date and place of birth of parents, names of children in family, marital status, occupation of patient, names of relatives, and previous employment record; also includes health record, showing previous diseases of patient, physical examination report, mental condition, medical history in home, recommendations, and date of final discharge. Arranged alphabetically by names of patients. No index. Handwritten on printed forms. 11 x 16 x 24.

392. INDEX TUBERCULOSIS RECORD
1929—. 1 file box.
Card index record of tuberculosis patients, showing case number, name and address of patient, age, sex, color, and brief description of progress of case. Arranged alphabetically by names of patients. Handwritten and typed on printed forms. 11 x 6 x 17.

393. TUBERCULOSIS CASE FILE CARDS
1931—. 4 file boxes. (labeled by contained letters of alphabet).
Card record of tubercular patients reporting to Lake County board of health, showing date entered, case number, name and address of patient, age, sex, color, occupation, date of birth, history of present illness, manner of exposure to tuberculosis, service rendered and explanatory remarks, and records of visits. Arranged alphabetically by names of patients. No index. Handwritten on printed forms. 11 x 16 x 24.

394. REPORT, CLINIC
1931—. 1 volume.
Record of city and county clinic examinations, showing date of examination, case number, name and address of patient, x-ray results, physician's name, and record of clinic treatments and monthly attendance. Arranged chronologically by dates of examinations. Indexed alphabetically by names of patients. Handwritten. 200 pages. 11.5 x 9.5 x 1.25.

395. MONTHLY CLINIC SUMMARY, LAKE COUNTY TUBERCULOSIS AND HEALTH ASSOCIATION
1931—. 1 volume.
Monthly summary of clinic attendance and diagnostic record: attendance record, showing date of report, number of male and female adults and children attending clinics monthly, new, return, and total patients; diagnostic record, showing date of report, positive, negative, suspicious, incipient, and arrested cases, physician's name, and final disposition. Arranged chronologically by dates are reports. No index. Handwritten on printed forms. 72 pages. 14.25 x 11 x .5.

The Lake County Memorial Hospital is one of the few county hospitals in the country. It owes its existence largely to the efforts of the ladies of the New Connecticut Chapter of the Daughters of the American Revolution, who worked energetically to build up public opinion on this project, and raise funds for the purpose for several years. In 1902 the Painesville Hospital Association, consisting of over a hundred citizens of Painesville and vicinity, was organized, and from their number a board of 15 trustees was chosen. The ladies of the D.A.R. turned over to them their accumulated contribution, and more money was raised by subscription. Two years later a large old residence, at the corner of Washington and High Streets, in Painesville, was leased, and in July of the same year the hospital was formally opened and received its first patient. The total number treated that year was 39. Care of indigent patients was made possible by the appropriation of public funds by the Lake County commissioners and the Painesville Township trustees.

In 1907 the hospital property was purchased, and a new building was planned, since the old Matthews' residence was completely inadequate. It was completed in 1908, and the original home became the administration building. In that year also, a bill was passed by the legislature authorizing townships to levy a tax to meet the cost of caring for patients unable to pay their own expenses.[1] The trustees of Lake County Memorial Hospital drafted the bill and were instrumental in getting it passed.

The institution was still a private corporation. It did not become a county hospital until 1924, when a new building was erected from funds raised by a bond issue for $200,000 accepted by the Lake County voters in 1923. These successive enlargements made it possible for the hospital to receive 3,217 patients during the year of 1939. At present the building contains a total of 84 beds, including bassinets, and is provided with two surgeries, and one delivery room. It has X-ray and physical therapy departments, and an excellent, well-equipped laboratory. The work is somewhat hampered, however, by crowded conditions, and further increase in space and facilities is very much to be desired.[2]

The institution does not maintain a training school for nurses. The training school opened in 1906 was discontinued in 1932 because of the cost of operating it, and all student nurses were replaced by graduate nurses.[3]

---

1. *Laws of Ohio,* XCIX, 72.
2. *Speaking of Your Hospital* (Painesville, 1939) 7 pages.
3. *Ibid.*

All records are located in Memorial Hospital, East Washington and High Streets, Painesville, Ohio.

396. [REGISTER OF PATIENTS]
1924—. 3 volumes.
Record of patients admitted to the hospital, showing case number, date and time of admittance, name and address of patient, occupation, religion, nationality, civil status, name of attending physician, provisional diagnosis, room number assigned, ward and bed numbers assigned, and date of discharge. Arranged chronologically by dates of admissions. No index. Handwritten on printed forms. Average 300 pages. 12 x 9 x 2.5. Business office.

397. CASE RECORDS
1924—. 20 cartons, 5 file boxes. (Labeled by contained case numbers).
Complete record of hospital cases consisting of the usual hospital case forms for recording clinical information, showing name of patient, date of admission, original diagnosis, x-ray results, laboratory reports, physiotherapy reports, medical and surgical report of services rendered, progress report of patient, and final disposition of case, showing date of death or discharge. Arranged numerically by case numbers. No index. Handwritten and typed on printed forms. Cartons, 6 x 12 x 14.5; file boxes, 12 x 16 x 24. 20 cartons, 1924-1932, stenographer's office; 5 file boxes, 1933—, Business office.

398. CENSUS
1924—. 1 volume, 1 file box.
Record of movements of patients from midnight to midnight, showing date of census, name of patient, case number, page and line number of [Register of Patients], entry 396, room number, ward or division number, rate, number of last admission, number of admissions during last 24 hours, time admitted, number of discharges during last 24 hours, number of patients admitted and discharged by transfers from or to other institutions, number of deaths during last 24 hours, and recapitulation. Arranged chronologically by dates of censuses. No index. Handwritten on printed forms. Volumes 350 pages 12 x 9 x 2.5; file box, 12 x 16 x 24. Business office.

399. [SUPERINTENDENT'S MONTHLY REPORT]
1924—. 1 file box.

Copies of monthly reports from the hospital superintendent to the board of trustees and the county commissioners, including detailed reports of expenses and receipts, showing date of report, amount expended, to whom, for what, and date paid; amount received, from whom, for what, and date paid into hospital fund; includes monthly statistical reports from the hospital superintendent to the board of trustees and the county commissioners, showing date of report and a detailed statistical report of services rendered during month, number of patients admitted, number discharged, number of births, and number of deaths; includes record of cases certified for aid by the relief administration, 1935—, showing date, name of patient, nature of case, amount approved for medical care by the relief administration, and total cost to the relief administration. Arranged chronologically by dates of reports. No index. Typed, some on printed forms. 12 x 16 x 24. Superintendent's office.

400. JOURNAL
1924—. 1 volume.

Record of monies received and disbursed, showing date received, from whom received, for what, amount, and what account; date paid out, to whom, for what, amount, and what account. Arranged chronologically by dates of entries. No index. Handwritten on printed forms. 700 pages. 12 x 9 x 3.5. Business office.

Care of the poor and infirm was recognized by state law as early as 1816 as a county obligation. It was in this year that the legislature authorized the county commissioners to build poorhouses in the counties and appoint boards for administering them.[1] The board of each county was directed to appoint a superintendent for the home, and to supervise his administration of the institution, on the condition of which it was required to report fully to the commissioners.

The administration was gradually simplified. There is now no board, but merely a superintendent responsible directly to the commissioners.[2] He is a civil service appointee, and is authorized to choose his own matron, also a civil service employee, as well as all other assistants.[3] Since 1882 the commissioners have been authorized to appoint a physician, who is required to report fully to them.[4]

The county home was first used to house various indigent classes, even children being confined there at one time. Children are not now regularly permitted within the county home, although some exceptions are made in the case of insane, idiotic, or epileptic children;[5] and in 1898 it was declared unlawful to confine adult insane and epileptics there.[6]

The original county home of Lake County consisted of the original farm buildings on a farm purchased at a cost of $4,000 in 1852,[7] and the first inmate was admitted and that year.[8] The site of 116 acres situated on Riverside Road has been subsequently added to until the present farm comprises 190 acres, of which 125 are tillable.

The contract for the present building was let in 1876, at $30,000.[9] It consisted of a two-story brick building, with administration accommodations in the front and rooms for the inmates in the rear. The original farm buildings were left standing and have been in used ever since the farm was purchased. The plant has since been enlarged and modernized. In 1897 a cottage hospital was added at a cost of $1421.95.[10]

---

1. *Laws of Ohio,* XIV, 447.
2. *Ibid.,* CII, 433.
3. G.C. sec. 2522.
4. G.C. sec. 2546.
5. *Walls of Ohio,* LXXXI, 92; G.C. sec. 3091.
6. *Ibid.,* XCIII, 274.
7. Commissioners' Record A (1840-1871, 142-143, entry 1.
8. Register of inmates, 1852, entry 401.
9. Commissioners' Record B (1871-1886), 106, entry 1.
10. *Ibid.,* D (1895-1900), 238.

Since 1924, however, when Lake County Memorial Hospital was built, inmates of the institution are taken there when their condition is such that they cannot be adequately cared for in the county home hospital. A fire escape was put on the main building in 1898.[11]

The home is administered by a superintendent and a matron, who are aided by a staff of six assistants. The superintendent is bonded for $5,000, and his salary has been set at $1,950 annually. The aggregate annual compensation of the staff for 1941 is $5,490.91.[12] In 1940 the total appropriation made by the commissioners for maintaining the county home was $14,540.[13]

Religious services are supplied to the inmates by inviting preachers of different denominations in succession to perform services for them.

The advent of old age pensions has not greatly affected the population of the county home since a large number of the inmates are foreigners who would not in any case be eligible.[14]

All records are located and the office at the county home, Riverside Drive and Route 84, Painesville, Ohio.

---

11. *Ibid.,* 330.
12. Record of Bonds, 1941, entry 306; Payroll, 1941, entry 283.
13. Appropriation Ledger, 1941, entry 269.
14. G.C. sec. 3138-1.

401. REGISTER OF INMATES
2 volumes. Title varies: Record of Paupers in Lake County Infirmary, 1852-1894, 1 volume.

Record of persons admitted to the institution, showing date admitted, name, age, sex, color, nativity, transported by, reason for admittance, date discharged, transferred, or date of death, where transferred, where buried, case history, and remarks. Arranged chronologically by dates of admittances. 1852-1894, indexed alphabetically by names of inmates; 1895—, no index. 1852-1894 handwritten; 1895—, handwritten on printed forms. Average 300 pages. 14 x 9.5 x 1.5.

402. DAILY MOVEMENT OF INMATES
1926—. 1 file folder.

Daily record of admissions and discharges of inmates, showing date admitted, date discharged, total days spent at infirmary, number of inmates at beginning of day, male and female, total number received during day, number discharged or died during day, total average for month, number of males and females continuously present for entire month, number of deaths during month, number received who were former inmates. Arranged chronologically by dates of entries. No index. Handwritten on printed forms. 9 x 11.5 x .5.

403. REPORT TO DIVISION OF AID FOR AGED [Division of Charities]
1923—. 1 file folder. Initiated 1923.

Financial reports of county infirmary to state division of charities, showing dates covered, itemized expenditures, amount for each listed item, total, gross cost per capita, net cost per capita, estimated total value of farm products, total acreage of farm, number of acres improved, amount spent for improvements, number of inmates, male, female, total, ages, color, place of nativity, physical and mental condition; also inventory of furnishings and equipment, with total value last year, and total value this year. Arranged chronologically by dates of reports. No index. Handwritten on printed forms. 9 x 11.5 x .5.

404. REQUISITIONS
1923—. 4 volumes.

Copies of requisitions to county commissioners for materials and supplies, showing date of requisition, requisition number, purpose, quantity, unit description, unit price, amount, order number, and code number. Arranged chronologically by dates of requisitions and also numerically by requisition numbers. No index. Handwritten on printed forms. Average 100 pages. 7.5 x 8.5 x .25.

405. PETTY CASH
1923—. 1 volume. Initiated 1923.

Daily record of money paid out from superintendent's office fund, showing date of entry, to whom paid, for what purpose, amount and total. Arranged chronologically by dates of entries. No index. Handwritten. 300 pages. 105. X 8.5 x 1.5.

406. CLASSIFIED RECEIPTS AND EXPENDITURES
1908—. 4 volumes. (1-4).

Record of money received and expended by infirmary; receipts, showing date received, from whom, for what purpose, whether from inmates or friends of inmates, names of persons donating money from Lake County or other counties, and from sources other than county treasurer, total receipts, payments into county treasury for infirmary use; also distribution of money received for purchase of farm stock, implements, produce, and other infirmary expenses by classification, showing date of entry, to whom expended, purpose expended, classified as salary of superintendent, matron, day laborers, repairs, provisions, fuel and light, clothing and footwear, drugs and medicine, tobacco, livestock, hay, grain, feed, vehicles, tools, implements, furniture, burial, miscellaneous, and total. Arranged chronologically by dates of entries. No index. Handwritten on printed forms. Average 230 pages. 17 x 15 x 1.5.

407. INVENTORY
1926—. 1 file folder.

List of material assets of county infirmary, showing date of inventory, name of department, location, description of materials, price or value, quantity, total value, extension, by whom priced or valued, entered, examined, checked, and extended. Arranged chronologically by dates of inventories. No index. Handwritten on printed forms. 9 x 1.5 x .5.

The child welfare board of Lake County was set up in 1924[1] under a state law passed in 1921[2] which authorized the establishment of such organizations in counties supporting no children's home. The program was supported out of county funds by the commissioners, and the four members of the board were appointed by them[3] and responsible to them. They served without compensation for an indefinite term, i, e., at the pleasure of the commissioners. In 1937 the number on the board was raised to five, no more than three to be appointed from one major political party.[4] They appoint trained social workers in the number justified by the work.[5] In Lake County one agent, as the administrator is called, assisted by one untrained worker and a stenographer, has so far proved adequate. The aggregate annual compensation allowed by the commissioners for 1941 is $2,670.[6] The total budget appropriated for child welfare board for 1941 is $23,270.[7] The amount of money allotted each year is the sum estimated as necessary in consideration of the amount required during the preceding year.

The children who are recommended to the care of the child welfare board are ordinarily cared for in one of three ways. They are boarded out in a boarding home; they are placed in a free home, i. e., the private home of a citizen who voluntarily undertakes the care of the child without charge to the county; or they are placed in adoptive homes. In each case the strictest examination of the home is made before committing the child to it, and frequent visits are made subsequently by the workers to determine whether or not the child is being properly treated and the conditions continue satisfactory. The only deviations from this rule are made in the cases of delinquent children, who are committed to delinquent homes, where the delinquency is regarded as not being entirely or largely due to poverty or neglect. The attempt is made, when it is considered at all likely to succeed, to treat any child as dependent, rather than delinquent. Most of the children naturally fall into the former group.

---

1. Journal, I, 1, 1924, entry 408.
2. *Laws of Ohio,* CIX, 533.
3. G.C. sec. 3092.
4. G.C. sec. 3092; *Laws of Ohio,* CXVI, 147.
5. G.C. sec. 3092; *Laws of Ohio,* CXVI, 147.
6. Appropriation Ledger, 1941, entry 269.
7. *Ibid.*

Lake County supports no detention home for children. Hence, children whose cases are under consideration are sheltered temporarily in the private homes of the juvenile probation officer, pending their permanent settlement.

The agency continues to supervise its charges until they come of age, frequently assisting them in securing both employment and higher education.

All records are located in the office of the child welfare board unless otherwise specified.

408. JOURNAL
1924—. 2 volumes. (1, 2).
Minutes of the child welfare board, showing date of meeting, appointments of committees, reports of committees, resolutions, action of board, and bills passed for payment; volume 1, page 1 contains record of organization. Arranged chronologically by dates of meetings. No index. Typed. Average 300 pages. 14.5 x 9.5 x 1.

409. CHILD WELFARE RECORD
1927—. 1 volume.
Record of wards of child welfare board, showing date recorded, name and age of child, name and address of boarding mother, period boarded, rate per week, amount paid for board, clothing, doctor, dentist, and miscellaneous items, and total amount. Arranged chronologically by dates of recording. Indexed alphabetically by names of wards. Handwritten on printed forms. 400 pages. 15.5 x 15 x 2.

410.[CARD RECORD OF WARDS]
1927—. 1 file box.
Card record of wards, showing name of ward, date of birth, birthplace, legal residence, information concerning parents, legal status, and record of placement. Arranged alphabetically by names of wards. Handwritten on printed forms. 4 x 6 x 17.

411. [REPORTS TO COMMISSIONERS AND DIVISION OF CHARITIES]

1927—. 1 bundle, 1 file drawer. Initiated 1927.

Copies of monthly reports of the child welfare board to the county commissioners and the state division of charities, showing date of report, an itemized report of expenses such as board of children, clothing, medical, dental, education, salaries of office staff, travel expenses, miscellaneous expenses, total expenses for month, and estimated budget for month; includes original and copies of monthly reports of the child welfare board to the county commissioners and state division of charities concerning the wards, showing name and age of child, names of parents or relatives, name of boarding mother, address of boarding home, amount paid towards support by relatives or parents; includes monthly census of wards, showing number of wards accepted and discharged, number of wards under the supervision of the child welfare board, number of wards boarded free in homes, number of wards boarded by contract in homes, number of local and out-of-town cases being investigated, and total cases for the month; copies of contracts with boarding homes, showing name of boarding mother, address of boarding home, amount of contract, how to be paid, amount of boarding mother's bond, and names of sureties; also miscellaneous correspondence and copies of telephone conversations, 1937—, in matters pertinent to the boarding of wards. Arranged chronologically by dates of reports. No index. Handwritten and typed on printed forms. Bundles, 9 x 12 x 3; file drawer, 10 c 16 c 24. 1 bundle, 1927-1932, attic; 1 file drawer, 1933—, Child welfare board office.

The board of county visitors, appointed by the court of common pleas, as provided by Ohio statute in 1892, was composed of six persons, three men and three women, not more than three of whom might be from the same political party.[1] The members of this board serve indefinite terms without compensation. By an act of the legislature passed in 1906, the appointive power was vested in the probate court, and the term was set at three years.[2] The board is bipartisan.

Necessary traveling expenses are paid to the members of the board, whose duty is to visit charitable and correctional institutions which are supported wholly or partly by municipal or county funds, and to report their findings and recommendations to the county commissioners, the state welfare board, and the prosecuting attorney.[3]

In Lake County the board is an active and effective organization. The members make careful examinations of the various institutions and propose improvements. The nature of their work can be seen from the kind of recommendations which they have made from time to time, such as that cells be removed from the rear of the infirmary building in order to provide an assembly room for the inmates; that an incubator be provided for the maternity ward of the hospital; and that a nurses' home be provided for student nurses.[4] All of these proposals were accepted by the commissioners, and duly put into effect.

The board keeps no separate records: for record of appointments, 1913—, see entry 169; for report to probate judge, 1913—, see entry 208.

---

1. *Laws of Ohio,* LXXXIX, 161.
2. *Ibid.,* XCIV, 70.
3. *Ibid.,* CIII, 173.
4. Commissioners' Record U (1927-1928), 49, entry 1.

The soldiers' relief commission as originally provided for by the act of May 19, 1886[1] was designed to assist veterans and the dependents of veterans, living or deceased, who were unable to provide for themselves. The county commissioners were authorized to determine the necessary appropriations and to levy a specified tax accordingly.[2] The court of common pleas was directed to appoint three persons, two of whom must be honorably discharged veterans of the Union Army, to serve for three years as a soldiers' relief commission.[3]

The law pertaining to this commission has been altered several times in respect to the personnel of the commission and the method of certification of those entitled to aid, the latest change taking effect in 1929. At that time the personnel of the commission which was charged to specify as one member the wife, widow, son, or daughter of a veteran of the Civil War, Spanish-American War, or World War, the other two to be honorably discharged soldiers, sailors, or marines of the United States, one of whom should, if possible, be a Spanish-American War veteran, the other a member of the American Legion.[4]

The salaries of the members of the commission are determined by the county commissioners, and in Lake County each member of the commission receives three dollars for each meeting held.[5] Individual applicants for relief are certified by local committees to the commissioners who investigate the case further and fix the amount of aid to be given. About 170 ex-servicemen and their dependents are now receiving aid from the commission in Lake County.[6] The annual amount of money expended for this purpose during the last five years has averaged about $11,500.[7]

---

1. *Laws of Ohio,* LXXXIII, 232.
2. G.C. sec. LXXXIII, 232.
3. *Laws of Ohio,* LXXXIII, 232.
4. *Ibid.,* CXIII, 466.
5. Commissioners' Record N (1918-1920), 134, entry 1.
6. Soldiers' Relief Reports, 1900-1922, entry 5.
7. Auditor's Docket of Bills Filed - Commissioners, 1935-1940, entry 274.

412. RECORD [Soldiers' Relief Commission]
1895—. 2 volume.

Minutes of soldiers' relief commission, showing date of meeting, names of members present, names of applicants and assistants, action taken by commission, amount granted, names of person dropped from rolls, names of appointees to commission by court, date of appointment, names of beneficiaries in different townships, record of monthly payments to beneficiaries giving name, date, and amounts of each payment. Arranged to chronologically by dates of meetings. No index. 1895-1931, handwritten; 1932—, typed. Average 300 pages. 12 x 8 x 1. Residence of Elmer Conklin, secretary of commission, 423 South St. Clair Street, Painesville, Ohio.

BLIND RELIEF COMMISSION

Provision for the relief of the indigent was made in 1805, but it was not until 1898 that the legislature provided separate relief for the indigent blind. The act authorized the township trustees to certify to the county commissioners an amount not to exceed $100 per person per annum for such relief, the certification to be made a record listing the name of the beneficiary in the amount required, and directed by the county commissioners to levy on the townships to the amount certified, this amount to be paid into the county treasury and thence to the township treasurer to be used for blind relief.[1]

Six years later, in 1904, certification authority was transferred from the township trustees to the probate judge, who was required to register the name and address of beneficiaries and to issue to each a certificate giving his name, address, and amount to be drawn. Persons eligible for relief were blind males over twenty-one and blind females over eighteen years of age, without property or means of support.[2]

---

1. *Laws of Ohio,* XCIII, 270.
2. *Ibid.,* XCVII, 392-394.

The act of 1904 was declared unconstitutional for the reason that it required spending for a private purpose public funds raised by taxation.[3] Hence, in 1908, an act was passed authorizing the county commissioners to levy a stipulated tax to create a fund for blind relief for the needy blind, the maximum benefits not to exceed $150 per person per annum to be paid quarterly; and authorizing the probate judge to appoint a blind relief commission consisting of three members to serve for a three-year term, directed to meet annually in the office of the county commissioners to examine applications recorded in order of their receipt in a book furnished by the county commissioners. This record was required to be kept open for public inspection.[4]

The blind relief commission was abolished by the legislature in 1913 and its powers and duties were transferred to the county commissioners.[5]

---

3. *Auditor of Lucas County v. The State, Ohio State Reports,* LXXV, 114-137.
4. *Laws of Ohio,* XCIX, 56-58.
5. See pp. 13-14.

413. BLIND RELIEF COMMISSION, LAKE COUNTY

1908-1913. 1 volume. Discontinued; commission abolished.
Minutes of blind relief commission, showing date of meeting, list of claims, action taken, application number, date filed, name and addresses of applicants for relief, date of action, amount allowed, and date order issued to auditor. Arranged chronologically by dates of meetings. Indexed alphabetically by names of applicants. Handwritten on printed forms. 280 pages. 15 x 10 x 2. Commissioners' clerk's office.

The " Old Age Pension" law proposed by initiative petition, was adopted by the people of Ohio in the general election of 1933.[1] The act, as amended in 1936, provided that any person sixty-five or more years of age may upon certain stipulated conditions, receive a pension, providing his total income does not exceed $360 annually. The applicant must be a citizen of the United States, and must have resided in Ohio not less than five years of a nine prior to making application for aid, or less than one year continuously in the county in which the application is made. He must be unable to support himself, and have no claim on any legally responsible person who is able to support him. In addition, the net value of all unencumbered property of the unmarried applicant must not exceed $3,000; if the applicant is married, the combined property of husband and wife must not exceed $4,000 in value.[2]

Such property may be transferred to the division of aid for the aged to be held in trust. An amendment in 1937[3] made this transfer of property optional, and not as originally ruled, a requirement to be compiled with before aid might be granted. Upon the death of the recipient of aid, this property, as well as life insurance over $250, less deductions for funeral expenses, claims of administrators, doctors, widow, and children, is used to defray in part or wholly the expense to the state of such aid as has been allowed. A bill for the amount of the aid is presented to the estate. If no funds are available for funeral expenses, the state allows $100 for the funeral, and $25 for a burial lot.[4]

The division of aid for the aged was set up as a part of the state department of public welfare in 1933 for the purpose of administering the old age pension law. In each county, however, the commissioners might operate as a local board if they so desired. If they declined to serve in this capacity, the chief of the division of aid for the aged was authorized to appoint, with the consent of the director of public welfare, a board of three or five members of the community who served without compensation. The board was required to come to keep complete records, and might employ, subject to the approval of the division, such agents and other assistants as proper administration of the act required.[5]

---

1. *Laws of Ohio,* CXV, pt. ii. 431-439.
2. *Ibid.,* CXVI, pt. ii, 216-221.
3. G.C. sec. 1359-6.
4. G. C. Sec. 1359-10.
5. *Laws of Ohio,* CXV, pt. ii, 431-439.

Since 1937 the chief of the division has been required to appoint such a board for each county, the commissioners no longer serving as the board in any county.[6]

Each case is thoroughly investigated, but the board is advised to make its inquiries not in a strictly formal way, but in the manner which seems "best calculated to conform to substantial justice." Its decisions may be appealed to the division.[7] After a case has been investigated, the applicant, if considered eligible, is granted a certificate of relief which is then passed on by the division,[8] and, once accepted by the division, need not be renewed.[9]

Under the social security act, the federal government contributes all administrative expenses and 50 percent of the amount contributed as aid to the aged, within a maximum of $20 a month for each person aided.[10] The remainder of the money is applied by the state.

The board of aid for the aged in Lake County does not meet regularly, but meetings may be requested at any time by the subdivision manager if its advice or authority should be required. A subdivision manager is appointed directly by the State Welfare Department and works under the supervision of a district supervisor who directs work in 10 counties. The manager has a staff of two assistants. In 1941, 600 persons were receiving aid, from this agency, the monthly grant to each person averaging $21.80.[11]

All records are located in the board of aid for the aged office.

---

6. G.C. sec. 1359-12.
7. *Laws of Ohio,* CXV, pt. ii, 431-439.
8. *Laws of Ohio,* CXV, pt. ii, 435.
9. G.C. sec. 1359-14.
10. *United States Code Annotated,* XLII, 303.
11. Subdivision manager for Lake County.

414. [REGISTER OF APPLICATIONS FOR OLD AGE ASSISTANCE] 1934—. 1 volume.

Register of applications for aid, showing date of application, application number, name and address, age, race, sex, marital status, citizenship, financial status, progress of case, and date of approval or rejection. Arranged numerically by application numbers. For index, see entry 415. Handwritten on printed forms. 25 pages. 17 x 12 x .5.

415. INDEX – CASE RECORDS
1934—. 1 file box.

Card index to [Register of Applications for Old Age Assistance], entry 414, Recipient of Aged Assistance, entry 416, and Old Age Assistance, entry 417, showing name, address, birth date, age, sex, and color of applicant, application number, certificate of aid number, date of application, and of approval or rejection. Arranged to alphabetically by names of applicants. No index. Typed on printed forms. 14 x 6 x 16.

416. RECIPIENT OF AGED ASSISTANCE
1934—. 2 file boxes.

Original applications made by aged persons for pensions, showing date of application, application number, name and address of applicant, date and place of birth, age, sex, color, financial status, date of approval or rejection, and all correspondence pertaining to case. Arranged chronologically by dates of applications. For index, see entry 415. Handwritten and typed on printed forms. 12 x 16 x 24.

417. OLD AGE ASSISTANCE
1934—. 1 file box.

Complete case records of each aid for the aged case, including original application, certificate of grant, if granted, investigator's report, physician's report, copy of report to state office, and all other papers, showing date of application, application number, certificate number, name and address of applicant, amount granted, or reason denied. Arranged chronologically by dates of filing. For index, see entry 415. Handwritten on printed forms. 12 x 16 x 24.

418. [CASH BOOK]
1936—. 1 volume.

Record of all money received and disbursed; receipts, showing date, source, and amount; disbursements, showing date, amount, and for what purpose expended. Arranged chronologically by dates of entries. No index. Handwritten on printed forms. 150 pages. 12.5 x 7.5 x .5.

The office of county surveyor was an important one in the early years of Ohio history when titles and boundaries were often in dispute. As early as 1803 the legislature authorized the common pleas court to appoint a qualified person to serve in this capacity. Commissioned by the governor and bonded for faithful performance of his duties, he was required to survey lands subject to sale for taxes and was authorized to appoint chainmen. His surveys were the only ones accepted as evidence, and fees collected were his sole remuneration.[1] An act passed in 1816 fixed his term at five years, and authorized him to appoint deputies, for whose official acts he was made civilly liable, as well as for his own.[2] The law provided also for his removal by the court for negligence or incompetence.

The act of 1831 consolidated the previous acts, redefined his duties, increased his bond, and authorized him, if directed by county commissioners, to procure from the surveyor general's office a certified plat with all fields notes and other data establishing boundaries and corners in his county, to be kept in the county auditor's office for the use of the landowners in the county. This act also required the surveyor to keep an accurate record of surveys made by his office. It made the office elective for three years, a term which was reduced in 1906 to two years, and increased again in 1927 or to four years, which it has since remained.[3]

Subsequent development of the office has imposed a number of additional duties. In 1842 the surveyor was charged with asserting and reporting trespasses upon public lands,[4] and an act passed in 1854 conferred upon him the authority to acknowledge instruments affecting real estate, and to administer oaths and take affidavits.[5] In 1867 he was authorized, when so directed by the county commissioners, to transcribe dilapidated maps, plats, and field notes of surveys of his own and other counties.[6]

With the automobile came a need for more efficient road construction and maintenance. An act passed by the legislature in 1906 required the surveyor to serve in the capacity of civil engineer in the construction and repair of bridges, roads, culverts, and other public improvements, except buildings, over which the county commissioners had authority. He was responsible for the inspection of such public

---

1. *Laws of Ohio,* I, 90-93.
2. *Ibid.,* XIV, 424-431.
3. *Ibid.,* XXIX, 399; XCVIII, 245-247; CXII, 179.
4. *Ibid.,* XL, 57.
5. *Ibid.,* LII, 70.
6. *Ibid.,* LXIV, 216-217; LXXVIII, 285.

improvements and was required to keep a complete record of estimates, bids, and contracts.[7] A measure passed in 1919 authorized him to appoint as maintenance engineer a deputy in whose charge all county road maintenance and repair work were placed.[8] In 1923 he was directed to assist the county planning commission, where one existed in the county.[9]

In 1935 the name county surveyor was changed to county engineer by an act restricting eligibility for the office to registered professional engineers and surveyors licensed to practice in Ohio.[10] This act, however, was amended to permit incumbents to continue in office even though they may not meet the new requirements.[11]

Construction of new roads and the maintenance and repair of the existing 195 miles of road and 132 bridges of Lake County constitute by far the largest part of the work of the engineer's department at the present time. This office staff including the engineer himself who is bonded at $2000,[12] and draws a salary of $3080,[13] received in 1940 a total aggregate compensation of $19,848.88;[14] this with a small additional allowance for office supplies constituted the entire office expense. The payroll for road work on the other hand, amounted to $104,915.69[15] for the sane period. A permanent maintenance staff of road workers of around 75 men is retained, though the number fluctuates somewhat from season to season. The total cost of road work for 1940, was $195,760.81.[16] The money for office expense and salaries of the office force is appropriated by the county commissioners from the general county tax receipts. Only a small amount of the money for road upkeep is derived from this source, the remainder being appropriated from automobile license receipts and gasoline taxes.[17]

---

7. *Ibid.,* XCVIII, 245.
8. *Ibid.,* CVIII, 497.
9. *Ibid.,* CX, 312.
10. *Laws of Ohio,* CXVI, 283.
11. *Ibid.,* CXVI, pt. ii, 152.
12. Record of Official Bonds, 1941, entry 348.
13. Payroll, 1940, entry 283.
14. *Ibid.*
15. *Ibid.*
16. Auditor's Docket of Bills Filed- Commissioners, 1940, entry 374; Payroll, 1940, entry 283, and Appropriation Ledger, 1940, entry 269.
17. G.C. secs. 5537, 6309-2.

Surveys, Maps, Plats

419. RECORD OF SURVEYS
1840—. 5 volumes. (1-5).
Record of surveys of land tracts made by county surveyors, showing date of entry and title of survey, description of tract surveyed, calculations, and name of owner of tract; also plat sketch of surveyed tract, showing boundary lines, length of each boundary line, area of tract, streams, roads, and location of landmarks, and names of flagmen, markers, and surveyors. Prepared by county surveyor. Arranged alphabetically by names of entries. Indexed alphabetically by titles of surveys. Handwritten on printed forms. Plats hand drawn. Scale varies. Average 200 pages. 12 x 9 x 1.5. Engineer's drafting room.

420. FIELD BOOKS
1840—. 227 volumes. (1-117).
Survey data and field notes of surveys of lands, showing date and number of survey, name of owner of tract, location of tract, notes of landmarks on boundary lines, bearing of boundary lines, location of benchmarks, monuments, watercourses, obstructions, buildings and roads, area of tract, and names of surveyors. Arranged numerically by survey numbers. For index, see entry 421. Handwritten. Average 150 pages. 7.25 x 5 x .75. Engineer's drafting room.

421. [Index to] FIELD BOOKS – ROAD RECORDS
1840—. 1 file box.
Card index to Field Books, entry 420, Road Record, 1915—, entry 424, Record of Estimates, 1911—, entry 430, showing name of township, name and number of road, number and title of survey, and volume and page numbers of records. Arranged alphabetically by names of townships and alphabetically thereunder by names of streets or roads, and numerically thereunder by survey numbers. Handwritten on printed forms. 5.5 x 7 x 16.5. Engineer's drafting room.

422. MAPS
1910—. 24 volumes. Subtitled by names of townships.
Plat maps of taxing district subdivisions of Lake County from which Tax Map, entry 239, are prepared, showing townships by sections with boundary lines of sections and townships, boundary lines of land tracts with name of owner of each tract, acreage, roads, railroads, and streams; also villages, towns, and city wards,

showing streets, alleys, streams, railroads, lot lines, and lot dimensions. Prepared by county engineer's office. Arranged alphabetically by names of taxing districts. No index. Ink tracings and blueprints. Scale varies, 1 inch equals 40 feet to 1 inch equals 500 feet. Average 125 pages. 18.5 x 31 x 1.25. Engineer's drafting room.

423. PROJECTS
1908—. Estimate 400 items in 1 tube and 1 duplicate set.
Engineer's plats of surveys of finished or abandoned projects including paving plans, tentative layouts of proposed and finished sewer and water line projects; complete line drawings; working details; profiles and pencil memos, showing name of township, property boundary lines, road and street names, curb lines, routes of sewer and water lines, hydrant and valve locations, bench marks, landmarks, and elevations and grades. Prepared by engineer's office. Arranged alphabetically by names of townships and alphabetically thereunder by names of projects. No index. Pencil, pen, ink tracings, and blueprints. Scale varies, 1 inch equals 40 feet to 1 inch equals 1000 feet. Tubes, 6.5 x 36; drawings, 6 x 10 to 24 x 26. Engineer's drafting room.

Improvements

424. ROAD RECORD
1806—. 7 volumes. (1, 1, A, A-D).
Record of surveys of proposed routes for the establishment of county roads and highways, including petitions to the county commissioners, showing name and description of proposed route, and signatures of petitioners; includes copies of surveyor's reports on survey with sketches of route and data on elevation and grade; appointments of appraisers, showing name and address of appointee, date appointed, and term of office; appraisers' reports and orders to survey, showing appraisers data on elevations and grades, locations of roads, bridges, and other landmarks, and complete description of route, including length, depth, width, and type of road or highway; records of establishment, alteration, vacation, and renaming of county roads. 1840—, compiled from Commissioners' Record, entry 1; 1806-1840, compiled from various commissioners' Records of Geauga and Cuyahoga Counties. No data shown when records were compiled from Geauga and Cuyahoga Counties; 1806-1887 were transcribed in 1924-1929. Arranged

chronologically by dates of establishment of roads. For index, 1806-1914 see entry 425; 1915—, entry 421. 1806-18878 typed; 1888-1908 handwritten; 1909—, typed. Average 475 pages. 16.5 x 11.5 x 2.5. Engineer's stenographer's room.

425. INDEX TO COUNTY ROADS

1806-1914. 1 volume. Discontinued.

Index to Road Record, entry 424, showing name of township, location, name, description, and number of road, volume and page numbers of record, date of establishment, alteration, vacation, and renaming of county roads. Transcribed in 1894 from Road Record, entry 424, and Commissioners' Record entry 1, and continued until 1914. Arranged alphabetically by names of townships and alphabetically thereunder by names of roads or highways. Handwritten on printed forms. 150 pages. 18 x 13 x 1. Engineer's stenographer's room.

426. ROAD IMPROVEMENTS

1911—. 8 file boxes. Subtitled by names of townships.

Originals and copies of documents pertaining to building and repairing county roads and bridges, including petitions to county commissioners by taxpayers for improvements, showing date of petition, type of improvement, and signatures of petitioners; claims for damages to commissioners from taxpayers, showing date, amount claimed, damage claimed, name and address of taxpayer, and final disposition; record of appointments of appraisers and committees, showing name and address of appointee, date of appointment and term of office; reports of committees and appraisers to county commissioners, showing date, recommendation or rejection of proposed improvement, appraisers' data on elevation and grade, location of landmarks, complete description of proposed improvement, and orders to the engineer to survey the tract; copies of surveyors' reports on surveys with sketches of routes, data on elevation and grades, and complete topography of tract; minutes and proceedings of meetings of council and county commissioners in matters pertaining to improvement; copies of specifications prepared by county engineer with copies of bids received, showing date, name of bidder, labor and material estimate, and total cost; record of proposals and agreements between contractor and engineer; contracts to bidders for improvements with bonds of contractors attached, showing date, amount of bond, name of contractor, and specifications; miscellaneous correspondence to and from the county commissioners and the engineer in matters pertaining to road and bridge construction and improvements. Arranged alphabetically by names of townships and alphabetically thereunder by names of improvements. No index. Handwritten and typed, some on printed forms. 11 x 16 x 24. Engineer's drafting room.

427. DITCH JOURNAL
1863——. 10 volumes. Subtitled by names of taxing districts.
Minutes of the board of township trustees including matters related to locating, establishing, constructing, reopening, and cleaning township ditches, showing date, and number of ditch; copies of petitions to township trustees from taxpayers for ditch improvement, showing type of improvement, and signatures of petitioners; copies of trustees' bonds, showing date and term of appointment and names of sureties; record of survey of ditch, showing grade and elevation data, and full description of length, width, depth, and condition of ditch; record of assignments of sections of ditch to groups for work, showing date, section assigned, to whom, and estimated date of completion; record of money paid out for improvements with original estimates, and proposed cost of project. Arranged alphabetically by township and numerically thereunder by ditch numbers. For index, see entry 428. Handwritten on printed forms. Average 275 pages. 14 x 9 x 1. Engineer's drafting room.

428. CULVERT AND BRIDGE [Record]
1840——. 2 file boxes.
Card index record of culverts, bridges, and ditches of Lake County and also index to Ditches Old records, entry 429, and Ditch Journal, entry 427, showing type of improvement, name of road or street, number of improvement, location, size and length of improvement, materials used, and total cost; includes records of repairs and inspections, showing date, by whom inspected, condition, and recommendations of inspector. Arranged alphabetically by types of improvements and alphabetical thereunder by names of roads and streets. No index. Handwritten and typed on printed forms. 5.5 x 7 x 16.5. Engineer's drafting room.

429. DITCHES OLD RECORDS
1840——. 1 file drawer.
Original documents pertaining to the construction and repair of certain ditches, drains, and water courses, showing date and number of improvement; petitions to township trustees and county commissioners by taxpayers, showing date of petition, type of improvement, and signatures of petitioners; copies of advertisements for

bids and original bids received, showing date, name of bidder, amounts of bids for improvement according to specifications prepared by engineer; reports of trustees to commissioners commending or rejecting the proposed improvement; plats surveys prepared by the engineer, showing location, name of street or road, township where improvement is proposed, survey data on elevation and grade, and sketch of proposed improvement; and miscellaneous correspondence from township trustees, bidders, and petitioners to the engineer and county commissioners pertaining to proposed improvement. Arranged alphabetically by names of townships and numerically thereunder by improvement numbers. For index, see entry 428. Handwritten and typed on printed forms. 11 x 16 x 24. Engineer's drafting room.

430. RECORD OF ESTIMATES
1911—. 2 volumes. (1, 2).
Record of contractor's estimates for county road repair and construction, showing date of estimate, road number, title of improvement, dates advertised, bids received, names of bidders and amounts of bids, estimates of labor and materials, estimates for payment on work, and contractor's name and contract price. Arranged chronologically by dates of estimates. For index, see entry 421. Handwritten on printed forms. Average 250 pages. 16 x 11.5 x 1.5. Engineer's stenographer's room.

431. COUNTY CONTRACTS COMPLETED
1919—. 3 file boxes.
Copies of contracts, with papers pertaining to completed county contracts for repairing and constructing roads and bridges and other county engineering work, including individuals or corporations, showing dates, name or number of road or bridge, specifications of contract, amount of contract, date contract to be completed, and name and address of contractor; engineers pencil memorandum and tentative estimates; estimates sent to commissioners from the engineer, showing date, name or number of road, contractor, labor estimate, material estimate, and total estimate; copies of advertisements for bids, estimates and awarding of contracts; engineer's preliminary surveys on grade and elevation; and data on length, size, and type of project. Arranged alphabetically by names of projects. No index. Handwritten and typed, some on printed forms. 11 x 5 x 17. Engineer's drafting room.

Miscellaneous

432. REQUISITIONS
1938—. 12 volumes. Prior records destroyed.

Carbon copies of requisitions sent to county commissioners for materials and supplies used by the engineer's office, showing date, requisition number, item, and quantity. Arranged numerically by requisition numbers. No index. Handwritten on printed forms. Average 100 pages. 8.5 x 7 x .25. Engineer's stenographer's room.

433. COUNTY GENERAL [Correspondence]
1927—. 1 file box.

Copies of incoming and outgoing mail of the county engineer's office including notices sent to the auditor from the engineer regarding the budget of the engineer's office; notices from the engineer to electric illuminating and city light plants regarding moving street light poles; data from the engineer to the commissioners regarding enclosing the transformer in the courthouse basement; data to the engineer from the telephone company regarding their conduits and lines; printed reports to the engineer from various state and federal bureaus regarding road mileage by counties; notices sent to commissioners from the engineer regarding estimate data and tentative estimates for fairground improvements; and catalogs and illustrations of traffic lights from manufacturers and agents to the engineer. Arranged alphabetically by subjects. No index. Handwritten and typed, some on printed forms. 11 x 16 x 24. Engineer's drafting room.

The county commissioners ordinarily delegate the duties of sanitary engineer to the office of the county engineer, they are authorized to engage a sanitary engineer as a separate and distinct unit of county government for the design, construction, operation, and maintenance of sanitary sewers and water mains in county sanitary districts.[1] This office was established in Lake County in September 1924,[2] and has never been a department of the county engineer's office.

Although the sanitary engineer cooperates closely with the county engineer and health department, he is responsible only to the commissioners, by whom he is appointed. He may choose and appoint his assistants, subject to their approval. In Lake County there are six on his staff, one assistant sanitary engineer, one office clerk, one demographer, and three others. The sanitary engineer is paid $2700 annually and the staff is paid at aggregate salary of $7405.[3]

The duties of this office are particularly associated with those of the board of health, which has issued a code of regulations with 16 sections, each a sanitary measure, which Lake County authorizes fully enforce.[4] While enforcement measures may be the function of the health officials and the prosecuting attorney, they necessarily require the closest cooperation of the sanitary engineer. His duties and responsibilities are more readily understood when it is recognized that Lake County is unlike any other county in the state. As in most counties where industry is not greatly developed, there are no large cities or towns, but the chief activity of the community is horticulture, not agriculture. The population includes an unusual number of wealthy families, who wish to enjoy the advantages of living in the country and yet demand the sanitary conveniences of the city.

Lake County, having no county sewer system, was compelled to protect its water supply by establishing a central control regulating the installation and operation of individual water and sewer systems. In a county where hundreds of private sewer systems are in use, it becomes a most important function of the government to ensure an adequate supply of pure water and to enforce such measures as are designed to protect it, whether the water supply be public or private. This is the chief purpose and responsibility of the Lake County sanitary engineer.

All records are located in office of sanitary engineer.

----

1. G.C. sec. 6602-1.
2. Commissioners' Record Q (1923-1924), 529, entry 1.
3. Payroll, 1941, entry 283.
4. G.C. sec. 4414.

Sanitary Improvements

434. GENERAL (Proceedings in Water Line and Sewer Construction]
1922—. 2 file boxes.

Transcripts of minutes of board of county commissioners in matters pertinent to water line and sewer construction, showing dates of meetings and members present, includes: resolutions passed creating districts or declaring improvements necessary; resolutions instructing sanitary engineer to prepare general plans and reports on proposed projects, showing name of project and sewer district, approval of preliminary plans and reports; certificates of the sanitary engineer of filing general plans with the state department of health; certificates of the sanitary engineer to commissioners that the territory to be improved is in Lake County, and outside any incorporated municipality; approval of projects by the state department of health; resolutions instructing sanitary engineer to prepare detailed plans and specifications of project; sanitary engineer's estimates of cost and tentative assessments of improvements; approval of estimates and assessments; sanitary engineers certificates of filing detailed plans for inspection; resolutions passed for construction and maintenance projects; sanitary engineer's certificates of mailing notices of hearings to every property owner affected by improvement and certificates that no person appeared to object to projects; resolutions passed for issuance of notes and tender of the notes to sinking fund trustees; original petitions from property owners to commissioners, showing purpose and date of petition, location of improvement, type of improvement, and signatures of petitioners; statements of property owners for claims for damages sustained during progress of projects, showing date, amount claimed, by whom, for what, and final disposition of claim; certificates of county engineer of itemized amounts to be assessed against property for improvements, showing name of owner, lot number, foot frontage, and amount assessed; copies of advertisements for bids published and local newspapers; copies of contracts, showing title of improvement, conditions of contract, and estimated dates of starting and completion, names of contractors; contract bonds, showing names of principles, names of sureties, amount of bond, inclusive dates, conditions of bond, and signatures of parties; and record of actual cost of labor and materials. Arranged alphabetically by names of sewer districts and numerically thereunder by project numbers. No index. Handwritten and typed on printed forms. 11 x 16 x 24.

435. CONTRACTOR'S ESTIMATES, ENGINEERING AND DISTRICT COMMISSIONER'S FEES

1922—. 16 file boxes. Subtitled by names of subdivisions.

Copies of estimates of costs in water line improvements submitted by the sanitary engineer to county commissioners, including papers and correspondence pertaining to water line and sewer improvements, showing date, estimate number, type of improvement, labor cost, material cost, and total cost estimates; copies of notifications to county commissioners of fees due and allowed the sanitary engineer on sewer and water line projects; copies of letters to county auditor, showing amounts due and payable to the commissioners and sewer and water districts. Arranged alphabetically by names of subdivisions and numerically thereunder by estimate numbers. No index. Typed on printed forms. 10 x 4.5 x 13.5.

436. BIDS

1922—. 1 file box.

Original bids received on proposed improvements and repairs to water and sewer lines, showing date, estimate number, name of sewer district, name and address of bidder, labor calls, material cost, and total cost estimate on specifications set by the county sanitary engineer. Arranged alphabetically by names of sewer districts and chronologically thereunder by dates of entries. No index. Typed on printed forms. 11 x 16 x 24.

437. TENTATIVE ASSESSMENTS, WILLOUGHBY SEWER DISTRICTS

1929. 1 file box.

Original estimates of assessments on real property for proposed sewer improvements by the sanitary engineer for Willoughby sewer district, showing date, type of improvement, location, name and address of property owners, description of property, and amount of assessment to be paid by each property owner. Arranged alphabetically by names of property owners. No index. Typed on printed forms. 11 x 16 x 24.

438. SEWER PERMITS

1922. 1 file box.

Sewer permits issued by the sanitary engineer to property owners to make connections with the main sanitary sewer, showing date, name of subdivision, name and address of owner, lot and block numbers, and permit number. Arranged alphabetically by names of subdivisions, and numerically thereunder by permit numbers. No index. Typed on printed forms. 11 x 16 x 24.

Water Service

439. [KARDEX INDEX FILE]
1931—. 1 file box.
Index to Applications for Water Service, entry 440; Consumers' File, entry 441, and Meter Setting Record, entry 443, showing name and address of consumer, date of application, account number, and meter and code numbers. Arranged alphabetically by names of consumers. Typed. 6 x 7 x 24.

440. APPLICATIONS FOR WATER SERVICE
1922—. 1 file drawer.
Original applications for water service, showing water district, lot and block numbers, name and address of applicant, date and number of application, billing address, and acceptance by sanitary engineer. Arranged alphabetically by water districts and numerically thereunder by application numbers. 1922-1933, no index; for index, 1934—, see entry 439. Handwritten on printed forms. 11 x 16 x 24.

441. CONSUMERS' FILE
1934—. 60 file drawers. (labeled by contained account numbers). Subtitled by names of service districts.
File of water consumers, showing account and permit numbers, name of sewer district, name and address of consumer, date connected, meter record, consumers record, and consumption record. Arranged alphabetically by names of sewer districts and numerically thereunder by accounts numbers. For index, see entry 439. Typed on printed forms. 11 x 16 x 24.

442. METER RECORD
1922—. 3 file boxes. Subtitled by names of manufacturers or makes. Initiated 1922.
Record of the registration of water meters, showing date, make, size, date purchased, from whom, account number assigned to meter, meter number, date of test, reason for test, and remarks. Arranged alphabetically by names of manufacturers or makes and numbers thereunder by meter numbers. No index. Typed on printed forms. 5 x 7 x 13.

443. METER SETTING RECORD

1929—. 5 file boxes. Subtitled by names of subdivisions. Initiated 1929. Record of water meters set by Lake County water department, showing name of water district, lot and block numbers, name and address of consumer, permit number, application number, type and size of meter installed, quantity and cost of materials used, labor cost, and total cost to county, date turned on and date turned off, account number assigned to consumer; includes meter record care and meter reading slips. Arranged alphabetically by names of water districts and numerically thereunder by application numbers. 1929-1933, no index; for index, 1934—, see entry 439. Handwritten and typed on printed forms. 6 x 8 x 18.

444. METER SLIPS

1936—. 1 file drawer. Prior records destroyed. Record of water meter readings, showing dates of readings, account number, name and address of consumer, name of sewer district, route number, meter number, make and size of meter, date installed, by whom installed, consumer's references, and name of meter reader. Arranged alphabetically by names of sewer districts and numerically thereunder by route numbers. No index. Handwritten on printed forms. 5 x 11 x 16.

445. WATER DEPARTMENT, SERVICE BOOK

1925-1934. 1 volume. Discontinued. Sanitary engineers record of water service to consumers, showing name of sewer district, inclusive dates of period covered, account number, name and address of consumer, amount of regular charge, delinquencies (if any), amount of rebates (if any), present meter reading, and amount and date paid. Arranged alphabetically by names of sewer districts and numerically thereunder by account numbers. No index. Handwritten on printed forms. 300 pages. 18 x 16.25 x 2.25.

446. PAYMENT STUBS FOR WATER BILLS

1934—. 1 file box. Prior records destroyed. Stubs detached from water bills and returned with remittance quarterly, showing district number, account number, name and address of payer, date and amount paid. Arranged chronologically by dates of payments. No index. Handwritten on printed government postal cards. 11 x 16 x 24.

447. CHANGE OF RECORD
1936—. 1 file box. Prior records destroyed.
Records of change of data on various records such as ownership, mailing address, temporary address agency, spelling correction, account number, and changes on Kardex card ledger, Kardex visible index, addressograph stencil, meter reading slip, meter record card, showing date, account number, old record, new record, change requested by whom, and change made by whom. Arranged chronologically by dates of changes. No index. Handwritten on printed forms. 5 x 7 x 13.

Field Books and Maps

448. FIELD BOOK, SURVEYOR [Sanitary Engineer's]
1922—. 50 volumes. (1-50).
Record of surveys made by the county sanitary engineer, showing date of survey, level, staking, final measure, location of meter boxes, valves, and manholes, and general topography of the district. Arranged chronologically by dates of surveys. Indexed alphabetically by subjects. Handwritten. Average 140 pages. 7.5 x 5 x .65.

449. SEWER AND WATER DISTRICTS
1922—. Estimated 500 maps in 20 file drawers. Subtitled by names of sewer and water districts
Physical maps of sewer and water lines of Lake County, showing water and sewer districts and detailed meter box locations. Prepared by county engineers. Arranged alphabetically by names of sewer and water districts. Black on white and blueprints. Scale varies, 1 inch equals 100 feet to 1 inch equals 1000 feet. Maps average 36 x 20; file drawers, 3.5 x 28 x 45.

450. MAPS, METER BOX LOCATION
1935—. Estimated 377 maps in 2 volumes. Subtitled by names of subdivisions.
Physical maps of Madison, Mentor, and Willoughby sewer and water districts, showing sewer and water lines, location of water meters, subdivisions, lot number, streets, and boundary lines. Prepared by the sanitary engineer's office. Arranged alphabetically by names of sewer and water districts. Black on white. Scale, 1 inch equals 40 feet. Maps, 10 x 29.5; volumes average 200 pages. 12 x 34 x 1.5.

451. MAPS OF LAKE COUNTY

1938. 2 maps.

Physical maps of Lake County, showing townships, corporations, and city wards with boundary lines of subdivisions, roads, highways, streets, and alleys, with names of streets and alleys, and highways numbers, streams, bridges, and railroads. Prepared by A. B. Wilson, County Engineer. Blueprint. Scale, 2 inches equals 1 mile. 51.5 x 38.5. Framed.

Fiscal Accounts

452. MAINTENANCE LEDGER

1924—. 1 volume.

Record of money received and disbursed on sewer and water accounts and general maintenance, showing name of account, date of entry item, debit, credit, and balance. Arranged chronologically by dates of entries. No index. Handwritten on printed forms. 100 pages. 12.5 x 10 x 1.

Miscellaneous

453. [MISCELLANEOUS]

1928—. 1 file box.

Copies of annual reports from the sanitary engineer to the county commissioners relative to the operations and proceedings of the county water supply and county sewage systems, showing dates of reports and including record of amounts of salaries paid to the personnel of both divisions with recommendations for increases in salary, showing name of employee, position, and amount of salary paid; record of installation of equipment, showing date installed, where, by whom, and total cost; record of collections upon delinquent accounts, showing date, name of payee, amount paid, and balance; balance sheet giving itemized report of expenditure and receipts for each department, showing department, reason for expenditure, to whom, and amount; source of receipts, for what, and amount. Arranged chronologically by dates of reports. No index. Typed on printed forms. 11 x 16 x 24.

According to the county planning law of April 17, 1923, the commissioners of any county may provide for the organization and maintenance of a county planning commission to consist of themselves and eight other persons appointed by them for three-year terms. At least three of the appointive members must be taken from the planning commission of any city in the county having more than 50 percent of the county's population. The members serve without pay, but expenses may be allowed.[1] They may demand the services of the county engineer, who is required to assist them if so requested.[2] The commission is empowered to make and certify to the county commissioners, and to the city planning commissioners, plans and maps showing their recommendations for systems of transportation, highways, park and recreational facilities, water supply, garbage and sewage disposal, civic centers, and other public improvements which affect the county as a whole.[3] After a plan has been adopted, the construction of no public building, roadway, bridge, viaduct, or other public improvement or utility which would constitute a departure from the plan may be authorized except by the unanimous vote are the county commissioners. [4] Lake County organized such a commission in 1927, but it was not very active and was dissolved in 1931.[5]

454. [PLANNING COMMISSION]
1927-1931. 1 volume.

Minutes of planning commission, showing resolutions passed, proposed improvements, reports on proposals, reports of committees and officers, and dates of meetings; includes March 1931 resolutions to dissolve commission. Arranged chronologically by dates of meetings. No index. Typed. 250 pages. 12.5 x 9.5 x 1.5.

---

1. G.C. sec., 4366-14.
2. G.C. sec., 4366-18.
3. G.C. secs. 4366-15, 4366-16.
4. G.C. sec., 4366-17.
5. [Planning Commission]. 1927-1931, entry 454.

The Lake County agricultural society was founded in 1850. The first fair was held in 1851 at Painesville and from that time on annually until 1894, when, because of financial difficulties, the directors dissolved the society.[1]

Many attempts were made to revive the society, but without success, until April 1911, when a bond issue of $40,000 was authorized by the voters.[2] A new site was purchased and buildings were erected, and a fair was held in the fall of the same year. The reestablishment of the institution of the county fair was enthusiastically welcomed by the people, and fairs have been held every year since.

Items to be exhibited or classified in separate groups, including poultry, livestock, seeds, fruit, flowers, vegetables, domestic and household handiwork, farm implements, flour and meal, baked goods, and the like, with special emphasis, as would be expected in Lake County, on the horticultural exhibits. Premiums not to exceed $10, are awarded at the fairs for the best and the second best of the various items shown.

455. [RECORD BOOK]
1851-1894, 1911—. 3 volumes. (1-3).

Minutes of regular and special meetings held by the Lake County agricultural society, showing date of meeting, names of members present, resolutions passed, and bills approved for payment. Volume I, 1851-1894, contains a record of organization original constitution and by-laws; volume II contains a record of reorganization, 1911. Arranged chronologically by dates of meetings. No index. 1851-1894, handwritten; 1911—, typed. Average 300 pages. 12 x 10 x 2. 1 volume, 1851-1894, attic; 2 volumes, office of clerk of society in residence, Mentor Avenue, and Fairgrounds Road, Painesville, Ohio.

---

1. Painesville *Telegraph,* December 19, 1894.
2. Commissioners' Record, I (1910-1912), 180, entry 1.

In 1914 the federal government provided for agricultural extension agencies in the states qualifying for certain specialized services of the United States Department of Agriculture and the state agricultural colleges. The purpose was to bring to those unable to attend such colleges practical demonstrations in agricultural and home economics, as well as publications, bulletins, and lectures not otherwise available. To provide this service the federal government proposed to supply part of the funds if the states would supply the remainder.[1]

In 1915 the Ohio legislature accepted the federal plan. It provided that when 20 or more persons organized and incorporated in agricultural society under the supervision of the trustees of Ohio State University, the state would allow $175 to enable the dean of the college of agriculture to provide speakers and demonstrations for each annual meeting. Additional expenses and costs were to be allowed if the county commissioners should provide $1000 or more or county agricultural extension, in which event the state would contribute an equal amount. A resident agent, appointed by the county commissioners and approved by the dean of the agricultural college, is required to make studies of soils and marketing methods in cooperation with the United States Department of Agriculture and the state agricultural colleges. If the commissioners do not act, the electorate may require them to do so by a referendum vote.[2] In 1919 and 1929 the legislature amended the law to include in the program, home demonstration agents and boys' and girls' 'club supervisors.[3]

The first agricultural extension agent of Lake County was appointed in 1917.[4] By 1940 the staff included, besides the agent, one home demonstration agent and one secretary.[5] There were 45 4-H clubs under the supervision of 50 adults, with an enrollment of 464 boys and girls.[6] Because of the great number of nurseries in Lake County, particular attention is paid to horticulture, and the demonstration work is carried on chiefly at the nurseries. It is the only county in which classes are conducted in nursery work.

---

1. *United States Code Annotated,* Title 7, sec. 343.
2. *Laws of Ohio,* CVI, 356-359.
3. *Ibid.,* CVIII, pt. I, 364; CXIII, 82-83.
4. Information secured from agency office.
5. *Ibid.*
6. Annual reports, 1940, entry 460.

The cost of agricultural extension is shared by the county and the state, as provided by law. Lake County's contribution in 1940 was $2590.[7]

All records are located and county agent's office, Federal Building, 25 North Park Street, Painesville, Ohio.

---

7. Appropriation Ledger, 1940, entry 269.

456. INDIVIDUAL PROJECT
1938—. 632 pamphlets. Subtitled by names of projects.
Record of individual projects, showing name of project, names of members, their ages, addresses, club number, name of club advisor, and study of the particular type of project, including planning the project, preparation of soil, cultivation, insect and disease control, harvesting, storing, marketing, soil, and crop management; also labor record, final summary with cost and profit of project. No obvious arrangement. No index. Handwritten on mimeographed forms. 15 pages. 11 x 8 x .25. On bookshelves.

457. LISTING SHEETS
1936—. 1 bundle.
Soil conservation summary, including total listing sheets of farm lands, crop lands, and goals, showing name of township, date of report, farm number, name of owner, acres in farm, acres of crop land, indicated goal, derived goal, recommended goal, total soil-depletion, corn yield, spatial crop productivity, and statistical information relating to same. Arranged by townships and chronologically thereunder by dates of reports. No index. Handwritten on printed forms. 10 x 18 x 6.

458. FARM REPORTS
1935—. 51 file drawers (Dated). Subtitled by names of townships.
Township statistical reports of AAA projects, active and inactive, including computation sheets of plan for farm participation, showing allotment and piece, adjustment payments, soil-building payments, maximum payment for farm, map of farm, giving pencil sketch of plot, farm number, number of acres of soil-depleted crops, number of acres of soil-conserving crops, soil-building practices and units, non-allotment provisions of conservation program, guide for classification of crops and land uses under program. Arranged by townships and numerically thereunder by farm numbers. No index. Handwritten on printed forms. 11.5 x 13 x 24.

459. CLUB RECORD
1938—. 43 pamphlets (labeled by contained club numbers).
Record of club activities, showing club pledge, name and number of club, names of secretary and other officers, project, minutes of meetings, annual summary; number of members enrolled, both boys and girls, and their ages; number of homes, both farm and village, represented; competitions in health programs, in raising produce, and livestock, and in home furnishing. Arranged numerically by club numbers. No index. Handwritten on printed forms. Average 20 pages. 11 x 8 x .25.

460. ANNUAL REPORTS
1918—. 38 volumes (Dated).
Annual reports issued by 4-H clubs, showing organizations of club, program work, projects, results, club activities, such as recreation, planting, junior fair board, and festivities, enrollment and growth, sketch of location of club in county, location of projects, planning of meetings, reports of educational tours, work planned and work accomplished by each project. No obvious arrangement. Indexed alphabetically by names of projects. Typed. Average 80 pages. 11 x 8 x 1.

461. ARIEL PHOTOGRAPHS
1937—. Estimated 250 photographs in 16 file boxes. (labeled by contained map numbers).
Ariel photographs of territory in Lake County, showing name of territory, flight lines, and map number; also contains enlargements of aerial maps. Prepared by federal operations. Arranged by flight lines. Indexed by master map giving flight lines and map numbers. 2 x 18 x 23.

Archival Materials and Published Documents

Acts of the General Assembly, 1803-1941 (119 volumes, published annually under
    state authority).
Annual Report of County Superintendent of Schools, 1912—, 1 file drawer, entry
    364.
Annual Reports [Agricultural Extension Agents], 1918—, 38 volumes, entry 460.
Appearance Docket [Court of Appeals], 1913—, 2 volumes, entry 154.
Appropriation Ledger, 1919—, 5 volumes, entry 269.
Auditor's and Treasurer's Financial Reports, 1931—, 9 file boxes, entry 304.
Auditor's Tax List, 1940—, 308 volumes, entry 246.
Baldwin, William Edward, ed., *Throckmorton's Ohio Code Annotated* (certified
    ed., Banks-Baldwin Company, Cleveland, 1936).
Carter, Clarence Edwin, ed. and comp., *The Territorial Papers of the United States*
    (8 volumes, United States Government Printing Office, Washington, D. C.
    1934, in progress). Volumes II and III treat of the Northwest Territory.
Cash Book [Clerk of Courts], 1873—, 22 volumes, entry 116.
Cash Book [Recorder], 1907—, 21 volumes, entry 80.
Chase, Salmon P., ed., *Statutes of Ohio and of the Northwestern Territory . . . 1788-*
    1833 . . . (3 volumes, Corey and Fairbanks, Cincinnati, 1833-1835).
Commissioners' Record, 1840—, 28 volumes, entry 1.
Coroner's Inquest, 1880—, 16 file boxes, entry 124.
Criminal Appearance and Execution Docket [Court of Common Pleas], 1894—, 7
    volumes, entry 129.
Curwen, Maskell F., comp., *Public Statues at Large of the State of Ohio* . . . (3
    volumes, published by the author, Cincinnati, 1853-1854).
Daily Register of Deeds, 1896—, 9 volumes, entry 42.
[Financial Reports, Board of Education], 1912—, 1 file drawer, entry 356.
General [Weekly Report of County Dog Warden, County Commissioners].
Jail Register, 1868—, 6 volumes, entry 228.
Journal [Child Welfare Board], 1924—, 2 volumes, entry 408.
Journal [Court of Appeals], 1913—, 1 volume, entry 156.
Journal [Court of Common Pleas], 1840—, 48 volumes, entry 131.
Jury Book, 1842-1856, 1864—, 7 volumes, entry 91.
Juvenile Appearance Docket, 1908—, 5 volumes, entry 214.
Juvenile Journal, 1906—, 5 volumes, entry 215.

Laning, Jay F., comp., *Revised Statutes of the State of Ohio* (3 volumes, The Laning Company, Norwalk, Ohio, 1905).

Laws of the Territory of the United States Northwest of the Ohio River (3 volumes, Published by authority, Philadelphia and Cincinnati, 1792-1796).

"Legislature of the Northwestern Territory, 1795," *Ohio State Archaeological and Historical Quarterly,* XXX (1921), 13-50.

McCook, G. W., Emilus O. Randall, and J. L. W Henney, *et al.,* reps., *Reports of Cases Argued and Determined in the Supreme Court of Ohio* (New Series, 137 volumes, various publishers, Columbus, New York, and Cincinnati, 1853-1941).

Ohio Auditor of State, *Annual Report,* 1836-1939 (published annually under state authority).

Ohio Secretary of State, *Annual Report,* 1836-1936 (published annually under state authority). Some volumes titled: *Ohio Statistics.*

Ohio Tax Commission, *Annual Report,* 1910-1938 (published under state authority).

Payroll [Auditor], 1924—, 8 file boxes, entry 283.

Pease, Theodore Calvin, ed., *The Laws of the Northwest Territory, 1788-1800* (Illinois State Historical Library, *Law Series,* Springfield, 1925, I).

[Planning Commission], 1927-1931, 1 volume, entry 454.

Receipts Journal [Auditor], 1937—, 2 volumes, entry 279.

[Record Book, Agricultural Society], 1851-1894, 1911—, 3 volumes, entry 155.

Record [Declaration of Intention, Court of Common Pleas], 1907—, 14 volumes, entry 136.

Record of Bonds Issued [Auditor], 1909—, 15 volumes, entry 309.

Record of Chattel Mortgages and Bills of Sale, 1893—, 2 volumes, entry 72.

Record of Deeds, 1840—, 191 volumes, entry 40.

Record of Leases, 1865—, 12 volumes, entry 44.

Record of Mechanics Liens, 1843—, 6 volumes, entry 51.

Record of Mortgages, 1850—, 136 volumes, entry 46.

Record of Official Bonds [Auditor], 1840-1904, 1926, 2 volumes, entry 306.

Record of Official Bonds [Treasurer], 1840—, 7 volumes, entry 348.

Register of Inmates [County Home], 1852—, 2 volumes, entry 401.

Report of Judicial Statistics to Secretary of State, 1927—, 5 pamphlets, 7 folders, entry 122.

Sayler, J. R., comp., *The Statutes of the State of Ohio* (4 volumes, Robert Clarke and Company, Cincinnati, 1876).

Smith, J. V. Rep., *Official Reports of the Debates and Proceedings of the Ohio State Convention . . . held at Columbus, Commencing May 6, 1850, and at Cincinnati, Commencing December 2, 1850* (Scott and Bascom, Columbus, 1851).

United States, Bureau of the Census, *Fifteenth Census of the United States, 1930, Agriculture* (4 volumes, United States Government Printing Office, Washington, D. C. 1931-1932).

— *Fifteenth Census of the United States, 1929, Manufacturers* (3volumes United States Government Printing Office, Washington, D. C., 1933).

— *Fifteenth Census of the United States, 1930, Population* (6 volumes, United States Government Printing Office, Washington, D. C., 1931-1933).

— *Fifteenth Census of the United States, 1930, Unemployment* (2 volumes, United States Government Printing Office, Washington, D. C., 1931-1932).

— *Religious Bodies*, 1926 (2 volumes, United States Government Printing Office, Washington, D. C., 1929-1930).

— *Twelfth Census of the United States, 1900, Population* (2 volumes, United States Census Office, Washington, D. C., 1901-1902).

United States Code Annotated (65 volumes, Edward Thompson Company, Northport, Long Island, and West Publishing Company, St. Paul, Minnesota, 1927, in progress).

United States Statutes at Large, 1789-1940 (54 volumes, United States Government Printing Office, Washington, D. C., 1848-1941).

Diaries and Memoirs

Burnet [Jacob], *Notes on the Early Settlement of the Northwestern Territory* (Derby, Bradley and Company, Cincinnati, 1847).

[Crary, C. B.], *Pioneer and Personal Reminiscence* (Marshall Printing Company Marshalltown, Iowa, 1893).

General Histories and Reference Works

Ayer, N. W, and Son, Inc., eds., comps., *Directory of Newspapers and Periodicals, 1937* (N. W. Ayer and Son, Inc., Philadelphia, 1937).

Channing, Edward H., *A History of the United States* (6 volumes, Macmillan Company, New York, 1905-1925).

Sutherland, Edwin H., *Principles of Criminology* (J. B. Lippincott and Company, Chicago, 1934).

Willoughby W. F., *Principles of Judicial Administration* (The Brookings Institute, Washington, D. D., 1929).

Regional and Local Histories, Treaties, and Monographs

Bond, Beverley W., Jr., *The Civilization of the Old Northwest: A Study of Political, Social, and Economic Development, 1788-1802* (Macmillan Company, New York, 1934).

Fess, Simeon D., ed., Ohio Reference Library (4 volumes, Lewis Publishing Company, Chicago and New York, 1937).

Galbreath, Charles B., *History of Ohio* (5 volumes, American Historical Society, Inc., Chicago and New York, 1925).

Heiges, R. E., *The Office of Sheriff in the Rural Counties of Ohio* (Published by the author, Findlay, Ohio, 1933).

Hillis, L. B., comp., Lake *County, Illustrated* (Herald Printing Company, Painesville, 1912).

Howe, Henry, comp. *Historical Collections of Ohio* (2 volumes, published under state authority, Norwalk, Ohio, 1896).

Jenkins, Warren, *The Ohio Gazetteer and Travelers' Guide* . . . (1st revised edition, Isaac N. Whiting, Columbus, 18 37).

Kilbourne, John, *The Ohio Gazetteer* . . . (10th edition, published by the author, Columbus, 1831).

Lake, D. J., *Atlas of Lake and Geauga Counties Ohio* (Titus, Simmons and Titus, Philadelphia, 1874).

McCarty, Dwight G., *The Territorial Governors of the Old Northwest: A Study in Territorial Administration* (State Historical Society, Iowa City, Iowa 1910).

Mills, William C., *Archaeological Atlas of Ohio* (Ohio State Archaeological and Historical Society, Columbus, 1914).

Ohio Geological Survey, *Reports,* Series ii (8 volumes, published under state authority, 1869-1888).

— Reports, Series iv (41 volumes, published understate authority, 1903-1940).

Ohio Study of Local School Units, *A Study of the Public Schools of Lake County, with Recommendations for Their Future Organizations* (Ohio State Department of Education, Columbus, 1937).

Ohio Tax Commission, *Financing State and Local Government in Ohio, 1900-1932* (published under state authority, 1934).

Randall, Emilus O., and Daniel J. Ryan, *History of Ohio: The Rise and Progress of a Great State* (5 volumes, Century History Company, New York, 1912).

The Reorganization of County Government in Ohio: Report of the Governor's Commission on County Government (n. pub., n. p. submitted to the governor, December 1934).

Rice, Harvey, *Pioneers of the Western Reserve* (2nd edition, Lee and Shepard, Boston, and Charles T. Dillingham, New York, 1888).

Roseboom, Eugene Holloway and Francis Phelps Weisenburger, *A History of Ohio* (Prentice Hall, Inc, New York, 1934).

Stranahan, H. B. and Company, and G. C. Cory, pub., *Atlas of Lake County, Ohio* (Cleveland, 1898).

Upton, Harriett Taylor, *History of the Western Reserve* (3 volumes, Lewis Publishing Company, Chicago and New York, 1910).

Williams Brothers, pub., *History of Geauga and Lake Counties . . .* (Philadelphia, 1878).

Articles in Periodicals

Atkinson R. C. "County Home Rural Developments in Ohio," *National Municipal Review,* XXXIII (1934), 235.

Atkinson R. C., "Ohio–County Charter Elections," *National Municipal Review,* XXIV (1935), 702-703.

— "Ohio–Optional County Legislation," *National Municipal Review,* XXIV, (1935), 228.

Boyd, W. W., "Secondary Education in Ohio Previous to the Year 1840," *Ohio State Archaeological and Historical Quarterly,* XXV (1916), 118-134.

Davis, Harold E., "Religion in the Western Reserve, 1800-1825," *Ohio State Archaeological and Historical Quarterly,* XXXVIII (1929), 475-501.

Downes, Randolph Chandler, "Evolution of Ohio County Boundaries," *Ohio State Archaeological and Historical Quarterly,* XXXVI, (1927), 340-477.

Dykstra, C. A., "Cleveland's Effort for City-County Consolidation," *National Municipal Review,* VIII, (1919), 551-556.

Gates, Charles M., "The Administration of State Archives," *The Pacific Northwest Quarterly,* XXIX, (January 1938), No. 1; also in *The American Archivist,* I (July 1938), 130-141.

Kaplan, H. Eliot, "A Personal Program for County Service," *National Municipal Review,* XXV, (1936), 596-600.

King, I. F., "Introduction of Methodism in Ohio," *Ohio State Archaeological and Historical Quarterly,* (X), 1902, 165-219.

Miller, Edward A., "History of the Educational Legislation in Ohio from 1803 to 1850," *Ohio State Archaeological and Historical Quarterly,* XXVII (1918), 1-271.

Mills, William Stowell, "Lake County and its Founders," *Ohio State Archaeological and Historical Quarterly,* X (1902), 361-371.

Stone, Donald C., "The Police Attack Crime," *National Municipal Review,* XXIV, (1935), 39-41.

Stout, Wilbur, "Early Forges in Ohio," *Ohio State Archaeological and Historical Quarterly,* XLVI, (1937), 25-41.

Van Cleef, Eugene, "The Finns in Ohio," *Ohio State Archaeological and Historical Quarterly,* XLIII (1934), 452-460.

Newspapers

Ohio State Journal, 1840; 1933.
Painesville *Telegraph,* 1894.

Commissioners**

Jonathan Stickney	1840-1842	Charles A. Moodey	1887-1892
Hezekiah Furguson	1840-1843	George H. Morse	1890-1896
John Kellogg	1840-1844	Raymond Freeman	1891-1895
Scribner Huntoon	1842-1848	John E. Post	1892-1902
Samuel Tomlinson	1843-1849	Charles W. Searls	1895-1895
Eliphalet Stratton	1844-1847	Frank P. Miller	1895-1901
Erastus Crocker	1847-1850	James C. Campbell	1897-1903
Jonathan Willard	1848-1851	Elmer Manchester	1901-1907
Seleck Warren	1549-1852	C. H. Stocking	1902-1909
John McMurphy	1860-1856	Clayton C. Cottrell	1903-1911
George Everett	1851-1851	Clinton A. Phelps	1907-1914
Solomon D. Williams	1851-1854	G. E. Stevenson	1909-1915
Orson St. John	1852-1855	Clarence A. Hine	1911-1917
Homer F.Griswold	1854-1866	E. H. Williams	1912-1915
Christopher G. Crary	1855-1861	J. G. Phillips	1913-1919
Eber D. Howe	1856-1859	Fred P. Freshley	1917-1919
Henry Paine	1859-1868	W. E. Thompson	1919-1924
Abner Parmalee	1861-1876	Herbert J.Wright	1919-1924
Simeon D. Hickok	1866-1872	C. A. Hine	1919-1923
Eli Olds	1868-1874	C. P. Rose	1923-1924
Alonzo P. Barber	1876-1882	F. O. Reynolds	1924-1933
Joseph Jerome	1877-1886	C. M. Grauel	1924-1931
Edward B. Griswold	1878-1884	Charles O. Manchester	1925-1937
Samuel C. Carpenter	1882-1890	Charles Alexander	1931-1937
Stephen B. Barber	1884-1890	Charles D. Clark	1933—
Henry C. Rand	1885-1891	Emmet R. Sweeney	1937—
Charles T. Morley	1886-1887	L. E. Hull	1939—

*Compiled from" Ohio Secretary of State *Annual Report*, 1836-1936, some volumes titled *Ohio Statistics;* Common Pleas Journals, A-Z, 1-51; Commissioners' Journals, D-AA; *Atlas of Lake County, Ohio* (H. B. Stranahan and Co., Cleveland, 1898); Painesville *Telegraph*.

**The board of county commissioners, with three members each serving a three-year term, was established in 1804 (*Laws of Ohio*, II, 150). In 1906 the term of office was changed to two years (*Laws of Ohio*, XCVIII, 271); in 1920 it was increased to four years (*Laws of Ohio*, CVIII, pt. ii, 1300).

Recorders*

Harry F. Shepard	1840-1844	William D. Mather	1893-1893
Benjamin D. Chesney	1844-1850	Frederick T. Pyle	1893-1906
Flavius J. Huntington	1850-1856	Frank G. Salkeld	1907-1908
Franklin Paine	1856-1862	Geo. A. Bates	1909-1916
Harry F. Shepard	1862-1865	A. J. Goldsmith	1917-1922
Isaac Everett	1865-1874	Mary Weixel	1923-1924
Silas A. Tisdel	1874-1880	A. J. Goldsmith	1925-1928
Henry B. Green	1880-1892	Gertrude H. Andrus	1929–1930
Harley Barnes	1892-1892	Lew S. Miller	1931-1940
John R. Clague	1892-1892	Daniel Jenkins	1941—

*Under the law of 1803, the associate judges of the court of common pleas appointed the recorder for a seven-year term (*Laws of Ohio*, I, 136). The office became elective for a three-year term in 1829, a two-year term in 1905, and a four-year term in 1936 (*Laws of Ohio*, XXVII, 65; *Ohio Const. 1851.* Art. XVII, sec. 2; *Laws of Ohio*, CXVI, pt. ii, 184).

Clerks of the Court of Common Pleas**

John W. Howden	1840-1846	B. Crofoot	1891-1904
Chas. D. Adams	1846-1854	J. C. Barto	1904-1913
Christopher Quinn	1855-1863	J. R. Williams	1913-1914
Perry Bosworth	1864-1872	Ford W. Andrus	1914-1921
Franklin Paine, Jr.	1873-1881	H. Clark Cozadd	1921-1926
R. A. Moodey	1882-1885	Elizabeth S. Murphy	1927—
J. C. Ward	1885-1890		

*Called prothonotary under the laws of the Northwest Territory and appointed by the governor. Under the Ohio constitution of 1802 the court appointed its own clerk for a seven-year term (Art. III, sec. 9). The constitution of 1851 made the office elective for a three-year term (Art. IV, sec. 16). Under the constitutional amendment of 1905 the term was changed to two years and to four in 1936. (*Laws of Ohio*, XCVII, 641; *Laws of Ohio*, CXVI, pt. ii, 184).

ROSTER OF COUNTY OFFICIALS
1840-1941

Judges of the Court of Common Pleas*
*President judges under the constitution of 1802 in the districts which included
Lake County*

John W. Willey	1840-1841	Benjamin Bissel	1842-1849
Reuben Hitchcock	1841-1841	Philemon Bliss	1849-1851

Associate judges under the constitution of 1802

Zenas Blish	1840-1846	Jonathan Lapham	1847-1848
William C. Matthews	1840-1846	Aaron Wilcox	1847-1847
David R. Paige	1840-1846	Milo Harris	1848-1851
Warren A. Cowderey	1846-1847	Henry Munson	1849-1850
William W. Branch	1847-1851	John P. Markell	1850-1851

*Judges under the constitution of 1851 in the districts which included
Lake County*

Reuben Hitchcock	1852-1855	Laban S. Sherman	1881-1891
Eli T. Wilder	1855-1855	William P. Howland	1891-1899
Horace Wilder	1856-1861	J. P. Cadwell	1900-1902
Norman L. Chaffee	1862-1871	W. S. Metclfe	1901-1909
C. E.Gliffen	1872-1872	Theodore Hall	1903-1904
Milton C. Cafield	1872-1875	J. W. Roberts	1905-1910
H. B. Woodbury	1875-1884	Arlington G. Reynolds	1909-1912
Delos W. Canfield	1875-1900		

Resident judges under the constitutional amendment of 1912

Arlington G. Reynolds	1912-1928	Winfield S. Slocum	1929—

*The president and associate judges under the first constitution were appointed for seven-year terms by joint ballot of both houses of the general assembly (*Ohio Const. 1802* Art. III, sec. 8). The constitution of 1851 made the office elective for five-year periods and required the incumbent to be a resident of the district in which elected (*Ohio Const. 1851*, Art. IV, sec. 12). The amendment of 1912 changed the term to six years, and required the election for each county of at least one judge, who must be a resident of the county in which elected (Art. IV, sec. 12, as amended September 3, 1912).

ROSTER OF COUNTY OFFICIALS
1840-1941

Judges of the Probate Court*

Jerome Parmer	1852-1855	Arlington G. Reynolds	1891-1897
Lord Sterling	1855-1861	Clinton D. Clark	1897-1902
Charles S. Waring	1861-1862	Clark H. Nye	1903-1920
Perry Bosworth	1863-1864	Addie Nye Norton	1921-1932
Moses S. Harvey	1864-1870	Ross Sweet	1933-1940
Grandison N. Tuttle	1870-1879	Elton L. Behm	1941—
Geo. H. Shepherd	1879-1891		

*The probate court established under the laws of the Northwest Territory in 1788, consisted of a probate judge and two judges of the court of common pleas (Pease, *op. cit.,* 99). Under the constitution of 1802 it lost its identity completely in the court of common pleas. It emerged with its present form and functions, with a single judge serving a three-year term, under the constitution of 1851 (Art. IV, secs. 7, 8). On September 3, 1912, the term was changed to four years (Art. IV, secs. 7, 8, as amended, 1912) as at present.

Prosecuting Attorneys**

William L. Perkins	1840-1840	Clinton D. Clark	1879-1886
C. Case	1840-1842	Homer Harper	1886-1895
Charles B. Smythe	1842-1844	Harry Pl. Bosworth	1895-1903
Salmon B. Axtell	1844-1848	E. F. Blakely	1904-1910
William Matthews	1848-1853	Homer Harper	1911-1914
Alva L. Tinker	1853-1857	Geo. C. Von Beseler	1915-1918
Charles J. Bomer	1857-1859	R. N.Whitcomb	1919-1920
William L. Perkins	1859-1863	Ralph M. Ostrander	1921-1922
W. W. Nevison	1863-1867	Morgan Giblin	1923-1924
Jerome B. Burrows	1867-1869	Seth Paulin	1925-1928
Alva L. Tinker	1869-1873	J. Frank Pollock	1929-1932
John W. Tyler	1873-1875	Howard U. Daniels	1933-1936
E. J. Sweeney	1875-1877	Lester W. Donaldson	1937—
Lord Sterling	1877-1879		

**At first appointive by the supreme court and later by the court of common pleas, the office of prosecuting attorney was made elective for a term of two years by a law passed January 23, 1833 (*Laws of Ohio*, XXI, 31). In 1881 the term was increased to three years, in 1906 reduced to two, and in 1936 increased to four (*Laws of Ohio*, LXXVIII, 260; *Laws of Ohio*, XCIII, 271; *Laws of Ohio*, CXVI, pt. ii, 184).

Coroners*

Clark Parker	1840-1842	Lester H. Luce	1873-1877
Stephen Sherman	1843-1845	Franklin Parker	1877-1879
Samuel E. Carter	1845-1847	Harry W. Grand	1879-1881
Joseph Waldo	1847-1849	Henry M. Mosher	1881-1891
Samuel Brown	1849-1851	J. N. Winans	1891-1897
Nathan Corning	1851-1855	A. G. Phillips	1897-1900
Henry Paine	1855-1857	H. E. York	1901-1906
Samuel Butler	1857-1859	H. N. Amidon	1907-1910
Henry Paine	1859-1859	Dr. M. J. Carmody	1911-1912
Moses H. Colby	1860-1861	Geo. F. Barnett	1913-1916
Jonathan Cooledge	1861-1863	J. N. Black	1917-1920
Franklin Parker	1863-1865	M. H. Bradley	1921-1922
Benjamin K. Cranston	1865-1867	James McMahon	1923-1924
Nathan Corning	1867-1869	O. O. Hausch	1928-1934
James H. Taylor	1869-1873	Dr. James G. Powell	1935—

*Established in 1788, the officer of county coroner was made appointive for a twoo-year term by the territorial governor (Pease, *op. cit.,* 24-25). The Ohio constitution of 1802 (Art. VI, sec. 1) made the office elective without changing the term of office, which remained at two years until 1936, when it was increased to four years (*Laws of Ohio*, CXVI, pt. ii, 184).

Sheriffs**

L. P. Bates	1840-1844	C.T. Morley	1877-1880
Jabez A. Tracey	1845-1848	A. D. Barrett	1881-1887
Dan Parker	1848-1852	John Austin	1885-1888
William Clayton	1852-1856	Albert Button	1889-1892
A. P. Axtell	1857-1860	Sanford Barber	1893-1896
J. V. Viall	1861-1864	Sultan St. John	1897-1900
John M. Benjamin	1865-1868	Frank G. Hughes	1901-1904
Samuel Wire, Jr.	1868-1872	J. W. Hunter	1905-1908
H. M. Mosher	1873-1876	W. M. Baker	1909-1912

**Under the territorial government the sheriff was appointed by the governor from the time the office was created in 1792 (Pease, *op. cit.,* 8). Under the first constitution the office was made elective for a two-year term (*Ohio Const. 1802*, Art. VI, sec. 1) and so remained until 1936, when tenure was increased to four years (*Laws of Ohio*, CXVI, pt. ii, 184).

Sheriffs (continued)

Ora M. Shink	1913-19116	James Maloney	1929-1932
D. L. Phelps	1917-1920	T. J. Kilcawley	1933-1936
Ora M. Shink	1921-1924	James Maloney	1937—
E. T. Rasmussen	1925-1928		

Treasurers*

Solon Coming	1840-1845	Harcoy Armstrong	1887-1889
Harry Woodworth	1845-1849	William D. Mather	1889-1891
Silas A. Tisdel	1849-1853	Solon Rand	1891-1893
John L. Batchelor	1853-1855	Robert C. Bates	1893-1895
William Lockwood	1855-1857	Samuel J. Potts	1895-1897
Samuel E. Carter	1857-1859	William A. Coleman	1897-1898
Lewis S. Abbott	1859-1861	C. L. Kimball	1899-1900
Caleb W. Ensign	1861-1863	E. V. Sawyer	1901-1902
Robert A. Moodey	1863-1865	Geo. H. Kellog	1903-1904
Samuel R. Houde	1865-1867	Sam Lorr	1905-1908
Thomas King	1867-1869	C. L. Kimball	1909-1910
Peter F. Young	1869-1871	J. S. Warren	1911-1912
Irwin S. Childs	1871-1873	E. M. Orcutt	1913-1916
Purhand G. Hrt	1873-1875	R. N. Whitcomb	1917-1920
Horace Norton	1875-1877	Chester C. Little	1921-1922
Harvey Woodworth	1877-1879	Francis J. Fuller	1923-1924
Henry H. Coe	4879-1881	Lynn J. Fuller	1925-1928
Hzro A. Hoskins	1881-1883	F. N. Shankland	1929-1932
Theodore h. Burr	1883-1885	Abel Kimball	1933—
Edward E. Gould	1885-1887		

*Omitted from the constitution fo 1802, the office of treasurer was created by legislative act in 1803 (*Laws of Ohio*, I, 98). It was appointive by the associate judges in 1803, and annually by the county commissioners from 1804 to 1827, when the office became elective for a two-year term (*Laws of Ohio*, I, 98; *Laws of Ohio*, II, 154; *Laws of Ohio*, XXV, 25-32). The constitution of 1851 provided that no person should hold the office for more than four years of any six (Art. X, sec. 3). In 1859 the general assembly made the term two years (*Laws of Ohio*, LVI, 105). In 1936 it was increased to four years which it has remained (*Laws of Ohio*, CXVI, pt. ii, 184).

Auditors*

Daniel Kerr	1840-1845	Walter C. Tisdel	1880-1898
Geo. Everett	1845-1851	E. D. Heartwell	1898-1910
Benjamin D. Chesney	1851-1853	W. Albert Davis	1911-1920
William A. Blair	1853-1855	L. J. Spaulding	1921-1923
Reuben P. Harmon	1855-1856	Cora Agnes Carrel	1923-1926
Benjamin D. Chesney	1856-1880	Henry Z. Pethetel	1927—

*The office was established by legislative act February 19, 1820 (*Laws of Ohio*, XVIII, 70). At first appointive, it was made elective annually by an act of February 2, 1821, the person elected taking office March 1 each year (*Laws of Ohio*, XIX, 116). In 1831 the term was set at two years, in 1877 at three years, in 1906 at two years, and in 1919 at four years (*Laws of Ohio*, XXIX, 280; *Laws of Ohio*, LXXIV, 381; *Laws of Ohio*, XCVIII, 271; *Laws of Ohio*, CVIII, pt. ii, 1294).

Infirmary Directors**

Harvey Woodworth	1852-1854	Carlas Mason	1876-1882
Collins Morse	1852-1859	Nicholas Brink	1878-1881
John T. Doolittle	1852-1864	Eleazer Burridge	1880-1889
Eber D. Howe	1854-1857	John H. Murray	1885-1885
Homer Higley	1857-1857	Carlas Mason	1883-1888
George Everett	1857-1858	John W. Crocker	1888-1894
Milo Harris	1857-1862	Charles M. Thompson	1889-1889
Invie P. Axtell	1858-1863	Eleazer Burridge	1889-1894
Asa Childs	1862-1871	Wallace L. Baker	1890-1899
Dates E. Able	1863-1866	J. W. Crocker	1891-1893
Harvey Craine	1864-1867	L. L. Morris	1894-1912
Franklin Rogers	1866-1878	David Law	1895-1902
John McLelland	1867-1874	S. T. Woodman	1899-1908
Silas T. Ladd	1871-1873	Albert F. Howe	1903-1904
Dates E. Able	1874-1875	W. E. Taylor	1904-1908
B. H. Woodman	1873-1875	W. B. Blair	1909-1912
Dates E. Able	1875-1876	M. E. Crofoot	1909-1912
Alva T. Brown	1875-1880		

Infirmary Directors (continued)

**This office was authorized by a legislative act in 1816, providing for the appointment by the commissioners of seven directors, to have charge of the county infirmary and choose its superintendent (*Laws of Ohio*, XIV, 447-448). By an act of 1831, the membership of the board was reduced to three and in 1865 the members were made elective for terms of three years (*Laws of Ohio*, XXIX, 317; *Laws of Ohio*, LXII, 24-25). The board was abolished by law in 1913, and its powers and duties were transferred to the board of county commissioners and the infirmary superintendent (*Laws of Ohio*, CII, 433).

Surveyors***

Jarvis S. Pike	1840-1843	Horatio N. Munson	1876-1894
Colbert Huntington	1843-1849	Frank M. Barker	1894-1899
Moses S. Harvey	1849-1853	J. C. Ward	1899-1910
Edward Huntington	1853-1856	H. P. Cummings	1911-1916
Daniel Kerr	1856-1859	Caspar A. Harris	1917-1918
Horatio N. Munson	1859-1862	Clyde C. Hadden	1919-1922
Edward Huntington	1862-1865	R. O. Burtch	1923-1924
Horatio N. Munson	1865-1872	A. C. Holden	1925-1932
Edward Huntington	1872-1876	Arthur B. Wilson	1933—

***From 1803 to 1831 the surveyor was appointed by the court of common pleas and commissioned by the governor (*Laws of Ohio*, I, 90-93) From 1831 to 1906 he was elected for a three-year term, from 1906 to 1928 for a two-year term, and since 1928 for a four-year term (*Laws of Ohio*, XXIX, 399; *Laws of Ohio*, XCVIII, 245-247; *Laws of Ohio*, CXII, 179).

Engineers****

Arthur B. Wilson   1935—

****An act of 1935 changed the title of surveyor to engineer (*Laws of Ohio*, CXVI, 382).

All addresses refer to Painesville, Ohio, unless otherwise noted

Auditor
https://www.lakecountyohio.gov/auditor/
105 Main Street

Board of Elections
https://www.lakecountyohio.gov/boe/
105 Main St. Ste. 107

Clerk of Courts
https://www.lakecountyohio.gov/coc/
105 Main Street

Commissioners
https://www.lakecountyohio.gov/commissioners-office/
105 Main Street

Common Pleas
https://www.lakecountyohio.gov/common-pleas/
105 Main Street

Coroner
https://www.lakecountyohio.gov/coroner/
5966 Heisley Rd. #200
Mentor, OH 44060

Dog Shelter
https://www.lakecountyohio.gov/dog-shelter/
2600 North Ridge Road
Painesville, Ohio 44077

Engineer
https://www.lakecountyohio.gov/engineer/
105 Main Street, Suite A205

Health Dept.
https://www.lcghd.org/
5966 Heisley Road
Mentor, Ohio 44060

Juvenile Court
https://juvenile.lakecountyohio.gov/
53 East Erie Street

Probate Court
https://www.lakecountyohio.gov/probate-court/
105 Main Street

Prosecutor
https://www.lakecountyohio.gov/lakecountyprosecutor/
105 Main Street

Recorder
https://www.lakecountyohio.gov/recorder/
105 Main Street

Sheriff
https://www.lakecountyohio.gov/sheriff/
104 East Erie Street

Treasurer
https://www.lakecountyohio.gov/treasurer/
105 Main Street

Veterans Service
https://www.lakecountyohio.gov/veteran-services/
105 Main Street

Non-governmental

FamilySearch
https://www.familysearch.org/search/catalog
FamilySearch is a free website with digitized records. Records for Lake County include Auditor, Board of Equalization, Clerk of Courts, County Assessor, Court of Common Pleas, Probate Court, Recorder, Sheriff, Supreme Court, and Treasurer Each of these headings contain a listing of records, many of which date to the beginning of the county.

Morley Public Library
https:morleylibrary.org
184 Phelps Street, Painesville, OH 44077-3926
Knowing the genealogy of the county helps in research. Lake County was part of Trumbull County from 1800-1806 and Geauga County 1806-1840 when Lake was formed. Many of the records located at the library are transcriptions of published court records. Records available are vital records, cemetery transcriptions, census records, city and telephone directories, military records, naturalization, newspapers (and obituary index). An added feature is the collection of high school and college yearbooks. The genealogy and local history department may be reached at: **genealogy@morleylibrary.org** See website for hours of operation.

Western Reserve Historical Society
https://www.wrhs.org
10825 East Blvd., Cleveland, Ohio
See website for hours of operation.
Located in the Cleveland History Center, WRHS has an extensive collection of works pertaining to Lake County in their books and manuscript collections. Records also include those for the parent counties of Lake being Trumbull and Geauga.

www.ingramcontent.com/pod-product-compliance
Lightning Source LLC
Chambersburg PA
CBHW050702280326
41926CB00088B/2426